Checklist for Starting a Freelan...

_____ 1. Create a freelance business that suits your skills and abilities.

_____ 2. Write a business plan.

_____ 3. Check all zoning regulations.

_____ 4. Get all necessary licenses and permits.

_____ 5. Select a business structure (sole proprietor, partnership, incorporation).

_____ 6. Find space in your home or rent outside space.

_____ 7. Set up an office. Buy equipment, furniture, and office supplies.

_____ 8. Set up a budget.

_____ 9. Establish a bookkeeping system.

_____ 10. Set up a billing system.

_____ 11. Buy adequate insurance.

_____ 12. Name your business.

_____ 13. Establish a work schedule.

_____ 14. Advertise and promote your business.

_____ 15. Create a public relations and publicity campaign.

_____ 16. Decide if you need an agent.

_____ 17. Establish a savings account.

_____ 18. Establish a retirement plan, preferably including a Keogh and/or IRA.

_____ 19. Calculate the amount of your estimated tax payment.

_____ 20. Continue to solicit work, learn new skills, and network.

alpha
books

Additional Resources

➤ **National Business Exchange**
http://www.director.nex/lexis-nexis/sba

➤ **Network Marketing Mall**
http://network-marketing.com/nmm/nmm.html

➤ **Networking Marketing Yellow Pages**
http:// network-marketing.com/nmyp/nmyp.html

➤ **PROFITS Online Magazine**
http://profit$online.com

➤ **Small Business Administration**
http://www.sbaonline.sba.gov

➤ **Small Business Administration software**
http://www.sbaonline.sbagov/shareware/
starfile.html

➤ **American Express**
http://americanexpress.com
(free ads for small businesses)

➤ **U.S. Treasury Department**
Internal Revenue Service
Washington, DC 20224
(Tax Guide for Small Businesses
Tax Guide for Depreciation
Tax Calendar and Check List)

➤ **National Small Business Association**
160 K Street, N.W.
Washington, DC 20006

➤ **American Entrepreneurs' Association**
2311 Pontius Avenue
Los Angeles, CA 90064

➤ **American Federation of Small Businesses**
407 South Dearborn Street

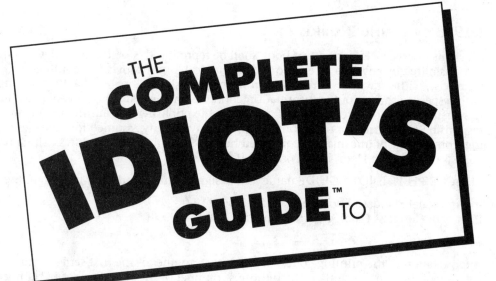

THE

COMPLETE IDIOT'S GUIDE™ TO

Making Money in Freelancing

by Laurie Rozakis

alpha books

A Simon & Schuster Macmillan Company
A Division of Macmillan General Reference
1633 Broadway, New York NY 10019

THE COMPLETE IDIOT'S GUIDE name and design are trademarks of Macmillan, Inc.

International Standard Book Number: 0-02-862119-0
Library of Congress Catalog Card Number: 97-80972

00 99 98   8 7 6 5 4 3 2 1

Interpretation of the printing code: the rightmost number of the first series of numbers is the year of the book's printing; the rightmost number of the second series of numbers is the number of the book's printing. For example, a printing code of 98-1 shows that the first printing occurred in 1998.

Printed in the United States of America

Brand Manager
Kathy Nebenhaus

Executive Editor
Gary M. Krebs

Managing Editor
Bob Shuman

Senior Editor
Nancy Mikhail

Development Editor
Mary Russell

Editorial Assistant
Maureen Horn

Production Editor
Michael Thomas

Copy Editors
Jeanne Lemen/Lynn Northrup

Cover Designer
Mike Freeland

Cartoonist
Judd Winick

Designer
Glenn Larsen

Indexer
Nadia Ibrahim

Production Team
Betsy Deeter, Brad Lenser

Contents at a Glance

Part 1: There's No (Work) Place Like Home   **1**

1 What Is Freelancing?   3
Find out what freelancing is, learn about today's freelancers, and get the lowdown on the freelance revolution.

2 Nightmare on Wall Street   17
Learn why freelancing looks like a great option to so many people these days, and hear some of their stories.

3 It's Half Full: The Upside   27
Discover the advantages to freelancing and learn how freelancers feel about their craft.

4 It's Half Empty: The Downside   37
Discover the disadvantages to freelancing and read some first-hand accounts of freelance hell.

5 Do You Have What It Takes?   47
Explore your attitudes toward freelancing and see if you have the skills, background, and personality to be a freelancer. Then weigh your options.

Part 2: The Ultimate Out-of-Office Experience   **59**

6 Nothing Ventured, Nothing Gained   61
Learn how to avoid common mistakes people make when they think about becoming freelancers, and start finding the right freelance career for you.

7 Mission Possible: Writing a Business Plan   75
Write a business plan and evaluate your chances of success as a freelancer.

8 No Guts, No Glory: Getting Work   87
Explore ways to get clients for your freelance business.

Part 3: Setting Up Shop   **99**

9 Space: The Final Frontier   101
Get the scoop on zoning laws, learn how to carve out office space, and start furnishing your home office.

10 Hard-Wired for Success   115
Assess the impact of technology on your freelance business and learn the basics of buying computer hardware and software, fax machines, photocopiers, and scanners.

11 Don't Stay Home Without It: Tools of the Trade   127
    Learn all about telecommunications systems for freelancers,
    stock up on office supplies, get the scoop on courier services,
    and explore office security.

Part 4: Crossing the Road: The Business of Freelancing   **141**

12 Money Business 1: Setting Your Rates   143
    Find out how to calculate your rates and negotiate fees.

13 Money Business 2: Getting Your Rates   155
    Learn about working on speculation and consignment,
    dealing with deadbeats, and deciding when to give yourself
    a raise.

14 Legal Beagles: Business Structure and Contracts   165
    Discover the three ways to structure your business, select the
    legal structure that's right for your freelance business, and
    explore contracts and letters of agreement.

15 In the Groove: Bookkeeping   179
    Learn how to keep financial records that would make an
    accountant proud (or at least satisfied that you're not going
    to get creamed by the IRS).

Part 5: Take It on Home: Survival Skills   **191**

16 Alert the Media   193
    Name your business, develop a marketing plan, and learn to
    advertise and market yourself.

17 Still Spreading the Word   207
    Explore advertising promotions, get into public relations, and
    polish your networking skills.

18 The Professional Edge   223
    Learn how to build, and keep, a good reputation, deal with
    clients (both naughty and nice), and decide if you need an
    agent.

19 Home on the Range: Running Life as a Freelancer   237
    Discover how to deal with the twin freelancing perils of
    procrastination and overwork, and learn how to protect your
    work time.

20 Working Without a Net   247
    Learn ways to square family and freelancing, combat loneli-
    ness, and balance the cash flow.

Part 6: Economics 101   257

21 Cry Uncle: Taxes   259
All you never wanted to know about taxes. See why it's important to clearly define your freelance status, learn about estimated tax payments, and discover the wonderful world of deductions.

22 Plain Talk About Protecting Yourself: Insurance   275
Learn about all the different kinds of insurance no freelancer should be without.

23 Caveat Investor   287
See why you need a nice, big, fat retirement account. Then learn how to get one through savings, thrift, and tax-deferred Keogh and IRA accounts.

Part 7: Top of the Heap   299

24 Expansion League   301
Learn how to deal with changing conditions, find out how to hire the help you need, and see if it's time to leave home.

25 Keep That Sparkle in Your Step   311
Discover ways to keep yourself challenged, and evaluate whether freelancing is really for you.

Index   319

Contents

Part 1: There's No (Work) Place Like Home   **1**

1 What Is Freelancing?   **3**

The Workplace War Zone 4
   Join the Revolution 5
   Making the Break 6
Learn the Lingo 7
   The Name of the Game 7
   A Rose by Any Other Name 9
A Fine Line 10
Who Are These People? 10
   The World's My Oyster 11
   Free to Be You and Me 12
How It All Adds Up 12
   Declare Your Independence 13
The Least You Need to Know 14

2 Nightmare on Wall Street   **17**

What's Wrong With This Picture? 18
Fear and Loathing 19
   The Blame Game 21
   I'm OK, but You're Really Screwed 21
Stressed and Pressed 22
   Life on the Edge 22
   Inquiring Minds Want to Know 23
You *Can* Get There From Here 24
   Crisis 24
   Chance 25
   Choice 25
The Least You Need to Know 25

3 It's Half Full: The Upside   **27**

To Dream the Possible Dream 28
Whose Life Is It Anyway? 29
   Live Free or Die 30
   And Baby Makes Overload 31

Eager Beavers 32
  Variety Is the Spice of Life 32
  Know Thyself 33
There's No Place Like Home 34
Master of Your Domain 35
The Least You Need to Know 35

4 It's Half Empty: The Downside   37

Going It Alone 38
Playing With the Big Kids 39
  The Cheese Stands Alone 40
  Working Nine to Nine 40
  Record Breakers 41
  One Is the Loneliest Number 41
Don't Give Up Your Day Job 42
Control Freak 43
  Who's on First? What's on Second? 44
  Promises, Promises 45
If You Can't Stand the Heat, Get Out of the Kitchen 45
The Least You Need to Know 46

5 Do You Have What It Takes?   47

Know Thyself 48
What You Know, Not *Who* You Know: Skills and
  Background 50
  Who Ya Gonna Call? 51
  Person Overboard! 51
Personality Plus 52
  In the Driver's Seat 53
  Critical Condition 54
Who Do You Think You Are? 55
The Least You Need to Know 57

Part 2: The Ultimate Out-of-Office Experience   59

6 Nothing Ventured, Nothing Gained   61

Gotcha! Traps to Avoid 62
  Shooting Blanks 62
  Getting Burned by What's Hot 62
  Stuck in a Rut 63

Connect the Dots 63
   What *Could* I Do? 63
   What *Should* I Do? 64
   What's the *Best* Freelance Career for Me? 64
   Putting Two and Two Together 64
   Cross at the Green, Not In-Between 65
Scratch a Niche 66
   Cleaning Up 67
   Write Away: Freelance Writing, Editing, and Desktop
    Publishing 68
   Life Lines 69
   Rent a Yenta: Consulting and
    Providing Services 70
   This Little Piggy Went to Market:
    Marketing and Selling 71
In the Home Stretch 72
The Least You Need to Know 73

7 Mission Possible: Writing a Business Plan   75

Getting Down to Business: Crafting a Business Plan 76
Hit the Books 77
Put It in Writing 78
   1. Overview 79
   2. Customer Profile 80
   3. Competitor's Profile 80
   4. Sales Forecast 82
   5. Location 82
   6. Organizational Plan 83
   7. Marketing Plan 84
   8. Financial Plan 84
The Least You Need to Know 85

8 No Guts, No Glory: Getting Work   87

Going Out for Business 88
People Who Need People 88
The Thrill of the Hunt 90
   Working the Web 91
   Hit the Bull's Eye 92
Like a Virgin 93

First Contact 93
  Story Hour 94
  Bosom Buddies? 94
  Talk Soup 95
  Dot the I's and Cross the T's 96
  Sometimes It's Over *Before* the Fat Lady Sings 96
  The Least You Need to Know 97

Part 3: Setting Up Shop   99

9 Space: The Final Frontier   101

Zoned Out 102
  Boning Up on Zoning.. 102
  Tattle Tale, Ginger Ale 103
  Twilight Zone 104
A Room of One's Own.. 105
  And in This Corner… 105
  Head Space 106
  Up Against the Wall 107
  Possession Is 9/10 of the Law 109
  Home Improvements 109
A Loaf of Bread, a Jug of Wine, and a $1,500 Chair? 110
  The Best Seat in the House: Something to Sit On 110
  Join the Desk Set: Something to Work On 111
  Darkness Visible: Lights.. 112
  File It: Storage Space 113
  Special Needs 113
The Least You Need to Know 113

10 Hard-Wired for Success   115

Hello, Dave 116
  Cyberphobia Strikes!... 117
  Techno Time 118
The Well-Equipped Freelancer 119
  Two Sides of the Same Coin:
    Hardware and Software 119
  Just the Fax, Ma'am: Fax Machines 121
  Instant Gratification: Photocopiers 121
  Beam Me Up, Scotty: Scanners 122

The Rules of Acquisition 122
   1. Assess Your Needs 122
   2. Do Your Research 122
   3. Check Your Budget 123
   4. Shop 'Til You Drop 124
   Captain Hook-Up 124
   Use It or Lose It 125
The Least You Need to Know 126

11 Don't Stay Home Without It: Tools of the Trade   **127**

Reach Out and Touch Someone 128
   You Say Hello, and I Say Good Buy 128
   ET, Phone Home 129
Front Men: Stationery and Business Cards 130
   Card-Carrying Freelancer 131
   Card Me 132
   The Medium Is the Message 133
Supply-Side Economics 133
   Hey, Big Spender...Shopping Like an Expert 135
In the Nick of Time 136
Better Safe Than Sorry 137
   Lock Down 138
   Little Things Matter a Lot 138
The Least You Need to Know 139

Part 4: Crossing the Road: The Business of Freelancing   **141**

12 Money Business 1: Setting Your Rates   **143**

Gilt Trip 144
Dollars and Sense 144
   Penny Wise, Pound Foolish 145
   Figure It Out 147
   Profit from My Advice 148
   Comparison Shopping 149
   The Long and Short of It 149
Cash on the Barrelhead 150
   To the Virgins, Make Much of Time 151
   Reality Check 152

Talk the Talk and Walk the Walk 152
Pass the Bucks 153
The Least You Need to Know 154

13 Money Business 2: Getting Your Rates   155

Life on the Edge: Working on Spec 156
    The Good… 156
    …The Bad and the Ugly 156
Taking the Wind Out of Your Sales 158
    How Much Is That Doggy in the Window? 158
    Even Steven: Trading 158
Show Me the Money: Dealing With Deadbeats 158
    Ready… 159
    Aim… 160
    Fire! 161
    Just When You Thought It Was Safe to Go Back
        in the Water… 161
We're in the Money: Give Yourself a Raise 162
The Least You Need to Know 164

14 Legal Beagles: Business Structure and Contracts   165

Legal Aid 166
    O Solo Mio! (Sole Proprietorship) 166
    Pas de Deux (Partnership) 167
    You, Inc. (Incorporation) 168
Help Me, Rhonda: Deciding on a Legal Structure 170
Clause and Effect 172
    Terms of Endearment 173
    Warning: Contents Under Pressure 173
No Uncertain Terms 175
The Least You Need to Know 177

15 In the Groove: Bookkeeping   179

Fear of Finances 180
    True Confessions 180
    Money Maven 181
Spring Cleaning, Financial Style 182

Book It, Danno: Setting Up a Record-Keeping System 183
    In and Out 183
    Spread 'Em 184
    Fork It Over 186
    Compulsion 187
Budgets 187
    Singing the Blues 188
    Help Is on the Way 189
The Least You Need to Know 189

Part 5: Take It on Home: Survival Skills   191

16 Alert the Media   193

What's in a Name? 194
    The Name Game 195
    Going Global 195
    The Doublemint Twins 196
Foot in the Door 197
    Card-Carrying Freelancer 197
    Resumes 198
To Market, to Market 199
Advertisements for Myself 201
    1. Classified Ads 201
    2. Display Ads 201
    3. Program and Yearbook Ads 202
    4. Yellow Pages 202
    5. Radio 203
    6. Television 203
    7. Brochures and Pamphlets 203
    8. Direct Mail 204
    9. Postcards 204
    10. Balloons, Billboards, Bumper Stickers, Buttons,
        Blimps, and Other Bizarros 204
The Least You Need to Know 205

17 Still Spreading the Word   207

Toot Your Own Horn: Public Relations and Publicity 208
    1. What's the Buzz? News Stories and Press Releases 209
    2. Take a Letter, Maria: Newsletters 209
    3. Bread and Butter: Thank-You Notes 209

4. When You Care Enough to Send the Very Best:
    Greeting Cards 212
5. Charitable Events 212
6. Press the Flesh: Speaking Engagements 213
Something for Nothing? Incentives 213
    1. You Could Already Be a Winner! Contests 214
    2. Save Big Bucks: Discount Coupons 214
    3. Freebies 214
    4. Free Gifts (Are There Any Other Kind?) 215
    5. Cheaper by the Dozen: Multiple-Purchase Offers 215
    6. Samples 215
Finding the Right Strings and Pulling Them:
    Networking 215
    Let's Do Lunch 216
    Facts on File 219
    Play Nice 219
Drums Along the I-Way 220
    Charlotte's Web 221
Touch Down 222
The Least You Need to Know 222

18 The Professional Edge   223

Building a Reputation 224
Luck of the Draw: Dealing With Clients 224
The Beaver Is Not Happy:
    Dealing With Difficult Clients 227
    Liar, Liar, Pants on Fire 227
    Sorry, Wrong Number 229
    Up Close and Personal 229
Secret Agent Man: Agents 230
    First-Night Jitters 231
    Work It Out 232
    Hide and Seek: Finding an Agent 233
    Caveat Emptor 234
    Breaking Up Is Hard to Do 234
The Least You Need to Know 235

19 Home on the Range: Running Life as a Freelancer   237

Performance Anxiety 238
    Ritual Behavior 238
    Patterns Plus 239

Three Neat Ways to Get Started 240
Last-Ditch Efforts 241
All Work and No Play Makes Jack a Dull Boy 242
Excuse *Me* 242
Cat on a Hot Tin Roof 243
Save Yourself 244
Why Buy the Cow When You Can Get the Milk
for Free? 244
The Least You Need to Know 245

20 Working Without a Net   247

Family Matters 248
Kid's Play 248
Hired Help 249
Homecoming 250
Me, Myself, and I 251
Buns of Steel 252
Go With the Flow 252
Strategy 1: Doing the Hustle 253
Strategy 2: Temp Time 254
Strategy 3: Part and Parcel 255
Getting the Credit You Deserve 255
The Least You Need to Know 255

Part 6: Economics 101   257

21 Cry Uncle: Taxes   259

A Horse Is a Horse, of Course, of Course 260
Oooo, Wilbur 260
You Can Run but You Can't Hide 261
Vive La Difference? 262
One Hand Clapping: Sole Proprietorships 262
Me and My Shadow: Partnerships 263
Highway Robbery: Corporations 264
There Is Some Justice in the World: Deductions 264
Something for Nothing? 265
Home Is Where the Deduction Is 268
Nothing for Something 269

Child Labor 269
Fork It Over Early and Often: Estimated Payments 270
Grin and Bear It: Audits 271
Plan Ahead 272
The Least You Need to Know 273

22 Plain Talk About Protecting Yourself: Insurance   275

An Ounce of Prevention: Health Insurance 276
    The Bad News 276
    The Worse News 276
Finally, Some Good News 277
    Better Safe Than Sorry 278
    Dollars and Sense 279
Shall We Dance? 280
Don't Lose Your Head: Disability Insurance 281
The Game of Life: Life Insurance 282
Cataloging: Do You Know What You Own? 283
    Spring Cleaning 283
    You Could Look It Up 285
What Do You Mean It's Not Covered? 285
The Least You Need to Know 286

23 Caveat Investor   287

Wrinkled but Running 288
The Rich Are Made, Not Born 289
    Money Talks, Nobody Walks 289
    Ouch! That Smarts! 289
    Daddy Warbucks 290
Living on Easy Street 291
    The Most Bang for Your Buck:
      Keogh Retirement Plans 292
    The ABCs of IRAs 293
Wall Street Wizard 294
Field of Schemes 297
The Least You Need to Know 298

Part 7: Top of the Heap   299

24 Expansion League   301

Boomtown Meltdown 302
    Help Can Help 302
    Looking for Mr./Ms. Goodbody 303
    Headless Body Found in Topless Bar! 304
Sizing Things Up 304
    Squeeze Play 305
    Leaving the Nest 305
Not Waving but Drowning 306
    Growing Pains 307
    Onward and Upward 308
The Least You Need to Know 309

25 Keep That Sparkle in Your Step   311

The Sweet Smell of Success 312
    A Table for One 313
    All the Right Moves 314
Freelancer Overboard 315
    Hello, I Came to Say I Cannot Stay 316
    Jumping Ship 317
You Should Live and Be Well 318
The Least You Need to Know 318

Index   319

Foreword

In this brilliant, witty, practical book, Dr. Laurie Rozakis illuminates setting up a freelance business, complete with plenty of anecdotes and solid advice to help you avoid the pitfalls inherent in any startup. The book begins by introducing the concept of freelancing, and describes a typical workplace, or "war zone," as she calls it. Here you're asked to score yourself to see if your work life fits into the standard mold. Most do! Every day it's the same thing—beating your head against the wall trying to earn a living and hating just about every minute of it. Furthermore, as the author reminds us, the traditional guarantees of work are receding faster than Willard Scott's hairline. Long-time employees are given the boot or granted an unwanted early retirement. Family demands shift and people find themselves in a new set of circumstances. What should you do?

Dr. Rozakis invites you to join the freelance revolution, an inexpensive and environmentally friendly way to have your cake and eat it too. Freelancing is so alluring that millions of Americans are already doing it. And so can you—with a little help. For too many people, freelancing is something that just happens when their lives change. They jump on the bandwagon of a passing trend without figuring out what really suits them, and end up back in the corporate fold wondering what went wrong. With the aid of this indispensable book, however, you can plan a freelance career that will work for you.

With penetrating insight and a healthy mixture of humor, Dr. Rozakis explains how you can turn your strengths into the business of your dreams. However, she's quick to remind you that breaking into freelancing involves more than luck. You also need to take care of a few prerequisites. And she's got them covered, in convenient checklists that enable you to make sure you have the qualities—from training to self-discipline to the ability to work alone—that will make freelancing a good fit for you.

Then it's on to the business of freelancing, with everything you need to know about setting up an office and finding clients. She even covers record-keeping, a real drag of a subject until you read the fine print. More than half of all new businesses fail in the first year. It's not all because of poor record-keeping, although that has a lot to do with it, as you'll learn. Dr. Rozakis shows you how to avoid these and other potential pitfalls as you build your business, and walks you through the important steps you need to take to successfully run your business and keep it growing. There's even a section on how to balance your family life with your freelance business. What more could you ask for?

David Rye is a successful two-time entrepreneur, speaker, and author of several books including the national best-seller Winning the Entrepreneur's Game. *He is currently the CEO for Western Publications.*

Introduction

Freelancing.

The very word has a ring of romance to it, as sexy as a supermodel, a summer in Sumatra, or sufficient sleep.

Freelancing.

What could be more appealing in today's crazy world, where nine-to-fivers march double-time to maniacal corporate or government drummers? Where even the best and brightest are "downsized," "rightsized," or just plain axed? Where even a shiny watch can't compensate for 25 years of frustration?

Freelancing.

Be your own boss. Set your own hours. Do your own thing. Oooo—don't you just love it when I talk dirty?

Maybe you like what you're doing for a living, but you don't like *where* you're doing it. Or you don't like what you're doing *or* where you're doing it. In either case, this book is for you.

What You'll Learn in This Book

In *The Complete Idiot's Guide to Making Money in Freelancing*, I'll tell you how to make your dreams of independence come true. Without ignoring the problems of working without a net, I'll show you where you can get the facts you need and overcome obstacles so you can make freelancing work for you. You'll learn how to find (or make!) your niche, set up your home office, and get organized.

Remember how you cried when you discovered that Mary Martin was flying with strings? Remember how shattered you felt when the New York Jets went 1-15? Remember how you felt when your hair began to thin—just as your middle began to plump? Well, freelancing has its downside, too.

I can't promise you that if you work at home you'll experience heaven on earth (that's a pint of Rocky Road, a down comforter, and a Ginger Rogers-Fred Astaire movie), but I *can* guarantee that by the time you finish this book, you'll have the tools you need to decide if freelancing is right for you.

This book is divided into seven sections that teach you the practical, hands-on facts you need to become a freelancer. You'll learn how to choose a freelance field, create a business plan, equip a home office, find clients, advertise and market yourself, and deal with taxes. Most of all, you'll finish this book better equipped to decide if freelancing is right for you.

Part 1, There's No (Work) Place Like Home, first defines freelancing and shows you how to tell if you have what it takes to become a freelancer. Along the way, I discuss the skills, background, and personality traits that make people successful freelancers. I'll help you make one of the most important decisions of your life.

Part 2, The Ultimate Out-of-Office Experience, gets into specific freelance careers, including writing, publishing, consulting, service jobs, marketing, and selling. Here's where you'll learn how to create a business plan and why one is so important. You'll also learn how to make new connections and still keep contacts from your staff jobs. These contacts can help you find work and get your freelance business up and running.

Part 3, Setting Up Shop, explores the basics of setting up and equipping a home office. First, you'll learn all about zoning laws so you can make sure that your office is legal. Next, I'll teach you ways to find the space you need in your home or what to do if you absolutely, positively can't s-q-u-e-e-z-e out a single inch of space. Then comes equipping the office. I show you how to get the "tech touch" so you can shop for computers, software, fax machines, telecommunications systems, and other high-tech goodies with confidence. You'll learn about buying the right furniture, office supplies, and lighting, and how to select professional-looking stationery and business cards. By the end of this section, you'll be a smart shopper when you sally forth to get everything you need.

Part 4, Crossing the Road: The Business of Freelancing, covers the basics of any business: money. I'll teach you how to calculate your rates and negotiate fees. In addition, I'll show you how to deal with contracts and keep good financial records. You'll also learn about business structures, including sole proprietorships, partnerships, and incorporation. This information will help you decide which business structure fits your needs as a freelancer.

Part 5, Take It on Home: Survival Skills, describes how to survive in the day-to-day world of freelancing. You'll start by learning how to pick a name for your business—and why the right name is so important for success. Then I'll show you how to toot your own horn through advertising, marketing, and public relations. You'll learn all about networking, building and keeping a good reputation, and dealing with home, family, and difficult clients. There's even a section on agents: Do you need one? If so, how can you select the right one?

Part 6, Economics 101, shows you how to deal with the freelancer's financial facts of life: taxes, insurance, and retirement planning. I'll teach you the basics of taking care of yourself financially. In addition, you'll learn all about the importance of planning for your future—in dollars and cents.

Part 7, Top of the Heap, shows you how to manage your success and keep yourself happy, challenged, and growing as a freelancer. I'll show you how to deal with such growing pains as burn-out and boredom. You'll learn how to cope with increased business and how to stretch out into different fields. You'll also discover how to tell if it's time to leave the nest.

More for Your Money!

In addition to all the explanation and teaching, this book contains other types of information to make it even easier for you to learn the basics of freelancing. Here's how you can recognize these features:

Bet You Didn't Know

You could skip these tidbits, but you won't want to because they're much too tasty!

Take My Word For It

Like every other skill worth knowing, freelancing has its own terminology. Here's where I explain these useful terms so you can walk the walk and talk the talk!

Mind Your Own Business

These warnings help you stay on track. They can make it easier for you to avoid the little goofs...and the major pitfalls.

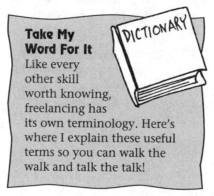

Home Alone

These are little expert tips that help you become a pro without all the fuss and muss.

Acknowledgments

To all the dear friends I have made freelancing: Janice, Paula, Ellen L, Mary Mac, Carroll, Meish, Nancy, Patricia L, Diane E, Kathy ("The Fox"), Drew, Mary Ellen ("Auntie EM"), Sharon, Steven Jay, and Hester. If I forgot anyone, please forgive me. You may not be on this page, but you're still in my heart.

A special thank you to my first editor, Linda Bernbach, who gave me my "big break" and has stood by me ever since.

Special Thanks to the Technical Reviewer

The Complete Idiot's Guide to Making Money in Freelancing was reviewed by an expert who double-checked the accuracy of what you'll learn here, to help us ensure that this book gives you everything you need to know to become a successful freelancer. Special thanks are extended to Sheila Buff.

Ms. Buff has been a freelance editor, writer, and picture researcher since 1981. She specializes in natural history, the outdoors, and health issues and is the author of more than 20 books. As co-executive director of the Editorial Freelancers Association, she has extensive experience with the problems and pitfalls that freelancers encounter.

Part 1
There's No (Work) Place Like Home

In My Fair Lady, *Eliza Doolittle knew exactly what she wanted:*

> *All I want is a room somewhere*
> *Far away from the cold night air.*

What about you? What do you want? Often, the answer to that question begins like Eliza's: "All I want is…" Of course that's not all you want, but it may be what's most important to you right now.

In these opening chapters, I'll give you the inside skinny on the freelancer's life. Then I'll help you decide what it is you really want from a freelance career—and show you how to make your dreams come true.

Chapter 1

What Is Freelancing?

In This Chapter

➤ So what is freelancing, anyway?

➤ Who are today's freelancers?

➤ The lowdown on the freelance revolution

A juggler, driving to his next performance, was stopped by the police. "What are those knives doing in your car?" asked the officer.

"I juggle them in my act."

"Oh yeah?" says the cop. "Let's see you do it."

So the juggler starts juggling the knives.

A guy driving by sees this and says, "Wow, am I glad I quit drinking. Look at the test they're making you do now!"

Does it feel like every day at the job is just another test? Are you sensing that the workplace hurdles are getting higher and higher? Are you juggling more than you can handle and enjoying it less? Are you ready to be your own boss? If so, it may be time to learn more about freelancing. That's what this chapter is all about.

First, I'll define "freelancing" so we'll all be on the same page. Then you'll get an inside look at today's freelancers from one of their own—me! Finally, I'll show you why so many smart people are going freelance.

The Workplace War Zone

As Lily Tomlin said, "We are all in this alone." *Or are we?* Below are ten situations the Typical Worker faces. Place a check next to every one that has happened to you. Let's see how typical *you* are.

_____ 1. The alarm clock sets off a buzz loud enough to wake the dead. A good thing, too, you think, as you fumble for the *off* bar. Your eyes are gritty and your head has that dull "I needed more sleep" ache. Your mouth feels like the inside of an inner tube. It's Monday—again.

_____ 2. As you lurch toward the shower, you remember that the car needs a brake job and you promised to be home early to watch your oldest child play soccer. You flip on the TV: The news is bad, the weather is worse. You feel a cold coming on...or maybe it's the flu?

_____ 3. You grab a cold, stale Pop Tart and it's hi ho, hi ho, off to work you go. The fog is as thick as your woolly socks. All you want to do is go back to bed.

_____ 4. Before you know it, you're on the parkway, moving as slowly as a cranky toddler. Horns blare; the radio drones on. Your brakes squeak, reminding you that they're on borrowed time. Great, you think. Saturday at the auto shop.

_____ 5. More than an hour after you've left the house, you finally arrive at the office. You're annoyed already, and it isn't even 9:00 AM. You wash down a few aspirin with some tepid coffee and gird your loins for a morning full of meetings.

_____ 6. At lunchtime the meetings finally break up, with nothing resolved. You're ready to smack a few heads together, but you don't have the time. Your phone is ringing and the fax is spewing out reams of paper.

_____ 7. Even though your belly's growling like a caged bear, the invoices have to be processed before you can get some lunch.

_____ 8. Someone is knocking on your door. It's the office manager, with a memo that demands an immediate response. "One quick meeting and we can resolve this entire issue," she says. "There's no such thing as a quick meeting," you mutter.

_____ 9. True to form, the meeting takes twice as long as it should—and accomplishes half as much. Oh, for a few minutes to work in peace, you think. And a little lunch, too.

_____ 10. Right before you leave, your boss pops in and says, "No raise this year. Profits are down, costs are up."

4

Bonus: Give yourself two points if you have to come in Saturday to finish (a) the year-end evaluations; (b) the audit; (c) a sales presentation. So much for the brake job.

Score Yourself

All checked	Keep counting...only 3,573 days to retirement.
7–9	You never forget that work is a four-letter word.
4–6	Dilbert is your patron saint.
1–3	May I have your job? Pleeeze?

Does this sound like your typical workday, Mouseketeer? And this day isn't even a disaster: No one's sick, nothing has broken down, and the boss isn't on a bender about something or other.

War may be hell, but work nowadays ain't no stroll in the park. Millions of today's workers look forward to a day in the office about as much as a root canal or a long drive with their children. Now, I'm not saying that the type of work you do is the problem. Actually, most people are quite satisfied with their chosen careers, be they doctors, lawyers, or snake charmers. No, what sets our blood boiling is getting to the job and then trying to get something done once we get there. *That's* the fly in the ointment.

Mind Your Own Business
If you commute just 20 minutes one way, five days a week, by the end of the year you could spend over 160 hours commuting.

Join the Revolution

What if I were to tell you that there is an inexpensive, environmentally friendly, hip way to have your cake and eat it, too? This method is time-tested and proven effective—over hundreds of years. The solution will let you arrive at your desk cool, calm, and collected—and work throughout the day without interruption. If so, would you consider it?

I'm no tease. There really *is* a way to do what you want, when and how you want, and get paid for it to boot. It's simple and practical. Here's the concept: Move the work instead of the worker. Freelancing is the wave of the future. Hear the buzz? All over the country, all sorts of people are working at home. They are freelancers.

Bet You Didn't Know

The term "freelance" likely comes from the Free Companies of the Middle Ages (*condottieri* in Italian; *compagnies grandes* in French), which were free and willing to lend themselves to any master and any cause, good or bad. Today's freelancers, by contrast, have the luxury of being a great deal more discriminating.

Bet You Didn't Know

According to government labor statistics, in the first three quarters of 1993 (the most recent year for which statistics are available), one out of every five new jobs added to the economy was created by people who put themselves to work.

Making the Break

Like many young, bright, and ambitious New York professionals, Pete had his sights set on a corner office, private assistant, and six-figure salary. To that end, every morning he took the subway from Brooklyn to Manhattan, standing Gucci to Gucci with other yuppies, working drones, and a few assorted creeps. When conditions were favorable—no water-main breaks, no panhandlers who hadn't bathed since the Roosevelt administration—Pete made it to the advertising office in about an hour. So what if he had to stand up all the way? So what if the subway was as steamy as a Turkish bath? Hey, it was a cheap way to sweat off a few pounds and Pete *was* getting a little porky, thanks to pizza grabbed on the run. Like other upwardly mobile young professionals, Pete was willing to endure his bruising commute for the sake of his Future.

Then he fell in love with Liz, another bright young thing with a shining future. Unlike Pete, Liz was a West Coast native. She hailed from Seattle, home of designer coffee, constant drizzle, and Birkenstocks. For Pete's sake, Liz left her damp but hospitable home to come to the Big Apple. As a compromise, the two bought a cute starter house in Long Island for a mere $250,000.

"What I did for love," said Liz. The couple now paid more than $4,000 a year to commute on the Long Island Railroad. "It made my subway commute seem like a piece of cake," said Pete. They had to buy a car to get them to the railroad station. Bills mounted.

Soon the strain of rising before the sun and returning home long after it had set took its toll on Pete and Liz. Pete was the first to make the break: He left his job and started his own freelance advertising company. For years, Pete had been designing flyers and promotional campaigns for local real estate firms, businesses, and individuals. "I had a state-of-the-art computer, some nifty software, and a small client roster. It was time to make the break—before I broke," Pete said. Liz left her job as a tech writer shortly thereafter to accept some freelance writing and editing assignments. The couple moved to Seattle, where they happily work at home. Life is sweet for Liz and Pete. It can be for you, too.

Learn the Lingo

What is...

➤ The most important social movement since the rise of the two-wage-earner family?

➤ The fastest-growing segment of the American job market?

➤ Estimated to increase by 50 percent (50 percent!) in the next six years?

It's freelancing.

Just because you're paranoid doesn't mean they're not out to get you. And just because a business trend has been hyped to death doesn't mean it isn't happening, maybe even faster than you imagine. An estimated 20 million Americans now make their living primarily as freelancers. What's a freelancer? Read on, buckaroo.

 **Bet You Didn't Know**

According to information gathered during the latest U.S. Census, about 33 percent of the U.S. work force is self-employed.

The Name of the Game

"When are you going to get a *real* job?" people often ask me. More than any other career, freelancing suffers from an identity crisis. Many people don't understand what sets a freelancer apart from any other worker. Sometimes even freelancers themselves have trouble trying to describe what they do.

How can you tell if someone is a freelancer? How are freelancers different from garden-variety everyday workers? How are they the same? I could argue that all workers are freelancers, given the state of the world today. I could also argue that baseball needs the designated hitter, all colas are the same, and pizza tastes best cold. But freelancing *is* different from everyday-ordinary-commonplace working.

Take a look at the following definitions. Which ones do you agree with? Circle the best definition of freelancing.

Freelancing is...

➤ Going to work in your jammies

➤ Using your cat as a paperweight

➤ Juggling on a tightrope without a net

➤ Nothing that a little Prozac wouldn't cure

➤ Working as a knowledge worker (writer, editor, accountant, etc.) or service provider under your own direction, finding your own work, and often but not always working at home.

They're all true, but the last one is the most complete definition: A freelancer is a knowledge worker or service provider who works under his or her own direction, finds his or her own work, and often but not always works at home. Another key ingredient is independence. A freelancer, according to Webster's, is "a person who acts independently, without being affiliated with…an organization; a person who pursues a profession without a long-term commitment to any one employer."

Most freelancers sell services rather than products. Here are three other ways to distinguish freelancing from a more easily understood career choice.

Freelancing is usually…

1. A one-person occupation, although some freelancers do hire assistants and other support staff

2. A home-based business

3. An unincorporated sole proprietorship, although some freelancers do incorporate (see Part 4 for a complete rundown on the legal business structure for freelancers)

Unlike small independent contractors, freelancers rarely want their business to grow to the point where they have to take on other employees and need an outside office. Most freelancers want to make money and keep busy, but they don't dream of creating their own corporate empire—in fact, getting away from those pressures is exactly why they've become freelancers in the first place.

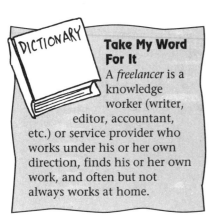

Take My Word For It

A *freelancer* is a knowledge worker (writer, editor, accountant, etc.) or service provider who works under his or her own direction, finds his or her own work, and often but not always works at home.

As you move from working for Big Daddy or Big Mama to working for yourself as a freelancer, the very nature of "work" changes in these five ways:

1. *What* you do

2. *Where* you do it

3. *When* you do it

4. *How* you do it

5. *For whom* you do it

So you're sure you'll know freelancing when you see it, I've charted some examples of the difference between working for others and freelancing:

Working for Others	Freelancing
Work is done by the clock	Work is done on your schedule
Hours are fixed	Hours are flexible
Schedule is fixed	Schedule matches the work
Workload tends to be constant	Workload varies
Work location is prescribed	Work location can vary
Work task is specific	Work task can vary
Job description defines role	Task defines role
Work and home are separate	Work and home are integrated
Work is monitored	Work is independent
Behavior at work is constrained by office ethic	Behavior at work is whatever you want it to be

A Rose by Any Other Name

Like the performer formerly known as Prince, the name for a freelancer has changed over the years. Once called independent contractors, today's freelancers have many different handles. Below is a list of some of the trendy terms for a freelancer. Put a check next to the ones you think best describe your personality.

```
_____    1. Consultant

_____    2. Contingency worker

_____    3. Contractor

_____    4. Free agent

_____    5. Lone eagle

_____    6. Lone ranger

_____    7. Lone wolf

_____    8. Open-collar worker

_____    9. Soloist

_____   10. Solo operator

_____   11. Telecommuter

_____   12. Teleworker (for the electronically savvy, especially in Europe)

_____   13. Virtual employee

_____   14. Virtual-business owner (very cool right now)

_____   15. Other (any handles *you* know?)
```

Mind Your Own Business

As independent agents, freelancers are free to accept as many assignments as they can complete, as long as they are not engaged in any conflicts of interest. For example, it is unethical for a freelance writer to work on competing projects, such as two books on the same topic for different publishers.

Home Alone

According to an article in the *New York Times*, about 7 million people telecommute at least one day a week, up from 4 million five years ago.

A Fine Line

The line between the employed and the self-employed is blurring as both large and small companies move away from the traditional nine-to-five-in-a-suit workplace. For example, more and more employees are *telecommuting*—working from home at least part of the time, tethered to an office by their phone and computer. They may look like freelancers as they shuffle to their desks in their bathrobes and furry slippers, but they aren't. In contrast to freelancers, most telecommuters work exclusively for one company. They remain on the company payroll, receive full medical and retirement benefits, and are expected to accomplish a set amount of work per day or week.

Many freelancers do use telecommuting tools, such as a computer, modem, and electronic mail. However, unlike freelancers, telecommuters usually get a fixed salary and corporate benefits. Freelancers are independent; telecommuters, in contrast, are tethered to the mother ship by a cable.

Who Are These People?

In the past, freelancers traditionally worked in the arts, such as acting, writing, or painting. There was also a small, hardy band of freelancers with intriguing occupations, the kind of work that led your parents to scream, "You're going to marry a man who makes beaded sandals/hand-dipped candles/homemade incense for a living? Over my dead body." Such freelancers were buying into a lifestyle as much as a career. They were happy to live on love, supplemented with a few handfuls of nuts and berries.

Like their more free-spirited kin of yesteryear, many of today's freelancers want to escape the highly structured and organized world of corporate business. They are likely to be independent people who don't like to take orders from others.

But there *are* some important differences between today's freelancers and freelancers of the past generation. While some of today's freelancers are indeed holdovers from the '60s, the contemporary freelancer is more apt to have the following characteristics:

➤ Businesslike

➤ Profit-oriented

➤ Well-organized

➤ Technologically literate

➤ Ambitious

➤ Enterprising

➤ Versatile

Today, more and more freelancers are techies who have escaped the corporate cocoon, such as accountants and computer specialists. There's also a generous helping of other professionals, such as lawyers. Even some medical professionals, traditionally not known as independent types, have turned to freelancing as they find their own work on a short-term basis.

The World's My Oyster

Today's freelancers are an amazingly diverse lot, working in nearly all fields. Here are some of the careers the "new" freelancers have entered:

➤ Accountants

➤ Attorneys

➤ Commercial artists

➤ Computer consultants

➤ Doctors

➤ Environmental engineers

➤ Fashion designers

➤ Financial advisors

➤ Insurance underwriters

➤ Librarians

➤ Media experts

➤ Nurses

➤ Nutritionists

➤ Personal trainers

➤ Photographers

➤ Professional shoppers

➤ Public relations specialists

➤ Real estate agents

➤ Security personnel

➤ Speech pathologists

➤ Technical writers

➤ Telecommunications advisors

➤ Telemarketers

➤ Word processors

Home Alone
Thanks to computers and other cutting-edge office technology, many new opportunities to freelance now exist. Many tasks that ten years ago had to be done in an office can now be done faster—and better—at home.

As with their ancient brethren, today's freelancers lend their experience and expertise to a particular job, but don't pledge their personal allegiance to a particular employer. When the job is over, they move on to the next position. And usually quite happily.

Free to Be You and Me

Freelancers can work as much or as little as they like.

Depending on the state of his or her trust fund, charge card balance, and children's orthodontics, a freelancer may decide to work 65 hours one week, but only 20 hours the next week. For example, I may decide to take a week to learn to tango, weed the lower forty, and hang the wallpaper. (As you can tell, I am a woman of not inconsiderable talents.) The next week, however, it's back to the grindstone to make up the time (and money) from the previous week off.

A freelancer's work schedule also depends on how much work is sitting in the *in* basket. Sometimes a freelancer doesn't have the luxury of taking a day off, much less a week, because the work is piled up higher than Newt's ego. Other times, however, there's not enough work to fill the day. More on getting work and allocating tasks in Chapters 8 and 19.

How It All Adds Up

According to legend, freelancers were knights who were not allied to any particular king. Instead, they hired out their lance—their services—to a prince in need.

Today, freelancers are still the hired guns, the independent employees you call when you need a job done. Who's a typical freelancer? Here's the inside skinny, according to *U.S. News and World Report*:

Male	53%
Female	47%
Average age	42.9 years
College graduate	44%
Married	85%
With children under 18	54%

How do freelancers fit when it comes to dollars and cents? According to a government survey, the median household income for freelancers is $55,100. Not bad for someone who has chucked Armani for Adidas.

No one does chicken like the Colonel, and no one does statistics like Uncle Sam. Here's the government's latest count of all self-employed workers, including home-based business people, farmers, and others:

Year	Number of Workers
1992	10,017,000
1993	10,335,000
1994	10,648,000
1995	10,482,000

Source: U.S. Bureau of the Census, Statistical Abstract of the United States.

Some private research firms have come up with considerably higher figures. One placed the number of primarily self-employed workers at around 14,200,000!

 **Bet You Didn't Know**

About 46 percent of all freelancers describe themselves as white-collar workers; 22 percent describe themselves as blue-collar workers; and 32 percent describe themselves as somewhere in-between. (IDC/Link)

Job growth in the category of self-employment increased at twice the rate of overall job growth through most of 1993 in the U.S. It's a change felt 'round the world. StatsCan, a Canadian statistical service, found that 2.2 million Canadians earned at least some income from self-employment in 1994, a 5.9 percent jump over the previous year.

But statistics don't tell the whole story. The actual number of freelancers may be much higher than the numbers suggest. That's because many employees freelance on the side for extra income; a fact they may prefer not to mention to statisticians (or the tax man).

Declare Your Independence

In 1776, Thomas Paine wrote a pamphlet titled *Common Sense* that helped convince the American colonists to revolt. Some of those free-spirited revolutionaries had more in common with today's freelancers than you might suppose. Take the simple quiz on the next page to see how much you know about the history of freelancing. Write *true* if you think the statement is true or *false* if you think it is false.

_____ 1. Freelancing is not a new movement.

_____ 2. Until the 1800s, most people lived on farms or in small villages.

_____ 3. Most workers made products in their homes; most service providers worked out of their homes.

_____ 4. The term "cottage industry" describes a work arrangement between a home-based worker and a company owner.

_____ 5. Under the cottage industry system, the company owner supplied the raw materials and the freelancer created the product at home.

_____ 6. In most cases, the freelancer could accept or reject work and was considered an independent contractor.

_____ 7. The Industrial Revolution of the 19th century initially spurred large growth in cottage industries.

_____ 8. By the early 1900s, better machines and assembly-line production led to the centralization of business within factories.

_____ 9. The cottage industry became uncommon, relegated to secondary income and pursuit of hobbies.

_____ 10. In the past 30 years, the structure of our economy has changed from an industrial base to a service and informational base.

_____ 11. As we entered the Computer Age, people found that the computer offered more freedom not only in the workplace, but also outside of it.

_____ 12. Home-based work is once again on the upswing.

Answers

Every statement is true.

Obviously, freelancing is nothing new. What *is* new, however, is the way freelancing is changing the face of the contemporary world. Increasingly, people are looking for a way to once again integrate their work with their lives—so they can have a life.

The Least You Need to Know

➤ A freelancer is a knowledge worker (writer, editor, accountant, etc.) or service provider who works under his or her own direction, finds his or her own work, and often but not always works at home.

➤ Freelancing is usually a one-person occupation, although some freelancers do hire assistants and other support staff.

➤ Today's freelancers are working in all fields, from the arts to technology.

➤ Thomas Jefferson envisioned a nation of independent merchants and workers. Today's freelancers are their heirs.

Chapter 2

Nightmare on Wall Street

In This Chapter

➤ Explore the new economic realities

➤ Find out how people react to them

➤ Learn why people choose freelancing: crisis, chance, choice

➤ Read some first-hand accounts of the freelance revolution

There was this fella with a parrot. The parrot swore like a sailor—a real pistol. The parrot could swear for five minutes straight without repeating himself. Unfortunately, the man who owned the parrot was a quiet, conservative type and the bird's foul mouth was driving him crazy.

One day, the parrot's blue streak got to be too much for its owner, so the guy grabbed the bird by the throat, shook it really hard, and yelled, "Quit it!" This just infuriated the bird and it swore more colorfully than ever.

The man said, "Okay, you—this is it!" and locked the bird in a kitchen cabinet. This infuriated the bird even more, so it clawed and scratched the wood. When the man finally released the bird, our fowl friend cut loose with a stream of vulgarities that would make a long-distance trucker blush.

At that point, the man was so angry that he threw the bird into the freezer. For the first few seconds there was a terrible din. The parrot kicked, clawed, and thrashed. Then the room suddenly got very quiet. At first the man just waited, but soon he got worried. What if the parrot was hurt?

After a few minutes of silence, the man was so worried that he opened up the freezer door. The parrot calmly climbed onto the man's arm and said, "Awfully sorry about the trouble I gave you. I'll do my best to improve my vocabulary from now on."

The man was astonished at the bird's transformation. Then the parrot said, "By the way, what did the chicken do?"

Are you feeling like the chicken, bunky? Does it seem like you've been frozen out of the career action? If so, you're not alone. That's what this chapter is all about.

What's Wrong With This Picture?

Quick—what do the following 14 terms have in common? Write your answer on the line provided.

---

1. Downsized

2. Restructured

3. Reengineered

4. Made redundant

5. Terminated

6. Dehired

7. Correct-sized

8. Rightsized

9. Selected out

10. Vocationally relocated

11. Payroll adjusted

12. Pink-slipped

13. Constructively dismissed

14. Given a career-change opportunity

These words all mean _____

The answer? Every one of these 14 terms means the same thing: *fired, canned, given the boot, dumped, kicked out, sent packing.* It means you're out on your ear, walking the line, collecting unemployment (if you're lucky). The enormous rise in job losses today has resulted in new terms to soften the harsh reality: people are losing their jobs and having trouble finding new ones.

Here are some facts to consider:

> ➤ In the past two years, there have been over ten million layoffs. (*New York Times*)

> ➤ During 1992, Fortune 500 companies slashed 50,000 jobs a month, mostly in middle management. (*New York Times*)

> ➤ In 1994, Dun & Bradstreet counted over 70,000 companies that went under with a loss to creditors. These failing companies left nearly $30 billion in unpaid bills and threw thousands of people into the unemployment lines.

Home Alone
Early (or forced) retirement is the reason some people turn to freelancing. Others decide to freelance because their spouse has a job that moves them around a lot, like fast-track corporate executives or military personnel.

> ➤ Nearly half of all workers witness layoffs in their own workplace every year. (*New York Times*)

> ➤ A growing number of traditional industries are simply going away and aren't coming back. (*U.S. News and World Report*)

> ➤ According to the *New York Times*, a young male high school graduate earns the equivalent of 30 percent less on a job today than his counterpart earned in 1979.

> ➤ Forty percent of workers say their employers expect them to work an unreasonable number of overtime hours. (*New York Times*)

> ➤ According to a number of studies, workers have a third less time for leisure and family activities than they did in 1969. (*Newsweek*)

The term *corporate anorexia* was coined to described the debilitating business disease resulting from excessive belt tightening. Some companies have trimmed so much fat that their ribs are showing.

Fear and Loathing

When my friend Lewis Morgan started looking for work in 1976, he expected his career to have some standard components: a job, an office, and a boss. Raises would be reliable, promotions routine. "My dad worked in the same company for 40 years," Lewis said. "That's pretty much what I expected to do." That was before Lewis was laid off from corporate jobs three times. Lewis is not a happy camper. He's suffering from a bad case of economic anxiety, a generalized fear that his head is going to appear on the chopping block next.

Take My Word For It
There's a term for our free-floating career worries: *economic anxiety.*

Home Alone
Some 2.3 million temps now head off to work every day, twice as many as four years ago. (*Newsweek*)

When did "economic anxiety" become the emotional bumper sticker for our coast-to-coast collective consciousness? Was it in March of 1996 when the *New York Times* ran a solid week of front-page stories on the downsizing of America? Was it the pictures of the ex-executives suddenly unable to pay their mortgages? Or does our pervasive job terror harken back to 1993, when employment-for-life missionary IBM announced its first ever five-digit layoffs? Was this when we began to feel the fear in the pit of our bellies, to realize that unemployment could happen to anyone?

By now the crisis of worker confidence is as omnipresent as the daily news, in headlines that glare at us every waking moment of every day. Corporate downsizing, mergers, and other belt-tightening measures leave us with a loss of jobs that seems like a hemorrhage. How many times have you seen stats like these?

➤ 37,000 jobs were cut every month in 1995.

➤ During the past two years, the seven regional telephone companies slashed about 125,000 jobs, on top of the 40,000 job cuts at AT&T.

➤ Real wages have fallen from a 1979 average of $24,000 for a high-school graduate to a 1995 average of $18,000.

➤ On any given day, more than 11 million workers report that they are not satisfied with their jobs.

➤ According to the U.S. Department of Labor, from now until the year 2025, college graduates will outnumber jobs available to them by 20 percent each year. (*Newsweek*)

People feel betrayed by the country's economy and its effect on real wage levels. The dire situation led former State Senator Bill Bradley to write: "Economic anxiety eats away at people who work in America." For laid-back ol' Bradley, this is the equivalent of pushing the panic button.

Bet You Didn't Know

Which jobs are most likely to lead to layoffs and bankruptcy? The riskiest industries (in order of risk) are coal mining, miscellaneous business services, holding companies, fishing, and apparel manufacturing. So don't start a freelance business that involves mining for fish in designer jeans. (*Newsweek*)

The Blame Game

Our parents believed in the American Dream, the notion that living standards will forever rise, that we'll do better than our parents, and that our children will do better than us.

Some say the dream is ailing; some say it's kicked the bucket. "The so-called security of a paycheck is an illusion," reports one worker. "Either you're answering what the market needs or you're not. If you're not, you're doomed, whether you're in an office at AT&T or an office in your basement."

The news stories lay the blame for our career uncertainty squarely at the feet of Big Business. Politicians and policy makers are quick to agree. When he was labor secretary, Robert Reich asserted that the implied social contract between employer and employee "has become undone" and must once again be knitted up. Elected officials have created legislation to once again get business to pull its weight.

I'm OK, but You're Really Screwed

According to a poll conducted by *U.S. News and World Report*, a person's age greatly influences how he or she reacts to today's career uncertainty. The survey revealed that younger workers are considerably more worried about their futures than their elders. For example, 55 percent of all workers under the age of 30 believe that Social Security will go bankrupt—but only 15 percent of workers over the age of 50 share their concern. Likewise, 24 percent of all workers under the age of 30 believe that Medicare won't pay their medical benefits, but only 5 percent of workers over the age of 50 are equally convinced that they'll be in the hole for their medical costs.

Younger workers these days realize that their working lives will be a patchwork of jobs, projects, and skills-gathering junkets. Most people find this a daunting prospect. Today, jobs come and go according to a company's changing needs. Now, this is fine for the company—but not so great for its employees, current as well as former.

As one disgruntled job seeker complained, "It seems that today there are three kinds of jobs: temporary, part-time, and overtime." Says William Bridges, author of *JobShifts: How to Prosper in a Workplace Without Jobs,* "Everyone is a contingent worker." The vast unknown breeds vast distress.

Bet You Didn't Know

In 1994, the most recent year for which statistics are available, the states with the highest number of business failures were California, Arizona, Washington, Maryland, and Nevada, respectively. (1997 *World Almanac*)

Stressed and Pressed

Paradoxically, even though it takes a college education to earn a good living these days, even college graduates aren't always finding jobs commensurate with their education and expectations.

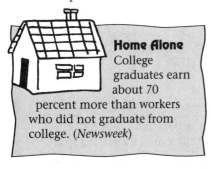

Home Alone
College graduates earn about 70 percent more than workers who did not graduate from college. (*Newsweek*)

But those who are fortunate enough to find full-time jobs aren't doing so well, either. They're putting in more hours, but they're getting fewer benefits and smaller raises. For many workers, the traditional 40-hour work week has become the 50-hour work week—or more. Executives put in an average of 60 hours a week.

But despite all the hours that people are working, the dollars aren't stretching far enough. Check out these facts, courtesy of *Newsweek*:

➤ One-third of all adults surveyed report they are having trouble paying their monthly bills.

➤ Three-quarters have trouble saving for their children's educations.

➤ Half have trouble saving for retirement.

Life on the Edge

Many single and two-career parents complain that they feel like one-armed paperhangers, hanging on by their fingernails. Chew on these stats, boys and girls:

➤ The average working parent has only 30 seconds a day of meaningful conversation with his or her child.

➤ Working couples have only four minutes of meaningful conversation with each other every day.

➤ Every day, 1,600,000 children ages 5 to 14 are left alone after school.

➤ Half a million children start their day without adult supervision. (Priority Management, Pittsburgh)

It's no wonder that we worry about our children and their future.

Inquiring Minds Want to Know

What do workers want? Based on a survey by the Gallup organization, the most critical factors in employees' satisfaction and job performance are the following:

Workers want...

1. To know that their jobs are important.
2. To use their skills and training to the utmost.
3. Materials and equipment to do their job properly.
4. Their jobs and concerns to be taken seriously.
5. Supervisors who care about them as people.
6. Opportunities to learn and grow.

It's clear that many workers aren't getting their needs met in the current economic climate—even if they have secure jobs. Thanks to cartoonist Scott Adams, we have a brand-new term for the misery that many people suffer at the hands of corporate tyrants: "Dilberted."

There are times when you have to cut your losses, even if your job is secure. No matter how ably you cope, dealing with the constant upheavals caused by a difficult boss, for instance, can become exhausting.

> **Take My Word For It**
> The term *Dilberted* has been coined to describe the state a worker is in after being abused by a cruel and capricious boss.

By the way, want to know what your supervisor is really saying about you in all those glowing performance evaluations? Here's a key to the secret meaning of the ten most frequently used terms. Has anyone said any of these about *you* lately?

Evaluation Term	Real Meaning
Character above reproach	One step ahead of the law
Spends extra hours on job	Miserable home life
Conscientious and careful	Terrified
Judgment is usually sound	Lucky
Enjoys job	Needs more to do
Average	Not too bright
Keen sense of humor	Knows a lot of dirty jokes
Happy	Overpaid
Will go far	Relative of management
Should go far	As far as possible, please

You Can Get There From Here

As stomach-churning as the economic news is, for those of you who want more autonomy, more flexibility, and more opportunity in your lives, these grim statistics can have a silver lining. Every layoff means that more work will be contracted to outside sources. You guessed it—that means freelancers. Some companies are actually laying off entire departments, whose functions will be contracted out. By crisis, chance, or choice, people can fashion new and better work for themselves.

Crisis

When writer Paula Hartz lost her job with a major Manhattan publishing firm, she decided to take three months off to enjoy New York. But things turned out differently. Here's her story in her own words:

> *As soon as the news got around that I was unemployed, people started offering me work. I did one freelance job, and when that was over, I thought "now I'll take those three months off," but the next day someone called with another freelance job. After about six months of this, one of the headhunters I'd registered with called. My heart just sank. I didn't want to go back to work full time. First of all, I'd learned that without the distractions of an office, I could do eight hours of work in five or six. I could make my own schedule. I certainly didn't miss office politics: An awful lot of my energy had been going into being nice to people I despised. People were just nicer to freelancers—they were grateful for the work I did! And said so! (As opposed to one of my last bosses, who, when told that people needed to feel appreciated, growled, "They're getting paychecks, aren't they?")*

Chance

Janice Race's decision to become a freelancer came about by chance rather than crisis:

My very first freelance job was given to me by Austin, my former employer. He flew in from Chicago one day, and we met for dinner, as we always did when he came into town. During dinner, he offered me a job writing two lessons for the reading program he was heading up. The work had to be done over a weekend; however, it paid $2,000. I was apprehensive because up until that point I had been a staff editor. I had never actually done a lot of writing.

Austin was full of encouragement and assured me I could do it. As I look back, I realize that he didn't care much how good my writing was, just that I get it done on time...which I did, and collected my check. That gave me the push to seriously consider freelancing.

Choice

Todd's move into the freelance life was a matter of choice. Employed as an artist by a major firm, he decided that it was time to make the break. Here's his story:

After years of working at the same job, I just got fed up. One grim morning, I thought, "There has to be a better life. I don't want to grow old in this job." I had enough of smelly subways, capricious delays, and office politics. At least half my job was making sure other people knew what I was doing. Some days, I spent most of my time blowing my own horn rather than working. Fortunately, my boss was understanding and gave me some freelance lettering and coloring assignments to get me started. Soon I had other clients, too. Even though I was making less, I was living better. No more commuting costs, $3 cups of coffee, and fancy clothing.

The Least You Need to Know

➤ Many Americans fear they will lose their job—with good cause.

➤ Most people these days can't expect to have a traditional, one-job career.

➤ For a growing number of people, freelancing provides a viable alternative to the no-longer-viable expectation of corporate job security.

➤ Many of those people find they are much happier as freelancers than they ever were working for someone else.

Chapter 3

It's Half Full: The Upside

> ### In This Chapter
>
> ➤ Test your FQ (freelancing quotient) to see how much you know about freelancing
>
> ➤ Discover the advantages of being a freelancer
>
> ➤ Learn how freelancers feel about their lifestyle

Just imagine. Your commute is cut to the time it takes to walk from the bedroom to your home office in the extension off the kitchen. For work, you dress in jeans and a T-shirt—sometimes even in a bathrobe. You can take a break whenever you want to jog around the block, pick up the kids, or call your mother. (You *do* call your mother, don't you?) And you never have to take time off to wait for a delivery to arrive.

The prospect of being a freelancer is so alluring that more than 12 million Americans have decided to do it. Being a freelancer has become the pet fantasy of millions of workers dismayed by glass ceilings, corporate layoffs, and paper-thin annual raises. In this chapter, find out what a career as a freelancer can offer you.

To Dream the Possible Dream

Every day it's the same thing: beating your head against the wall trying to earn a living—and hating just about every minute of it. Perhaps your job doesn't allow you to use many of your talents and capabilities, and you've become more tightly wound than the inside of a good Swiss watch. You need some space to stretch out and test your abilities. Freelancing can give you that space.

But before you jump ship, it's not a bad idea to put a toe in the water. How much do you know about freelancing? Find out now. For each statement, write *T* if you think the statement is true and *F* if you think the statement is false.

____ 1. If you run your freelance career in a professional way, you have a better than 50 percent chance of making enough money to support yourself comfortably.

____ 2. As a freelancer, there's theoretically no limit to how much money you can earn.

____ 3. In general, freelancers have more freedom than staff workers to turn down unwanted assignments.

____ 4. Freelancers can often plan their own work schedule. This is great for people who don't do well by temperament in the 9-to-5 mold.

____ 5. Freelancers don't have to worry about commuting and dress codes.

____ 6. As a freelancer, you don't have a supervisor to criticize your work.

____ 7. Freelancers set their own company policies.

____ 8. You can establish your own vacation and holiday schedule as a freelancer.

____ 9. As a freelancer, you can work in more than one field at a time, if you choose.

____ 10. Your family life will very often be better if you freelance than work a staff job.

Bonus: If you work at home, you don't face the prospect that every nut case in the city will try to sit next to you on the subway.

Answers

1. T	6. T
2. T	7. T
3. T	8. T
4. T	9. T
5. T	10. T

Bet You Didn't Know

According to *Newsweek*, about 30 percent of adult workers—40 million people—have never owned a business but dream of starting one. About 19 percent of those dreamers—nearly 8 million people—are currently in the process of going freelance. They are setting up contacts, learning new skills, and planning to quit their day jobs soon.

Do we see a pattern here, kiddos? Freelancing has a lot going for it, which is why so many people are flocking to it. Let's look at what freelancing can offer *you*.

Whose Life Is It Anyway?

I can't say how much the flexibility of freelancing has meant to me. Not long after I started freelancing, a friend of mine became seriously ill. I was able to adjust my schedule to nurse him, and that was worth more to me than any paycheck. That doesn't mean that I shirk deadlines to go off skylarking—I take my work seriously indeed. But sometimes personal priorities are more important than editing the next grammar lesson, and companies don't recognize that.

—Paula Hartz, freelance writer

Mind Your Own Business
Talent alone doesn't cut it in the freelance biz. Clients look for cheerfulness, dependability, promptness, and honesty. Think about it: If you have a choice between hiring someone who acts like they're doing you a big favor and someone who's cooperative and pleasant, who you gonna call?

People who become freelancers want a measure of control over their lives, a control that neither a job with a small company or a huge one will usually allow. When you become your own boss, you set the schedule for the number of hours you work every day and the days you work. You can adjust the schedule to suit your own needs. For example, you might stumble out of bed at 5:00 AM, get to work immediately, and wrap up before the kids get home from school. Or you can work a normal day until 3:00 PM, pick up the kids from school, stuff their faces with nutritious junk food, play a round of Super Mario Brothers, and make up the work time after they are tucked into bed.

Mind Your Own Business
As a freelancer, you may not actually have the total freedom you dream of. Remember, if you're not there for your clients in August, they may not be there for you in September.

Although I have children, I have always been a big fan of sleep. As a result, I trained my kids not to wake me up in the morning unless there's some national celebration, such as double coupons at the supermarket or a Mel Gibson sighting in the neighborhood. I like to start work at 9:00 AM, a most civilized hour, pound away until noon, and then enjoy a leisurely lunch. After lunch I try to take a walk for an hour, and then it's back to the keyboard until about 4:00 or 5:00. We do the dinner thing together as a family and very often I will be back in my office until 9:00 or 10:00, when I try to break for some mindless TV. If I'm on a roll, it's not uncommon for me to go back to work at 11:00 and keep going for another hour or so. Reread this carefully, kiddies, and you'll see that I work a *very* long day. Not all freelancers are as compulsive.

Home Alone
Since you are your own boss, the harder you work, the better you'll eat.

Many unmarried freelancers and married freelancers without offspring report having time to pursue a wide range of outside activities, including evenings at the opera, spiritual pursuits, and hobbies. A close friend of mine in the freelance biz is passionately involved in theater: He attends a Broadway or off-Broadway show at least five nights a week. In addition, he is a part-time performer. Another freelancer finds that her career affords her the time to pursue her religion. Still another is the finest pastry chef I've ever met. She turns out succulent fruit pies, creamy cheesecakes, and outrageous cookies that I generously devour for her.

Live Free or Die

As a person who grew up in a blue-collar community, all I heard was "Get a job with a big company, a good company. Civil service is great, too." That lifestyle never suited me. Fortunately, being a freelancer is much more culturally acceptable now than it was in the past.

—Sam Harris, freelance textile designer

Along with flexibility comes independence. To be able to work at home with no outside interference is a goal that many Americans cherish. As a freelancer, you make all the business decisions. You don't have to call central supply to requisition a new piece of office equipment or fill out a hundred forms (in triplicate) to order a new printer cartridge. You'll be in charge of deciding what you need and when. As a freelancer, the buck stops with you.

And Baby Makes Overload

The final straw came the evening my three-year-old son said, "Mommy, I swallowed a battery." "Battery, what battery?" I asked. "Was it a watch battery, a toy battery?" I found myself yelling. My son didn't know. After an evening in the emergency room and a round of x-rays, we discovered that he had not swallowed a battery. He had not swallowed anything. He had imagined the whole thing. By now, it was 3:00 AM. I was so wiped out with worry and fatigue that I couldn't function for a week. That's when I decided something had to give with my career—before I gave out.

— A convert to the freelance side

Family concerns are frequently cited as a reason to go freelance. I was typical of the many women in the workplace who struggled to juggle the conflicting demands of office and family. As with many of the freelancers I interviewed for this book, I discovered that running a household and maintaining an office-bound career is more difficult than it appears at first glance, second glance, and third glance. It's harder than sitting through reruns of *The Brady Bunch*, getting out of the Department of Motor Vehicles in under an hour, or flying coach with children.

As the following statistics show, this juggling act is only going to intensify.

➤ According to the latest U.S. Census figures, more than 70 percent of all mothers in two-parent households have jobs outside the home.

➤ According to a report by the Families and Work Institute (a nonprofit research and planning organization in New York City), between now and the year 2000, nearly 75 percent of all women entering the U.S. workplace will become mothers for the first time.

Some freelancers strike out on their own right after their children are born; some try to stick it out after the stork arrives, but find out within a few years that working 80-hour weeks and raising a family is less fun than a root canal without anesthesia. Juggling baby, toddler, or teen and a full-time office job quickly loses its charm.

Eager Beavers

Freelancers often cite increased productivity as one of the big pluses to working at home. This efficiency lets freelancers earn more money in less time. Here are two big reasons why:

➤ Freelancers are not as likely to be interrupted at home as they are in the office. No one "takes a meeting" at home, has any "face time" (the new term for face-to-face meetings with someone), or does a two-hour lunch.

➤ Freelancers can get a lot more done because they're not losing time commuting long distances.

 **Bet You Didn't Know**

According to *Time*, if a fraction of Los Angeles' carbound commuters, just 5 percent, worked at home one day a week, they would wind up driving 205 million fewer miles every year.

Variety Is the Spice of Life

When I lost my fourth banking job to industry mergers, I took a battery of assessment tests. The results led a counselor to suggest that I target jobs in technical writing and editing. This field would let me use my facility with words as well as my background in information technology. I decided the time was right to make a break to freelancing.

I called some friends and former colleagues and told them I was looking for work as a tech writer. A few months later, a company specializing in interactive videos hired me to write some manuals for CD-ROMs. This led to more jobs, including some from my former employers. My jobs have included manuals for many different products. I love the variety of my work!

—A freelance technical writer

Unlike most static office jobs, freelancing can offer tremendous variety. This is true even if you stay within one field. For example, I'm a freelance writer. That's just one job, yet within this field I've been able to explore the following different areas:

➤ English, language arts, grammar, usage, style

➤ Multimedia, including CD-ROMs and animation

➤ Science

➤ Math

➤ Foreign languages

➤ History

➤ Antiques and collectibles

➤ Public speaking

➤ Consumer economics

➤ Relationships and dating

➤ Educational theory

Home Alone
If possible, try to leave some work unfinished when you break for the day. That way, it's much easier to get started the next morning, since you're just picking up where you left off.

Each time I explore a new field of writing, I have to do research—which often leads to other areas to pursue.
Sometimes I take courses, especially where new technology is concerned. This year alone, I've taken four mini-courses on using the Internet. As a result, my job is anything but dull!

Know Thyself

This variety has another payoff: It helps you learn what you do and don't like to do. As you complete different jobs and tasks, you refine your interests as well as abilities. You'll see that your interests often change as you mature, too. Sometimes, even the worst freelance job can have unexpected positive benefits. Here's one freelancer's story:

> *Freelance jobs from Hell can definitely turn out to be positives. For instance, my Job from Hell caused me to reassess my priorities in life. To be more precise, it forced me to decide what role work played in my life. The Job was a pivotal one, for it did change my views and alter my behavior regarding work. After the Job I was even more selective than before of the assignments I would take. I realized that peace of mind and quality of life were more important than money. I also came to accept the fact that I didn't like managing, that the title of "manager" or "supervisor" was not all it was cracked up to be, because along with the title came more grief than I could ever be compensated for. I know that is contrary to the American way—climb the ladder of success and all. But, I don't care. I feel free because I am not a slave to money and I cannot be bought. I know who I am and what is important to me.*

Bet You Didn't Know

Successful freelancers report these three character traits:

1. I work well over the phone.

2. I like to control the pace of my work.

3. I enjoy working on my own.

There's No Place Like Home

How many times have you sat in the middle of a tornado in the office and wished that you could click your heels three times and return home? Working at home is like having an instant pair of ruby slippers.

When you're a home-based freelancer, you have all your favorite things— your couch, your recliner, your kitchen table, your refrigerator. You can play whatever music you want; you can turn the heat up and down at will. No more freezing in the summer and sweating in the winter.

Take a moment and list the six items that make you most comfortable at home. Which of these do you think you would place in your home office?

1. _____
2. _____
3. _____
4. _____
5. _____
6. _____

Here are my findings, based on a highly informal survey:

1. CD player/stereo/radio

2. TV with cable hookup

3. Plants, both real and artificial

4. Coffee maker

5. Personal pictures

6. Really good quality candy (stuff like Godiva that you'd never share with anyone in the office)

Working at home, there are none of the disadvantages of an often sterile office environment, with its paper-thin cubicle walls. Sometimes, you're not even allowed to decorate your office walls, or the Office Decor Police will cite you for making holes in the wall. Any deviation from office style can get you a citation for bad taste, too. And have you ever tried to make a private call from a cubicle? You're better off in a public phone booth in Penn Station. At least *there* no one pretends to ignore you!

Mind Your Own Business

Make your home office a room you want to be in. This makes it easier to motivate yourself to get to work every day.

Master of Your Domain

As we've seen, freelancing has a great many advantages over office-based work—advantages that can enrich your life in many ways. Your family life, personal satisfaction, and interpersonal relationships can all improve once the stress of commuting and office politics are removed. Here are a few more advantages to freelancing. Some may seem minor, but they all add up to one nice life, believe you me!

➤ You'll pay less in car insurance, thanks to no commuting.

➤ You'll have fewer days of misery in cold and flu season because no one is sneezing on you all day in the office.

➤ You'll have lower clothing bills since you're not dressing to impress. And the clothes you do buy can be the kind you actually *want* to wear.

➤ You'll have very pleasant lunches spent eating the delicious leftovers from dinner the night before while reading the newspaper. I do so like my lunch hour now!

➤ You'll be able to see doctors and dentists during the day. This saves hours of waiting time, since you'll no longer be a slave to crowded Saturday and evening hours.

Getting the message? Freelancing has a lot going for it. And I'll bet there's some special advantage I haven't even thought of that rosies up the glasses for you. But of course there's a downside. Read on to get some perspective back, you dreamer, you.

The Least You Need to Know

➤ Freelancing has many advantages, including flexibility, independence, and comfort.

➤ Many freelancers report increased productivity once they're on their own.

➤ Freelancing can improve your family life as well.

➤ Even if you stay in one field, freelancing can offer great variety.

➤ Freelancing has less flashy advantages, too, that combine to greatly improve your quality of life.

Chapter 4

It's Half Empty: The Downside

In This Chapter

➤ Discover the downside of freelancing

➤ Learn what upsets freelancers most

➤ Hear what happened to some hapless freelancers

Some days, being a freelancer can be about much fun as having a job with the Albanian Ministry of Tourism or doing business with the Gambino family.

You'll learn how difficult it can be to get a foothold in a freelance career and get the inside scoop on the long hours, the uneven work load, and the difficulty of maintaining a workable cash flow. Next, I'll describe the tsunami of record-keeping and paperwork and touch on the problem of setting up your own retirement account, medical insurance, and office insurance. Let's not forget the stress associated with keeping meticulous financial records, a task about as enjoyable as chewing aluminum foil. In addition, freelancing is a lonely occupation. But that's okay; freelancers are often so annoyed at one client or the other that they'd be lousy company anyway. Besides, most freelancers constantly worry about screwing things up. Ahh, the pleasures of being a freelancer!

Going It Alone

I love chocolate bars the size of national monuments, luxury vacations, and tabloid TV. But each of my passions has its downside: Chocolate is fattening, vacations are expensive, and trash TV rots my brain.

I love freelancing, too, but I also recognize that it has its downside. Freelancing can be lonely, frustrating, and just plain hard. After a day working, invoicing, and drumming up more business, my brain and backside hurt. I'm not alone in my love/hate relationship with freelancing. All freelancers experience this ambivalence toward their lifestyle.

 **Bet You Didn't Know**

No, silly, the Internet is not a fancy hairspray. Among other things, it *is* a great source of help for freelancers—newcomers as well as veterans. One new Web site called *About Work* (*http://www. aboutwork.com*) features discussions on such topics as changing careers, writing business plans, setting up a home office, and handling the kids while working at home. Whatever your problem, chances are you can find somebody somewhere on the Web who can help—or at least empathize.

In the previous chapter, you explored the upside of freelancing. Now, let's check out the flip side. How much do you know about the less delightful aspects of being a freelancer? For each statement, write *T* if you think the statement is true and *F* if you think the statement is false.

_____ 1. It can be very hard to get started in a freelance career.

_____ 2. Freelancers tend to work long hours, especially when they are first starting out on their own.

_____ 3. Many freelancers find that the workload is very uneven. They may work 90 hours one week and 20 the next. As a result, planning a life is as tricky as a New Age fruit bat channeling a 35,000-year-old sage named Ramtha.

_____ 4. Some freelancers experience difficulty maintaining a smooth cash flow. It's often economic feast or famine in the freelance biz.

_____ 5. Freelancers are often inundated with record-keeping and paperwork, sorta like December 26 at Toys R Us.

_____ 6. As a freelancer, you have to establish your own benefits package (retirement account, medical insurance, and so on).

_____ 7. You have to keep careful financial records for the IRS. You never know when Uncle Sam will come to visit.

_____ 8. Freelancing can be a lonely row to hoe alone. Many freelancers miss the camaraderie of office life, especially the easy give-and-take chatter of the lunchroom and water cooler.

_____ 9. Freelancers often lament their lack of control over their work—and with good cause. In truth, they often have very little control over it.

_____ 10. Freelancing carries a great deal of responsibility, because you're the head weenie at the roast. There's no one else to blame if things go up in smoke.

Answers

1. T	6. T
2. T	7. T
3. T	8. T
4. T	9. T
5. T	10. T

Score Yourself

All correct   You're on to me, aren't you?

6–9 correct   Still believe in the Tooth Fairy and the Easter Bunny, do we?

4–8 correct   May I borrow those rose-colored glasses? Mine have gotten a little cloudy.

1–3 correct   Is the glass half full, half empty, or half cracked?

Still haven't given up and thrown this book out the window? I'm not even warmed up yet. Hang on—and read on!

Playing With the Big Kids

Remember when you were a munchkin and you wanted to play with the big kids? Can't you still feel the butterflies setting up shop in your stomach as you gazed at the long shadows the big kids cast on the summer field? You never bothered to consider if the big kids were nice or nasty, or if they were really having any fun. *They* were the big kids and *you* were the runt.

Maybe you finally got to play and no one called you "squirt." Maybe you never screwed up the courage to approach them. The outcome isn't important—the lingering fear is. It's the same way you feel when you undertake any important venture, especially a major change in lifestyle such as a move from a staff position to freelancing. Let's look at this downside to freelancing and several other equally justified concerns, including the temptation to overwork, the seemingly endless record-keeping, and the bouts of loneliness.

The Cheese Stands Alone

Breaking into freelancing brings all your childhood anxiety bubbling back to the surface. Even though you're one of the big kids now, it's hard to forget what it felt like being the squirt. Besides, you're no fool; you know that if it were *that* easy to get started as a freelancer, everyone would be doing it. Hey, you bought this book in part to learn how to break into the business, didn't you?

Mind Your Own Business

The riskiest time in the life of a new business is the first five years. About 40 percent of all new businesses fail during this time. The number of failures drops to 27 percent in years 6–10 and rises to 33 percent after 10 years. (*Business Failure Record*, Dun & Bradstreet, 1995)

Getting started as a freelancer involves more than luck and pluck. What else do you need? Try these prerequisites:

➤ Training

➤ Talent (let's not fool ourselves)

➤ Equipment

➤ Connections (hey, they can't hurt)

➤ Desire

➤ Commitment

➤ Grit

➤ Discipline

See Chapter 16 for tips on specific ways to break into freelancing. And remember: This fear *is* justified. Breaking into freelancing isn't impossible, but it can be very difficult.

Home Alone

Talk to freelancers in any field, not just your own, for hints about breaking into the business.

Working Nine to Nine

Freelancers are often so grateful to be home, free from the usual encumbrances of office life, that they work harder than they ever have before. At first it's an exhilarating feeling. Then it's a tiring feeling. And before you know it, it's an exhausting feeling.

There's no denying that you work harder at your own business than at somebody else's, especially as you strive to get established and make a name for yourself as a freelancer. But even old hands, freelancers who should know better, can fall prey to overwork. My sainted editor, Nancy Stevenson, jokes that I write faster than the speed of light. I wish it were true. Instead, I just write all the time.

Because there's no official starting and stopping time when you're a freelancer, you can easily find yourself working without end. To combat this, establish regular working hours. Try to make a habit of starting and stopping on time.

Record Breakers

And then there's the drudgery of record-keeping, the seemingly endless paperwork of a freelancer. I have so many receipts, canceled checks, and stubs that I sometimes feel they must be asexually reproducing in their little shoeboxes and manila envelopes. I suspect they are planning to take over the world in a bloodless coup, smothering us all with their sheer bulk.

While we're on the paper chase, here are some more things that make a freelancer's life less than heavenly:

➤ The health insurance deduction is pitiful.

➤ You shoulder the burden of social security tax, not your employer (since you now *are* the employer).

➤ Having a home office sends a warning salvo to the IRS, which makes it much more likely that you're going to get audited. More on this in Chapter 21.

Mind Your Own Business
As you'll learn in Chapter 21, always check with your tax preparer before you take any deduction. You really don't want to operate your freelance business from the state pen. (But then again, you *would* always know where the phone was.)

And speaking of paperwork, don't forget to establish your own benefits package, including a retirement account and medical and disability insurance (tasks your supervisor used to do for you when you had a staff job). Many people I interviewed for this book didn't appreciate the benefits they received from their previous employer until they had to pay for their own coverage. It's costly and a nuisance, but it's necessary. Stay tuned for details in Chapter 22.

One Is the Loneliest Number

You really wanted to get away from the office. You thought you could get more work done, be your own boss, ditch all the yammering and office politics. Well, that's all true. Working at home as a freelancer, you're more productive than ever, and you even have some time for the kids, the pooch, and the garden.

But once you leave the office setting, you also leave the excitement of being with others. No doubt you're fascinating company, but how much can you talk to

Home Alone
If your spouse (or compan-ion, in certain instances) has a family insurance plan through his or her work , you may be covered. If you're both freelancers, however, you'll have to buy your own insurance.

Home Alone
To combat the loneliness of the freelance life, consider joining a professional organization. For proofreaders and copy editors, for example, there's the Editorial Freelancers Association. Journalists often link up with the prestigious American Society of Journalists and Authors. In addition to offering a sympathetic "we're-all-in-this-together" shoulder, these organizations can also offer job referral services and group health plans.

yourself before you've heard all your own stories? And how long before you're so lonely that you're even thinking fondly of your former co-worker and lunch pal—you know, the one who always started a conversation with his mouth full of egg salad? Let's not forget the woman who warbled on about the great deal she got on canned tuna, the desk-pounding political partisan, or the weekend conquistador with tales of love won and lost. Even *they* can seem appealing through the fog of freelancer loneliness. Yes, things can get that bad when you feel yourself adrift on Gilligan's Island without the Skipper or Mary Ann.

The loneliness that often comes with isolation can be a real shocker if you've longed for solitude. Being surrounded by colleagues who crunch their salads along with their numbers can make us yearn for the peace and quiet of home. But too much peace and quiet can be deafening. You'll hear the numbers change on the digital clock, the water drip in the sink, and the days of your life tick past.

Besides, isolation exacerbates bad habits. It's very easy to waltz over to the refrigerator when you're lonely and bored. And it's a snap to stay in your jammies all day. Just ask me.

Bet You Didn't Know

How can freelancers sit all day without moving?

Freelancers have powerful sitting muscles developed by evolution that enable us to sit for extended periods. In prehistoric times, the more successful hunters were able to sit still for days, thereby passing on this ability to their progeny. The fidgety types were all gobbled up by saber-toothed tigers. The end result? All successful freelancers have an innate ability to sit like lumps of lard.

Don't Give Up Your Day Job

OOOooooo...freelancing. The glamour, the excitement, the occasional hunger pang.

"Do what you love and the money will follow," the mantra goes. Yes, but when? Until you build up a base of reliable clients, freelancing can leave you with a serious cash-flow problem.

Even with plenty of clients, you still might not get paid for a long, long time. It's been a year since I wrote a (great) chapter in a book and I've yet to see a dime. Unfortunately, that's not uncommon in many freelance careers. Almost every freelancer I interviewed for this book has heard "the check is in the mail" more often than they find comfortable. You can always call the clerk in accounts payable; you can even go to small claims court to get your money. In the meantime, however, who's paying the rent?

In addition, there's the uncertainty of work. Freelancing gives new meaning to the phrase "feast or famine." Here's what one freelancer said about the uncertain work flow of his chosen field:

> *Financially, I've had good years and bad ones. On the whole, I earn less and often collect less, but I get to keep more of it, and I need less—fewer expensive clothes, meals out, commuting costs. More of what I do is tax deductible. I have to buy my own health insurance, but I consider health insurance a necessity, so I do it.*

Mind Your Own Business
The way your contract is written is crucial in matters of payment. See Chapter 14 for a detailed discussion of contracts and other legal matters that freelancers often face.

Home Alone
It's not a bad idea to set aside a little nest egg in a savings account before you strike out on your own. This way, you have some money on hand until your first checks start coming.

Control Freak

When I developed a book called Indian Terms, *I traveled to the publisher's home office to discuss the parameters for the book as well as the illustrations and cover. I paid for the illustrations, which were done by a respected scholar in the field. When the book was printed, it had acquired a new—and inaccurate—title,* Indian Terms of the Americas. *(It's not about South America. False implication.)*

To my amazement, the earth tones I had asked for were replaced with flagrant Pepto-Bismol pink. The cover now featured nondescript shapes that looked like melting blobs of strawberry yogurt, which the art editor insisted were the Black Hills of South Dakota. The spine was done in royal blue with lettering in green and orange—a truly despicable combination. I refused to autograph books at an annual convention of librarians. The acquisitions editor and I aren't speaking—and may never speak again.

—A freelance writer

Freelancers often cite lack of control over their work as one of the most frustrating aspects of their job. Sometimes the job is taken out of your hands and changes are made that violate your understanding of the assignment—or even the written agreement. You feel abused and misused—and you very often are. It's embarrassing to have your name linked to a shoddy product.

Worse than that, a job mangled by the Powers That Be can reflect badly on you. If people don't know the story behind the fiasco, they might assume that you completed the project too quickly or made the bad decisions that resulted in the shambles. And if you tell the story, you sound like a crybaby, which can further tarnish your reputation in the industry.

Who's on First? What's on Second?

Other times, the people in charge shift so often that you feel as if you're in an Abbott and Costello routine, as the following story shows:

> *I was writing an 8th grade social studies book, and every time I called my supervisor for help, it was a new supervisor—I never talked to anyone more than once—the previous one having quit in disgust, or been fired, or something. I only know that at one point I had three managers in one week. I was assigned Chapter 15, which seemed, from the one-sentence description in the Table of Contents, very much like Chapter 13. So I asked to see Chapter 13.*

> *This turned out to be a big problem, because the two chapters were in different parts of the book, with different writing teams and different managers. Finally, it emerged that labor had been divided so discretely that no one had ever read the whole outline (no one but me, apparently).*

> *When I finally got Chapter 13, it turned out to be a ringer for the one I was supposed to be writing, identical down to the subheads. I called my manager—a new one, of course—and was told to shut up and write. I said okay, but I did take the opportunity to point out that eventually someone was going to read the whole book and discover two nearly identical chapters, and then something unpleasant would hit the fan, and maybe this manager would like to be the one to point this out. I did write the chapter. I was paid. Fortunately for schoolchildren all over America, the project was canceled soon after.*

> —A freelance writer

Amid all the confusion, you've lost all control of your work. The frustration builds, especially if you don't have a strong contract to protect your interests.

Promises, Promises

It can be just as frustrating when promises are made but not kept. Recently, I interviewed a freelancer who trained as a movie grip (an electrician). When we met, he was working as a driver on the set of the Discovery Channel. He told me the following story of his experience:

I have a degree in Movie, TV, and Theater Production from Temple University, so I really know my stuff. I thought I knew the ins-and-outs of being a freelance grip, too, until earlier this year. That's when I was promised a fairly long-term job as a grip on a movie set. It looked like a great gig, right up my alley. And it would have been, too, if the producer had made good on his offer. It seems that he found someone he liked better, the friend of a friend of a friend. So now I'm working as a driver until I can get another shot at a job in my field.

If You Can't Stand the Heat, Get Out of the Kitchen

A guy went to a psychiatrist and said, "Doc, I keep having these alternating recurring dreams. First I'm a teepee; then I'm a wigwam; then I'm a teepee; then I'm a wigwam. It's driving me crazy. What's wrong with me?"

The doctor replied, "It's very simple. You're two tents."

Sometimes the freelance assignment is great and the people are honorable, but outside factors still get in the way. Perhaps the job really doesn't suit your talents and abilities, even though you thought the fit was perfect when you took on the assignment. Or maybe you're given too much work to handle in too short a time. Whatever the reason, control has been wrested from you. You feel like you're charging up Hamburger Hill without your bazooka.

> **Mind Your Own Business**
> Never underestimate the chaos factor. You could get your work done if (pick one): The puppy hadn't chewed the phone cord, your son hadn't lost the phone in that mess he calls his room, your neighbor hadn't had to use your phone because hers is out of order. Nothing eats up a freelancer's time faster than chaos and confusion.

IS THAT CLEAR?

This is a cruel cheat: After all, as a freelancer, you're supposed to be the captain of your ship. If you wanted to feel "two tents," you'd be working a staff job! The responsibility and pressure of certain freelance jobs (not to mention the entire freelance life) can be overwhelming.

Here's one freelancer's story:

> *The job was based in San Antonio, the project headed by two people whom I knew when I worked in the company in a staff position. When we got back to New York, they outlined for me the things I needed to do to get started. First I had to prepare schedules, hire staff—all things I had never done before. I was told I would need a staff of 12.*
>
> *It was hell. I worked ALL hours. I lived on Tylenol because I had a continuous headache, literally. I would get into bed and cry and shake, thinking about all that had to be done in such little time and knowing I was responsible. Then I would get out of bed, pour myself some Chambord, and watch Larry King (4 AM) until the dawn broke. I would then turn on the computer and start to work.*
>
> *I didn't know how to extricate myself from this situation. I also didn't know how I could continue without being hospitalized. I was afraid that if I bailed out, I would never be offered work again. I was equally afraid of being committed.*
>
> *Just when things seemed their bleakest, I was delivered from my ordeal. For reasons that I never knew nor cared about, the project was canceled. I swore I would never let myself get into that kind of situation again. NOTHING WAS WORTH IT!!!!!! NOTHING.*
>
> *This is still a standard against which I measure jobs.*

If all that isn't enough for you, here are six more often-cited problems with freelancing:

1. Lack of security
2. Lack of recognition
3. Rejection
4. Unreliable clients and suppliers
5. Stress on yourself and family members
6. Difficulty in keeping up with the latest developments in your field

Okay, now you know the downside to freelancing. Is it worth it to take the plunge? Only *you* can answer that question for sure, but I *can* help you make the decision. Read on. Chapter 5 will help you decide if you have what it takes to be a happy and prosperous freelancer.

The Least You Need to Know

➤ The primary drawbacks to freelancing include trouble getting started, overworking, and not earning enough money.

➤ Freelancers often experience difficulty keeping good records.

➤ Combating loneliness is another big problem when you're a lone eagle.

➤ Other problems include lack of security, rejection, unreliable clients and suppliers, and stress on yourself and family members.

Chapter 5

Do You Have What It Takes?

In This Chapter

➤ See if you're ready to make the break to freelancing

➤ Check out the skills and background a freelancer needs to succeed

➤ Learn about the personality traits that will ensure freelancing success

➤ Focus your thinking: What do *you* want from your career?

I think that to survive in this business, you have to be good. No job can be too small or too poorly paid to do and to do well. It takes a lot of really careful, punctilious, error-free, on-time work to build up the reserves of good will necessary to get repeat business. You have to be the one who will work over the weekend (or all night, if necessary) when your supervisor is up against it. You have to be the one who will fix it for nothing if it's not right. You have to care about your audience—the people for whom the work is eventually intended—and keep them continually in mind. If you don't care, you'd better not do it. There are easier ways to make a living.

—A savvy, successful freelancer

Fed up to here with the gauntlet of the daily work grind, an increasing number of people leave their office jobs. Some of the newly freed spend the first few months of their independence in a blind panic, convinced they've made a mistake. Desperately, they try to find their way back on the corporate hamster wheel. A few, though, collect their wits, print up a fistful of business cards, and go out on their own. Are you one of the foxy and the fit, ready to enter the fastest-growing segment of the U.S. job market? Read on to find out.

Know Thyself

The whole time I was growing up, every night I heard my father complain about how much he hated his job. When I heard myself saying the same thing, I knew I had to make a change. But no one would pay me to do what I wanted to do, so I had to go out on my own.

—A successful freelance filmmaker

For generations, a regular paycheck has been the main source of financial security. Supporting yourself and your family most often meant that you spent most of your waking hours working for someone else. As a result, most people's lives were organized and structured entirely around their eight-hour workday.

Home Alone
If you don't mind generic-brand shampoo and an occasional late notice from the phone company (at least in the beginning), you're on the road to being a freelancer.

The security and certainty gained as a result of this arrangement made it attractive, desirable, and comfortable. But it offered virtually no flexibility in terms of when to work, where to work, or how to work. Generations of workers spent their lives counting the days to retirement, when at last they could spend their time doing what they wanted to do.

Unfortunately, there are still droves of workers putting in their time. Even if you'd rather not be one of them, is the freelance life really for you? Before you decide to pursue a career as a freelancer, it's worth the time to do a little introspection. The following Interest Inventory can help. Place a check next to each statement you agree with.

Interest Inventory

Personality Issues

_____ 1. I would describe myself as self-reliant.

_____ 2. I often have the urge to build something from scratch.

_____ 3. I want the opportunity to control my own destiny.

_____ 4. I have always followed my own dreams.

_____ 5. I enjoy working on my own.

_____ 6. I set clear goals and objectives—and most often achieve them.

Growth Potential

_____ 1. I dislike the closed-in feeling of a staff job.

_____ 2. My current career is boring.

_____ 3. I've been looking for more creative work for a long time.

_____ 4. I've gone as far as I can with my present job; there's no promotion on the horizon.

_____ 5. I'm actively looking for chances to expand my horizons and learn new skills.

_____ 6. I have the backing of family, colleagues, and friends.

Economic Issues

_____ 1. I'm between jobs (i.e., unemployed).

_____ 2. I want to earn more money.

_____ 3. I want to reduce my overhead costs, such as lunches, commuting, and clothing.

_____ 4. If need be, I can live on a reduced income until my freelance career takes off.

_____ 5. I'm a good money manager, self-disciplined and practical.

_____ 6. There's space in my home for an office.

Quality of Life Concerns

_____ 1. I don't like my present work.

_____ 2. I hate to commute.

_____ 3. I want to wear inexpensive, comfortable clothing.

_____ 4. I'm fed up with office politics.

_____ 5. I want more time with my family and friends.

_____ 6. I want the convenience of being home.

Score Yourself

If you checked off most of these items, you're in pretty good shape to strike out on your own. But *should* you? Hold on there, buckaroo. To succeed as a freelancer, you need two more things:

➤ Skills and background

➤ The right personality

Let's look at these requirements in detail.

Bet You Didn't Know

When the Industrial Revolution began, many people feared that ordinary men and women would never be able to adjust to holding down a job in a factory. Before that time, most people worked at home on their own schedules. Sunday school classes were established to help adults learn the discipline required of the new on-the-job work ethic.

What You Know, Not *Who* You Know: Skills and Background

Mind Your Own Business

As a freelancer, you're not totally free from office politics. Even on your own, you still have to adapt to a huge range of personalities, management styles, and corporate cultures.

Ever feel that experience is something you don't get until just after you need it? That no one is listening until you make a mistake? That he who hesitates is probably right? These observations are especially true when it comes to freelancing.

As a freelancer, you can fool some of the people some of the time, but if you can't cut the mustard, people will eventually catch on to your inexperience and ignorance.

If you become a freelancer, you probably won't have the security of a union, tenure, or an iron-clad contract to help you ride out botched assignments and keep your employer's good will. As a result, you must acquire the necessary skills and background *before* you become a freelancer.

Who Ya Gonna Call?

Some fortunate freelancers have years of experience in their field before they leave the security of a staff position for the freelance life. In my case, I did a great deal of writing in my position as an English teacher. I churned out student recommendations, teacher evaluations, and scholarly articles. From these experiences I was familiar with such elements as grammar, usage, audience, tone, and publishing requirements. Many of my fellow freelance writers worked in staff jobs in large publishing companies and learned even more about the business.

> **Home Alone**
> Never under-estimate what we call the *schmooze factor*, the ability to get along with people of different personalities. It's a very important element to success as a freelancer (as well as an office worker).

Other prospective freelancers must acquire the skills and background they need without the benefit of on-the-job training. This is especially true if you change careers, becoming a freelance fen shui consultant, astrologer, or film cameraman after being a circus roustabout. Here are some ways to gain the skills and experience you need:

1. Do some freelance jobs on the side while you keep your day job.
2. Get some formal training in the field in which you hope to freelance by taking college courses or attending seminars and workshops.
3. "Shadow" people in the field to discover what skills you need to be successful.
4. Complete an apprenticeship to acquire the necessary background knowledge.

Remember that in addition to the specific skills required in your field, you are also going to need such general work skills as promptness, reliability, and initiative. You'll also need some sales experience (to market yourself) and managerial ability (to handle your books and records). If you lack business and managerial experience, consider taking a few formal courses in management and business before you set out on your own.

Person Overboard!

Take this simple quiz to assess whether you have sufficient skills and background to jump ship.

_____ 1. Have you worked for at least five years in the field where you hope to freelance?

_____ 2. Are you recognized for your skills? Do other people at work come to you for help?

_____ 3. Are your skills up-to-date?

_____ 4. Do you have business training?

_____ 5. Do you have experience with sales?

Score Yourself

Yes to all 5	It may be time to become You, Inc.
Yes to 3 or 4	Still a little wet behind the ears. Take some classes and get some training before you cut the cord.
Yes to 1 or 2	Keep reading—and training. You'll get there by the end of the book, bunky.

Personality Plus

There's no doubt that successful freelancers share common personality traits. First of all, to make a go of this business, you must have lots of self-confidence. Lots of it.

Mind Your Own Business
If you want to become a free-lancer in a technical field such as software design, animation, or computer design, it's crucial to have state-of-the-art skills.

Superlative staffers get praise through annual performance reviews and raises. Superlative freelancers, in contrast, find that praise is as rare as fat on a socialite. In the freelance world, you often know you did a good job when the check clears or the same client calls with another assignment.

You must also be able to negotiate with clients without feeling that you're selling your soul. (You may be selling your soul, but you don't want to *feel* like you're doing it.) And let's not forget the ability to be alone for long periods of time. If you're a social butterfly, freelancing is likely to really clip your wings.

Bet You Didn't Know

Even though freelancing tends to be a solitary pursuit, successful freelancers play well with others. They were the ones who shared their shovels in the sandbox and their Oreos at lunch. Team interaction is especially crucial when it comes to finding jobs and building a good reputation.

As a freelancer, you also have to be able to tolerate time and money pressures. Because the workload for the average freelancer is notoriously uneven, it's not uncommon for us to bite off more than we can chew in an attempt to make money while the work is available. When work is plentiful, I have to forgo something I want to do, like sleep, to finish my work—or I find I can't meet my deadline. I miss my deadline and my reputation is tarnished.

Home Alone
Successful freelancers tend to have keen analytical abilities and excellent oral and written communication skills.

Most freelancers cite the ability to withstand money pressures as one of the most important traits a freelancer must have. There are times when people owe you big bucks, but the check is most assuredly *not* in the mail. This can make for sleepless nights as the bills mount and the creditors pant at your door. You'll be gnawing your fingernails to the quick if you can't handle that type of pressure. (Check out Chapter 20 for tips on dealing with cash-flow problems.)

Here are some other key traits that freelancers need to be successful. Put a check next to each trait that you possess.

I am…

_____ self-motivated

_____ a risk taker

_____ ocused

_____ determined

_____ a "juggler" who can multi-task

_____ willing to learn

_____ adaptable and resourceful

_____ responsive

_____ creative

In the Driver's Seat

"A person who freelances has to be strongly organized and disciplined. You have to stay totally in control," says one freelancing telemarketer. I, as you might have guessed, am very well-organized. I'm *so* well-organized that my husband calls me "compulsive." (He calls me a lot of other things, too, but they're all *nice*.) How can you tell if you're equally compulsive, er…*well-organized*? Take the simple quiz on the next page. Write *True* for any statements that apply to you.

_____	1. If anything is wrong, I fix it.
_____	2. I believe that multiple projects lead to multiple successes.
_____	3. I start at the top and try to work my way up.
_____	4. I'll do it by the book…but only if I've written the book.
_____	5. If you can't beat them, join them…then beat them.
_____	6. Bureaucracy is a challenge to be conquered with a righteous attitude, a tolerance for stupidity, and a bulldozer (when necessary).
_____	7. When not faced with a challenge, I create one of my own.
_____	8. "No" simply means begin again at a higher level.
_____	9. I don't walk when I can run.
_____	10. When in doubt: Think!
_____	11. Perfection is not optional.
_____	12. The faster you move, the slower time passes, and the longer you live.

Bonus: When given a choice, I take both options.

Score Yourself

10–12	true	When's the last time you slept more than four hours a night? 1940?
7–9	true	I bet you line up your shoes in nice little rows, by color.
4–6	true	So depressingly normal.
0–3	true	You're so laid back they hold a mirror under your nose to see if you're breathing.

Critical Condition

If you answer *True* to any of the following items, think twice before you pursue a career as a freelancer.

1. You crave companionship. In a pinch, you'll talk to the gerbil.
2. You take rejection personally. Really personally.
3. You think a note that says "Not suited to our current needs" means you're fat, stupid, and ugly.
4. You'd rather be flayed alive than move back with the Parental Units.
5. You're too proud (shy, well brought up) to sell yourself.
6. You didn't go to college for four years so you could work as a temp when money gets tight.
7. If you can't play tennis every Wednesday at noon, you pout and stamp your well-shod foot.

8. You refuse to buy anything off the rack.

9. Your self-esteem fluctuates with your bank account.

10. You think "freelancing" means never having to miss an episode of *General Hospital*.

Who Do You Think You Are?

In general, making a major life change isn't as simple as changing your toothpaste, socks, or toaster pastries. (If it is, you must be *really* miserable at work!) Because moving from a staff position to the freelance world is such a radical change for most people, I've created another way to help you focus your thinking.

Rank each of the following items from one to five, with one being what suits you the least; five what suits you most. There's no right or wrong answer here. Rather, this assessment is designed to help you think more deeply about your likes and dislikes. I'll pick up on this again in Chapter 6 when I discuss freelance occupations.

> **Mind Your Own Business**
> If you're the kind of person who would die of shame before you'd shop at outlets or trim your own hair, being a freelancer is probably not for you.
>
> IS THAT CLEAR?

---

1. I feel best about myself when

   _____ I challenge my physical abilities.

   _____ I know that I'm helping others.

   _____ I know that my efforts are appreciated.

   _____ I'm organizing people to get something done.

   _____ I'm solving problems.

2. I feel more confident when I

   _____ make others feel comfortable.

   _____ overcome obstacles.

   _____ know that other people can't manage without me.

   _____ see my ideas taking form.

   _____ get things to work as they should.

3. I most enjoy

   _____ making something new.

   _____ getting things arranged as they should be.

   _____ taking charge.

   _____ helping out.

   _____ solving a problem.

---

4. I feel most comfortable when I am

_____ talking one-to-one with others.

_____ in the spotlight.

_____ following orders.

_____ getting outdoors and working with plants.

_____ working on my own.

5. The phrase that best describes me is

_____ intelligent and scholarly.

_____ social and talkative.

_____ practical and down to earth.

_____ kind and supportive.

_____ reliable and conscientious.

6. I am always anxious to

_____ explore new possibilities.

_____ lead the way.

_____ work with machines and tools.

_____ find the answers to baffling problems.

_____ follow through with what needs to be done.

7. Time flies fastest for me when I am

_____ repairing things.

_____ performing, directing, persuading.

_____ interacting with other people.

_____ helping others achieve their goals.

_____ exploring new possibilities and ideas.

8. I feel most energized when I

_____ am under pressure.

_____ am faced with a seemingly impossible problem.

_____ have to straighten out someone else's mess.

_____ give a public presentation.

_____ can see things taking shape.

Do you have what it takes to become a successful freelancer? Only you can make that assessment, but don't despair if things look a little bleak right now. It's still very early on and there's a lot more to come in this book. As you read on, you'll discover many ways to assess your skills and get the training you'll need.

The Least You Need to Know

➤ To be a successful freelancer, you need the skills and background to go it alone.

➤ Assess your skills fully before you make the decision to leap to the freelance side of life.

➤ Successful freelancers share some basic personality traits, including self-confidence and self-discipline.

➤ Assess your personality and work style to make sure freelancing is the right fit for you.

➤ Freelancing offers many advantages, but it's not for everyone. Think carefully before you make the break to freelancing.

Part 2
The Ultimate Out-of-Office Experience

➤ *Kathleen Dennis Kelly runs International Protocol Advisors, educating exporters and other people in the nuances of foreign cultures and business protocol.*

➤ *Jerry Moulden publishes photomaps for fishermen that show aerial views of the Texas bays and give information on water depth and channel markers.*

➤ *D. Ann Slayton Shiffler writes and desktop-publishes company newsletters, advertising brochures, and economic development booklets.*

What do these three people have in common? They are all former in-house wage slaves who developed their own freelance careers. In this section of the book, you'll learn how to discover and create the freelance career that's right for you. I'll also show you how to write a business plan—and how it can help you get your freelance career off the ground. Then you'll learn how to find work, and how to establish a professional image while you do it.

Chapter 6

Nothing Ventured, Nothing Gained

In This Chapter

➤ Lay the groundwork for a great freelance career

➤ Avoid common mistakes that can stop you before you get started

➤ Explore your strengths and examine your options

➤ Check out potential freelance careers

➤ Find the right freelance career for *you*

Three guys were about to be shot in a prison camp. The first one thought, "If I could just find a distraction, maybe I could escape."

Just as the squad leader said, "Ready, aim..." the guy shouted, "Tornado!" The members of the firing squad looked around and the prisoner ran away.

The second prisoner decided to try the same thing. The squad leader said, "Ready, aim..." and the second guy yelled, "Flood!" The members of the firing squad looked around and the prisoner ran away.

The third guy thought, "Hey, we're on to something here." But when the leader yelled, "Ready, aim..." the third guy yelled, "Fire!"

In this chapter, you'll learn how important careful thought and planning are to establishing a successful freelance career. Then *you* won't end up in the line of fire!

Gotcha! Traps to Avoid

Most of us never really give much thought to becoming a freelancer. Instead, we let our lives revolve around our school, job, or family demands. Now, this is not such a terrible thing—assuming that the status stays quo. But what happens when the earth shifts beneath us and everything changes? Today, school, job, and family are carved in sand, not granite.

As you learned in Chapter 2, the traditional guarantees of work are receding faster than Willard Scott's hairline. Long-time employees are suddenly given the boot or granted an unwanted early retirement. Family demands shift and people find themselves in a new set of circumstances. Even the most casual student graduates or runs out of money to complete that education. For many, freelancing is something that "just happens" when their lives change.

As a result, when some people make the break to the freelance life, they make some common mistakes:

1. They can't pick a freelance career.
2. They pick a trendy freelance occupation that doesn't suit their interests and lifestyle.
3. They get stuck in a new and different kind of rut.

At best, the unenlightened just lose some time as they get derailed for a while. At worst, these people conclude that freelancing just isn't for them and they go back to the grind they hated in the first place. Let's examine each of these missteps so you can avoid them as you lay the groundwork for a great freelance career.

Home Alone
Looking for more help laying the groundwork for a freelance career? Check out the National Association for the Self-Employed (800-200-6273).

Shooting Blanks

If you don't know what kind of freelance work suits your interests and abilities, you might come up empty and waste years trying to find the right career. The same thing happens to people who lack the confidence to pursue a field that does suit their talents. Does this sound like you? If so, read on.

Getting Burned by What's Hot

Not knowing what you want to do as a freelancer, you may be tempted to jump on a passing-trend bandwagon. It's the same impulse that led many of us to buy a Nehru jacket or white go-go boots. (Not to mention the pet rock, Ginsu knife, and all that exercise equipment gathering dust in my basement.) In the 70s, it was trendy to become a freelance marriage and family counselor; in the '80s, freelancing as a real estate guru wound many 'a clock. The early '90s? A lot of people decided it was hip to be a freelance financial advisor or tap into the 900-number business. Unfortunately, many of these freelance careers fizzled when people realized they just didn't like the work or they lacked the experience and training to be a success in the field.

Stuck in a Rut

If people don't know what they want to do, they sometimes end up duplicating the life they had at the office. They keep the same hours, work with the same clients, and sometimes even spend the same time commuting—only to end up wondering why their new life as a freelancer isn't any better than their former life as a staff employee. Why? It's because their life as a freelancer is virtually identical to their life as a staffer. If the freelance life you create for yourself is just as stressful, financially tight, or boring as the life you had, why go to all the trouble of becoming a freelancer?

Connect the Dots

In contrast to line dancers, lemmings, and politicians, freelancers tend to buck the tide. A notoriously individualistic lot, successful freelancers "do their own thing" with a vengeance. If you're stamped in this mold, here are three questions *not* to ask yourself as you consider your options:

Home Alone
Don't worry if you're having a hard time crystallizing your reasons for wanting to become a freelancer. It can take a while to put your thoughts into words.

1. What *could* I do?
2. What *should* I do?
3. What's the *best* freelance career for me?

Let's look at why these questions are about as useful as walking through the metal detector once too often.

What *Could* I Do?

If you ask yourself this question, chances are good that you'll get lost in a forest of possibilities. By my count, over 1,500 different freelance careers exist, but I stopped counting because I ran out of fingers and toes. Odds are that there are scores of careers you could do well, so asking yourself "What could I do?" is apt to simply make you dizzy.

What *Should* I Do?

Here's another potential swamp. This is especially dangerous if you ask other people for their input, because their private agendas can get in the way of their objectivity. Your spouse might want you to pursue a freelance career that will leave more time for you to do the chores; your mom might want you to go into a field that gives her something to brag about during her Monday night mah-jongg sessions.

This is not to say that relatives, friends, and co-workers won't sometimes be able to give you some solid career advice. But it *does* mean that you have to listen to all advice with a judicious ear. When you hear someone tell you that you "should" pursue a specific freelance career, ask yourself these questions instead:

➤ What authority does the speaker have to make this assertion?

➤ What will happen if I *do* pursue this field?

➤ What will happen if I *don't*?

What's the *Best* Freelance Career for Me?

The sticking point here is that little word "best." You don't have to find the very best freelance career; instead, you simply have to find the one that suits you at this point in your life. One of the greatest aspects of freelancing is the flexibility it gives you to modify or change careers as your life changes. For example, you might start as a freelance technical artist, doing charts and graphs. Later, however, you might turn to other freelance art careers, such as greeting cards, comic books, or fashion ads. Or, you might start teaching freelance art classes and some years down the road decide to become a textile designer.

Putting Two and Two Together

So how *can* you figure out what freelance career to pursue? Begin by listing your strengths, including education, training, and background. Then ask yourself what you're looking for in life. Here's a chart to help you pull all this together.

1. My education is in the field of

   _____

   _____

2. I am trained to

   _____

   _____

3. My previous jobs were

   _____

   _____

---

 4. My side jobs include

 _____

 _____

 5. My hobbies include

 _____

 _____

 6. Things I'm most often praised for include

 _____

 _____

 7. Things people ask me to help them with include

 _____

 _____

 8. My strongest talents include

 _____

 _____

 9. I most enjoy doing

 _____

 _____

 10. In five years, I see myself

 _____

 _____

It's amazing how much you know when you sit down and catalog all your accomplishments. Many freelancers launch successful careers by building on their life experiences and circumstances. Read on to find out how!

Cross at the Green, Not In-Between

You know that you should build on your job experience, education, and training as you consider what freelance career to pursue. You know that it's helpful to capitalize on your life experiences and circumstances as you make the break to the freelance life.

But did you know that it's equally useful to capitalize on other people's experiences? Work your contacts. Speak with other freelancers in person, on the telephone, or via e-mail. Getting a variety of opinions from people in the freelance biz (no matter what their specific careers) can help you finalize your thinking about your future as a freelancer.

Other freelancers can:

➤ Help you get ideas.

➤ Share their experiences.

➤ Serve as role models.

➤ Open doors you couldn't open on your own.

➤ Be your cheerleaders.

Home Alone
As you consider your freelance career options, try to incorporate the equipment you already have, such as computers, fax machines, and vehicles.

How can you find freelancers who might be willing to help? Start by checking the library for professional directories. You can also call professional organizations in the area as well as service groups such as Rotary and Lions. In addition, try contacting the Small Business Administration in your community. Many small businesses employ freelancers as contract workers and temps.

Scratch a Niche

"This is all well and good," you're thinking, "but I'm not really sure what I *can* do with my education, training, job experience, and interests." Relax. In this section, I'm going to outline and describe some careers that are well suited to freelancing. Just be sure to research each suggestion fully (and I mean *fully*) before you quit your day job.

Clearly, not everyone who wants to be a freelancer can make his or her dream come true. After all, it's pretty hard to freelance if your dream job is a slot on the Chevy assembly line. On the other hand, many jobs—including many you've probably never associated with freelancing—are good bets because they lend themselves to home-based work.

Traditionally, freelancing was reserved for writers, actors, photographers, artists, consultants, and other "creative types." But today, freelancing embraces a much wider spectrum of possibilities, such as:

➤ Landscape architect

➤ Astrologer

➤ Book indexer

➤ Medical transcriber

➤ Carpenter

➤ Construction worker hired by the job

➤ Pipe-organ technician

➤ Oil-well pumper

➤ Installer of vacuum systems

➤ Stagehand

➤ Engine rebuilder

➤ Specialist in aquarium maintenance

> **Mind Your Own Business**
> Beware of hitching your wagon to a star just because it seems to be soaring. Remember what you learned earlier in this chapter about selecting a freelance career that suits all aspects of your life.
>
> IS THAT CLEAR?

There are freelance accountants, agents, analysts, administrators, and auditors. Working our way through the alphabet, we have freelance bookkeepers, brokers, data-entry specialists, computer programmers, computer repairers (thank goodness!), engineers, personal shoppers, researchers, security consultants, tax preparers, telemarketers, and word processors. And that's just the beginning. The following sections describe in greater detail some of the leading candidates for freelance careers.

Cleaning Up

One result of the dramatic changes taking place in the way we live and work today is that people have less time for the chores of daily life. Now, speaking as a person who has no great fondness for cleaning the bathroom grout with a toothbrush, I find this particular lack of time no great sacrifice. But there *are* people who fret over dust bunnies the size of a Buick; in my house, we just give them names.

> OH!
>
> **Bet You Didn't Know**
>
> According to an article in *Newsweek,* almost a third of all Americans say they feel rushed for time and more than half say they almost never have spare time on their hands.

How many of these chores would you like someone to do for you? Check them off on the Chore List on the next page. Fill in the blanks with other chores you need to do but can't seem to find the time to complete.

Chore List

_____ ➤ Clean the house	_____ ➤ Mail packages
_____ ➤ Take the kids to activities	_____ ➤ Plan wedding
_____ ➤ Drop off and pick up cleaning	_____ ➤ Wash clothes
_____ ➤ Write social notes	_____ ➤ Garden
_____ ➤ Shop for gifts	_____ ➤ Walk the dog
_____ ➤ Decorate for holidays	_____ ➤ Cook
_____ ➤ Food shop	_____ ➤ Take car for tune-up
_____ ➤ _____	_____ ➤ _____
_____ ➤ _____	_____ ➤ _____

See the freelance career possibilities? The lack of time for cleaning alone has spawned a need for dozens of specialized cleaning services, and we still have those pesky errands to run. Now take another look at that list. Anything there you're particularly good at?

Write Away: Freelance Writing, Editing, and Desktop Publishing

Traditionally, freelancing has been to writers what kiwi and raspberry vinegar are to nouvelle cuisine. It's the nature of the beast—after all, who ever heard of a "staff novelist"? Most creative writers are forced into freelancing because there are very few staff positions in "creative" writing.

Many people who have the ability to sling words together in a pleasing and graceful manner find that freelancing offers a wide range of possibilities. Many of these "not creative" writing tasks turn out to be very creative after all. Here are some of them:

➤ Technical writer

➤ Freelance editor

➤ Script editor

➤ Business and commercial freelance writer for industry, associations, and government

➤ Resume writer

➤ Newsletter publisher

➤ Brochure writer

➤ Copywriter

➤ Freelance journalist

➤ Grant writer

IS THAT CLEAR?

Mind Your Own Business
In general, start-up costs for freelance writing are minimal beyond a basic computer system and some word-processing software, but desktop publishing may require a pricier system that costs $5,000 or more.

Let me take a minute to get you in your write mind. Before you set sail for the land of the literary, you should know that *90 percent* of freelance writers earn only about $5,000 a year from writing. That means that only *10 percent* of all freelance writers earn enough to buy a Happy Meal once a week (and maybe have enough left over for a flight or two on the Concorde).

Bet You Didn't Know

Two good sources for literary freelancers are *How to Start and Run a Writing and Editing Business*, by Herman Holtz (John Wiley and Sons), and *The Upstart Guide to Owning and Managing a Desktop Publishing Service*, by Dan Ramsey (Upstart Publishing Company).

Life Lines

Then there are freelance life-management careers, which are popular because our lives increasingly need someone to manage them. Below are 24 different careers to consider. See how many match your experience, interests, and training:

- ➤ Bill-paying service
- ➤ Color consultant
- ➤ Gift-basket business
- ➤ Image consultant
- ➤ In-home health care worker
- ➤ Massage therapist
- ➤ Medical claims assistant
- ➤ Pet-sitting service
- ➤ Personal shopper
- ➤ Private investigator
- ➤ Self-esteem coach
- ➤ Travel consultant

- ➤ Caterer
- ➤ Errand service
- ➤ Disc jockey
- ➤ Interior designer
- ➤ Makeup artist
- ➤ Photographer
- ➤ Plant caregiver
- ➤ Repair service
- ➤ Personal trainer
- ➤ Reunion planner
- ➤ Tour operator
- ➤ Yoga instructor

These are only a handful of the freelance career possibilities in the field of life management. As our lives get more frantic and time gets shorter, more and more of these careers will develop. Why not be the freelancer on the cutting edge?

Rent a Yenta: Consulting and Providing Services

Home Alone
Comic books and cartoons used to be colored by hand by staff artists. Today, much of the work is done on computers—by freelancers.

➤ Have a strong background in retail? *Freelance store-opening consultants* teach new specialty retailers how to open their stores. Their seminars include information on scouting locations, negotiating leases, planning store layouts, establishing credit, advertising, and marketing.

➤ Good with fashion, makeup, and interpersonal skills? *Freelance image consultants* present workshops on image, business protocol, and verbal and nonverbal communication.

Consulting is especially well suited to freelancing. The key to success in this field is having expertise that you can clearly explain (and sell) to a client. Income varies from $35 to $100 or more per hour. With consulting, it's vital to keep current in your field and listen to your clients.

Here are two good sources of information on this kind of career:

1. Independent Computer Consultants Association
   933 Gardenview Office Parkway
   St. Louis, MO 63141
   Phone: 800-774-4222, 314-892-1675

   This is a national organization that provides professional development opportunities and business-support programs for independent computer consultants. There is an annual membership fee.

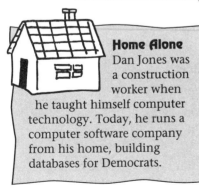

Home Alone
Dan Jones was a construction worker when he taught himself computer technology. Today, he runs a computer software company from his home, building databases for Democrats.

2. The National Entrepreneurs Opportunity Network, Information Exchange
   P.O. Box 373229
   Satellite Beach, FL 32937
   Phone: 407-777-0557

   This group offers matchmaking services for technical consultants seeking alliances. It also provides access to a database of freelancers in the same field. There is an annual membership fee.

Bet You Didn't Know

For further information, you may wish to consult *The Business Plan Guide for Independent Consultants*, by Herman Holtz (John Wiley and Sons), and *How to Start a Service Business*, by Ben Chant and Melissa Morgan (Avon Books).

This Little Piggy Went to Market: Marketing and Selling

"I can turn my hobby into a great freelance career," you may think. And indeed you may be able to—but do you *want* to? Your hobby may not be so much fun when you turn it into a 60-hour-per-week freelance job. I suggest you start slowly, and build up to a heavier work week if you decide this is really for you. Visit shops and craft shows regularly to stay on top of what's selling. Also consider diversifying into related crafts to tap broader markets.

Startup costs tend to be minimal, because as a craftsperson you should already have your tools. Regarding money: I've heard of freelancers who have earned as much as $50,000 a year, but then again, I've heard of teenagers who clean their rooms and give parents their telephone messages. When it comes to money, a lot depends on how much you can produce and how much you hustle.

Home Alone
Dennis Weaver is a freelancer who sells Earthship house technology. For the unenlightened, Earthships are homes dug into hillsides. Made of concrete and recycled tires, they can be heated with less hot air than is found in the average Senate subcommittee.

Savvy freelancers know that the horizon is practically limitless when it comes to marketing and selling. When I started researching freelance sales, I discovered hundreds upon hundreds of items to sell. Here are just a few:

➤ Junk metals
➤ Dog food
➤ Wind-surfing gear
➤ Cutlery
➤ T-shirts
➤ Sauna equipment

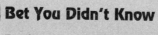

Bet You Didn't Know

For further information on freelance marketing and selling, you may wish to consult *How to Open and Operate a Home-Based Craft Business,* by Kenn Oberrechi (Globe Pequot Press).

In the Home Stretch

Now it's your turn. Complete the following personal inventory to zero in on possible freelance careers that suit you. On the left-hand side, list your relevant resources. On the right-hand side, list the freelance careers that match those resources.

You *Can* Get There from Here

Job experiences   Possible freelance careers

_____

_____

Education   Possible freelance careers

_____

_____

Training   Possible freelance careers

_____

_____

Life experiences   Possible freelance careers

_____

_____

Personal contacts   Possible freelance careers

_____

_____

Equipment, facilities   Possible freelance careers

_____

_____

Your three greatest assets and strengths	Possible freelance careers

How'd you do, bunky? Pleasantly surprised at how many options you have? Or did you come up a little short in the possibility department? There's a world of potential careers out there; the secret is knowing how to find out about them. "So," you're probably saying about now, "where *does* this amazing woman find all her information?" If you promise not to spill the beans, I'll give you the scoop. Here are my sources:

➤ *The public library.* Check the traditional sources (*Occupational Handbook*, newspapers, magazines) as well as the new whiz-bang online resources to see what's the buzz in your business.

➤ *Professional organizations.* Join! Join! Join! People in the game know what's happening far better than people on the sidelines. Get in the game yourself to find out what freelance careers suit your interests and abilities.

➤ *Conferences.* I attend local as well as national conferences to find out what's going on. This helps me forecast trends.

➤ *Community work.* Join a service organization such as Rotary, get elected to the school or library board, go on 5K walks for the Heart Fund. Get out there and see what's going on. I was a member of Rotary for years, I've been on the library board for more than a decade, and I'll walk for just about any good cause (I refuse to run, however).

The Least You Need to Know

➤ Remember that careful thought and planning are essential to establishing a successful freelance career.

➤ Assess your education, training, and background, and work with your strengths.

➤ Beware of picking a trendy freelance occupation that doesn't suit your interests and lifestyle.

➤ Don't pick the wrong career and get stuck in a different kind of rut.

➤ Network with other freelancers to get more information.

➤ Look for freelance opportunities in nearly every field, including the arts, consulting, marketing and selling, and technical fields.

Chapter 7

Mission Possible: Writing a Business Plan

In This Chapter

➤ Discover why a business plan is important to you

➤ Learn how to find the information you need to succeed

➤ Write a business plan

➤ Use your plan to evaluate your chances of success as a freelancer

It was a dark and stormy night. A drunk left a bar and decided to take a shortcut through a graveyard. The drunk failed to see an empty grave and fell into it. He tried to climb out of it, but the grave was too deep and the rain had turned the dirt to mud, making the walls too slippery to climb. The drunk finally gave up and decided to spend the night in the grave.

A little while later, another drunk left the bar and decided to take the same shortcut through the graveyard. He, too, fell into that open grave and tried to climb out but couldn't. The first drunk watched silently as his fellow lush staggered around the grave.

At last, the first drunk stood up, tapped the second drunk on the shoulder, and said, "Buddy, you'll never get out."

But he did. Immediately.

See, almost *anything* is possible if you have the right motivation. In this chapter, you'll learn how to start establishing yourself as a freelancer, a task that's not as difficult as it might seem. First, you'll discover the importance of crafting a business plan, no matter what freelance business you wish to pursue. Then you'll explore the different parts of the typical business plan in detail. Along the way, I'll prepare you to write one of your own. Follow the steps I describe (and stay out of bars and graveyards), and you won't get stuck in a hole.

Getting Down to Business: Crafting a Business Plan

"Me, write a business plan? Why would I need a business plan? It's just me, the dog, and a pair of pruning shears," you say to me incredulously. If you're like most freelancers, you wouldn't dream of writing a business plan. That's because most people associate a business plan with Big Business stuff like getting a loan. And since the great majority of freelancers don't need a loan to get started, you're likely to decide that you don't have to craft a business plan. Wrong.

Let me show you why. Place a check next to each statement you think is correct.

The Business of Business

As a freelancer, you should write a business plan to:

_____ 1. Figure out exactly what business you're in.

_____ 2. Clarify your goals.

_____ 3. Fine-tune your freelance plans.

_____ 4. Determine if your freelance plans are realistic.

_____ 5. Help you develop your freelance career as fully as possible.

_____ 6. Maximize your profits.

_____ 7. Explore who is going to buy what you have to sell.

_____ 8. Set the parameters for your life as a freelancer.

_____ 9. Consider the financial ramifications of your plan.

_____ 10. Aid you in tracking your progress in the future.

Answers

True, True, True, True, True, True, True, True, True, True.

Yup, every one is true.

Late at night when we let our imaginations soar, we all get to establish exactly the freelance business we want. Perhaps I'll make a ton of money writing the Great American Novel; perhaps you'll retire as a wealthy person thanks to your fabulously successful career as a freelance film producer. Whatever your freelance plans, reality rarely cooperates as eagerly as we'd like. Usually, we have to establish a freelance career that will actually generate enough income to pay the bills. Therefore, I mainly write textbooks and trade books rather than fiction; you might become a freelance film editor rather than a producer.

That's why you need a business plan. It forces you to consider whether or not your dream can become reality. A business plan can also help you find ways to have your cake...and eat it, too!

A solid, well-crafted business plan can help prevent you from:

➤ Jumping into a new career without considering all the ramifications.

➤ Pursing the wrong career.

➤ Incurring unnecessary debt.

➤ Biting off more than you can chew—or attempting too little.

➤ Getting sidetracked.

➤ Letting important career opportunities slip by.

➤ Not realizing your potential.

➤ Losing sight of your goals.

➤ Passing up potentially good ideas.

➤ Deciding that you can't make it—when you can.

Home Alone
Use your business plan to determine the feasibility of a full-time career as a freelancer. And remember, although you may conclude that now is not the time to go out on your own, don't rule it out for the future.

Hit the Books

"Just the facts, ma'am," the hard-boiled detective snarls out of the corner of his mouth. Researching the feasibility of your freelance business requires equally ruthless analysis and legwork. Your goal? To gather enough facts to enable you to construct a solid business plan. From these facts, you'll be able to form logical opinions and draw valid conclusions about your freelance career.

Your sources depend, of course, on the nature of your potential freelance career. If you want to be a freelance landscape architect based in your present location, for example, the local Chamber of Commerce can give

Mind Your Own Business
At the risk of further blocking you anal-retentive types, you're better off getting *too much* information than *too little*. This is not carte blanche to work on your business plan until Cal Ripkin retires—but *do* be complete in your research.

IS THAT CLEAR?

you valuable information on community demographics. If you're looking for a freelance career as a textile designer, you'll want to cast your net a bit wider. In that instance, you'll want to follow the news of your industry in the newspapers and trade journals. In addition, you might seek out the advice of people in the textile business who work in large urban centers.

Below are some sources of information to consider as you firm up your freelance career plans. Select the ones that best suit your career.

Get Information By...

1. Talking to friends in the same business.

2. Reading up on the business in journals, newspapers, and magazines. Pay special attention to the business section of the newspaper.

3. Taking polls of knowledgeable people.

4. Visiting the Chamber of Commerce.

5. Visiting small business centers at local colleges and universities.

6. Speaking to people at the Small Business Administration.

7. Checking with an accountant, preferably one with a working knowledge of freelancers' tax situations.

8. Talking to members of a business organization or a professional association in your field.

9. Seeking advice from experts, especially your competition.

10. Attending small business fairs.

11. Checking out business classes and seminars offered at local colleges and universities.

12. Asking local bankers for their input. They will often know how the competition is faring.

Home Alone
The Editorial Freelancers Association serves self-employed publishing professionals, including writers, editors, proofreaders, indexers, and photo researchers.

Don't neglect online sources as you research, especially the Internet. Often, you'll get the most up-to-date information and meet knowledgeable people in chat rooms and on bulletin boards.

Put It in Writing

When you've gathered enough information, it's time to start writing the actual business plan. Some of you (I won't point any fingers) are apt to put off this stage until you are altogether too well informed, but write you must. Actually setting your plans down on paper can be as intimidating as programming your VCR, but it need not be. Remember...

➤ Don't worry about how well you write. Miss Nelson isn't going to grade this, so you won't lose points for poor spelling.

➤ A business plan is a work in progress. You'll have many chances to refine it as you go along.

➤ You can easily add any additional information you discover.

➤ You can easily delete anything that proves extraneous.

> **Home Alone**
> Treat people to a business lunch while you interview them about their job and ask their advice on your freelance plans. Because no good deed goes unrewarded, chances are good you can deduct the cost of the lunch from your taxes.

A business plan is nothing more than a short report. It has the following main parts:

1. Overview
2. Customer Profile
3. Competitor's Profile
4. Sales Forecast
5. Location
6. Organizational Plan
7. Marketing Plan
8. Financial Plan

You don't necessarily have to write your business plan in this order. Start with the section that is easiest for you and go from there. Let's look at each step in detail.

1. Overview

Think of the overview as a sneak preview of the rest of the business plan. In a sentence or two, describe your freelance business and each of its major elements, such as customers, sales, location, and marketing. The overview helps you focus your thoughts and narrow your scope. Keep your focus as specific as possible.

Here's a sample overview:

I want to write trade books for general adult readers (Customer Profile) to compete with the Mediocre Trade Book series (Competitor's Profile) that will sell at least 10,000 copies each per year (Sales Forecast). I will work from my home (Location) as the sole proprietor (Organizational Plan). I will sell my books to major publishers such as Macmillan (Marketing Plan) and earn at least $50,000 per year (Financial Plan).

2. Customer Profile

For your freelance business to succeed, you must offer a product or service that others want. Sounds simple, yes? Well, so did the sacking of Troy, and look what happened *there*.

Home Alone
Once you have completed the overview portion of your business plan, consider whether you can accomplish these goals by a means other than freelancing. If so, you might try to stay on staff. This way, you can still accomplish your aims and avoid expending time and energy on the marketing and administrative parts of being self-employed.

Your task, if you choose to accept it, is to figure out in your business plan if there are real, live, breathing people who want to buy what you have to sell. Trying to sell people something they neither want nor need is likely to be as successful as the Edsel or *Plan 9 from Outer Space*.

To figure out if your product or service is in demand, and who is demanding it, create a customer profile. Include every relevant detail about your potential customers. Here are some of the elements to analyze:

➤ Customers' age

➤ Customers' income

➤ Customers' gender

➤ Customers' buying habits

This customer profile will help you decide crucial money issues, such as how much to charge for each task. There's more on this in Chapter 12.

If you are a knowledge worker like a writer or an editor, your customer profile will look a little different. You need to find out who uses freelancers in your field, what the pay is like for various kinds of work and with various kinds of employers, what qualifications employers are looking for, and so on. Writers, get thee to the library and pick up a copy of *Literary Market Place*. The rest of you, follow them in. A chat with the reference librarian will steer you in the right direction. And don't forget to check with professional organizations in your field.

Home Alone
You don't necessarily have to exceed the competition; sometimes there is an additional need for your product or service. Otherwise, why would one small community have five flourishing freelance accountants, lawyers, or nurses?

3. Competitor's Profile

Next, you've got to look at the competition to see how your plans measure up. Try to compare apples to apples: your proposed line of work to the same kind of business. If your service is unique, however, this might not be possible. In that case, examine competitors whose work is as similar to yours as possible. Use the worksheet on the next page as you complete this step in the process.

I'll Show You Mine If You Show Me Yours: Competition Analysis

1. How is the competition similar to your proposed business?

_____

_____

_____

_____

2. How is it different?

_____

_____

_____

_____

3. How long has the competition been in business?

_____

_____

_____

_____

4. Who are their primary customers?

_____

_____

_____

_____

5. What fees do your competitors charge?

_____

_____

_____

_____

Home Alone
Check out trade journals for mention of your competition's progress; talk to people who use their services. You may even be able to stop by their place of business and observe them first-hand.

Here's the crucial step: Ask yourself if your town or industry is big enough for one more business—yours. If so, continue to the following step. If not, refer to the worksheet you completed in Chapter 6, where you brainstormed additional freelance business ideas. See which of these alternate ideas are more likely to be successful.

4. Sales Forecast

Want to make the money roll in from all directions? Then take some time to make a "guesstimate" of your projected income. Try to be as accurate as possible. Too high and you're apt to be crushed when you fail to swim in the moolah. Too low and you're not likely to live up to your potential. To get a rough idea of projected income, see what other freelancers in your field make. If you're bold, come right out and ask them. If you're bashful, check reference sources in the library. Many trade journals do salary surveys, for instance.

If it seems likely that you'll make the money you need, forge ahead. If not, move back to GO (and do not collect $200). But don't be discouraged if your first plan doesn't pan out. You're much better off learning this now, before you invest your time, money, and energy in something that won't fly because of the time, place, or other factors.

5. Location

What's the biggest myth of the new economy? It's that geography no longer matters. Because the world is evolving into one big homogeneous marketplace, the story goes, freelancers can locate anywhere. Okay, maybe every city's mall looks like every other city's mall, but for many freelancers, location continues to matter a great deal. Why should this be? It's simple. Today, businesses need every competitive advantage they can get—especially freelancers. Location is one more edge that a smart freelancer can capitalize on. When it comes to freelancing, place can matter a great deal. Here are two reasons why:

Home Alone
Freelancers are roosting in small towns all over America. For example, the small town of Steamboat Springs in Colorado actively recruits freelancers. Consider location as you plan your freelance career.

➤ In a fast-changing economy, some cities and regions give a helping hand to certain businesses, no matter what their size.

➤ Some regions expect to experience greater growth than others. For example, Colorado's population is expected to grow twice as fast as Illinois' population between now and 2005.

It's not enough to go where the action is—you have to go where the action is in *your* business. For example, if you start a freelance film-services business, you're likely to be in

Los Angeles, New York, or North Carolina. Interested in some aspect of the country music industry? Nashville is the place to be. That's not to say you can't make it somewhere else. It *is* to say that you should give yourself every advantage.

Because most freelancers are home-based, there's also the location *within* your home to consider. The room you use for your office can be crucial to the success of your business. For example, will a client really be comfortable having a meeting in your bedroom, surrounded by your personal items? More on this in Chapter 9.

If you plan on opening an office outside your home, it's equally important to select the right spot. Most likely, you're going to plunk yourself right in the middle of the action. For example, if you're a freelance trial lawyer, you'll probably want to be near the courthouse. A freelance researcher, in contrast, will work most efficiently near the library.

Home Alone
You may wish to hire an interior designer to help you make the most efficient use of your space. See if you can swap services to help defray start-up costs.

6. Organizational Plan

No, you don't need a Time-Warner/AT&T/GM-type flow chart showing the 10,000 layers of responsibility from CEO to custodian. After all, you are the CEO *and* the custodian. You're also the sales and marketing staff, the bookkeeper, and the administrative assistant. As a result, your organizational plan will look like this:

all jobs ─────────────────➤ me

Since I've just finished your flow chart, how about *you* list all the responsibilities you envision as part of your freelance operation. Use the following worksheet:

Taken to Task

1. _____
2. _____
3. _____
4. _____
5. _____
6. _____
7. _____
8. _____
9. _____
10. _____

Now, study your list. How many of these tasks can you perform comfortably? Do you need to farm out some of them, such as bookkeeping and accounting? Do you need to hire an employee to handle some of these responsibilities? Now's the time to factor this expense into your business plan.

Home Alone
Consider hiring a high school student to help you with the routine office tasks that can eat up your day, such as photocopying and mailing. High school kids often welcome the experience for their work record and they charge reasonable rates. (Hey, I have two teenagers. *Someone* has to pay for all those CDs.)

7. Marketing Plan

In this part of your business plan, you decide how to attract your customers. People might find your product irresistible, but first you have to let them know it exists. That's where a marketing plan comes in. A marketing plan should address these three factors:

➤ Service

➤ Price

➤ Advertising

Your clients need to know what services you provide and what they cost. How they discover these fascinating facts is the advertising part. Here are some questions to ask yourself as you write your marketing plan:

1. Will my customers travel to me or me to them?

2. Do I need extensive mail service, couriers, and messengers?

3. Will I request payment at the time of the sale or will there be a grace period?

4. Will I accept credit cards?

5. How can I make customers aware of my product or service?

Now for those of you who think a marketing plan doesn't apply to *your* kind of business, think again. No matter what you do, you have to attract clients and you certainly want to get paid. More on marketing in Chapters 16 and 17.

8. Financial Plan

Mind Your Own Business
Most credit card companies charge between 4 and 9 percent of the total bill for their services. As a result, you must figure this cost into your analysis.

The financial plan shows whether you have enough money to start your freelance business and operate it for the time it takes to show a profit, generally within a year. Here are some elements to consider:

➤ How much money do you have in reserve?

➤ How much income comes in from other sources?

➤ How much money do you need to live?

➤ Subtract. Can you earn that much from your new freelance career?

Financial statements are described in detail in Chapters 12 and 13. In those chapters, I'll take you step-by-step through the process of figuring out how much to charge, working out a cash flow, and dealing with payment schedules. Financials are especially important for freelancers, because we tend to mingle our business and personal funds. As a result, you need to evaluate not only if you can afford to start the business, but also if you can put food on your table during the time it takes for the business to become profitable.

> **Mind Your Own Business**
> Don't omit the financial part of your business plan, even if you're not actively seeking a loan. It's especially important to complete this part if you're money-phobic like me and have to use your fingers (and toes) to make change.
>
> *IS THAT CLEAR?*

The Least You Need to Know

➤ Before you embark on your freelance career, you *must* have a business plan.

➤ Base your business plan on solid research.

➤ Your business plan should include these eight parts: 1. Overview; 2. Customer Profile; 3. Competitor's Profile; 4. Sales Forecast; 5. Location; 6. Organizational Plan; 7. Marketing Plan; 8. Financial Plan.

➤ Use your business plan to gauge the feasibility of your freelance plans.

➤ Take the time to plan completely; it will pay off.

GRRR...

Chapter 8

No Guts, No Glory: Getting Work

In This Chapter

➤ Learn how to ease your way into the freelance waters so you don't get bitten by the sharks

➤ Explore ways to find clients for your freelance business

➤ Get over your fear of selling yourself and make contact

➤ Learn how to maintain a professional image with your new employers

A burglar in Fairfax, Virginia, tried to break into a department store through a skylight. The police nabbed him on the roof. It seems he forgot to wait until the store was closed, and his error was reported by some of the many shoppers still in the store. Sometimes it's the little things that trip you up.

"The little things" can trip you up when you get started in the freelance biz, too. Knowing how to solicit clients correctly can make the difference between paying your bills from the very start or having to placate Peter to pay Paul, Pam, and Petunia. In this chapter, you'll first learn how important it is to remain on good working terms with your former supervisors and colleagues. Next, you'll explore different ways to get business, especially through personal contacts and the Internet. Finally, I'll give you some pointers on professionalism that will keep the work flowing into your office like Fabio's hair flows down his brawny shoulders.

Going Out for Business

Before you can actively seek work, it's important to get yourself oriented to the new realities of living life as a freelancer. Once you make the break to freelancing, you're not in Kansas anymore, Toto. When it comes to work, being a freelancer is *not* the same as holding a staff position.

Home Alone

Making It On Your Own, by Paul and Sarah Edwards (Jeremy P. Tarcher, 1991) offers some useful hints for freelancers. The authors also offer an on-line newsletter of the same name.

When you are a staff employee, the longer you work for someone, the greater your chances are of becoming a lifer, all things being equal. Do a good job, pay your dues, and you might just retire at a ripe old age with a gold watch and a luscious pension.

As a freelancer, in contrast, you don't have this assurance. Even though you will likely one day build a stable of clients who will hire you over and over, every freelance assignment is new and different from the last job—even if the work and the client are the same. Furthermore, no job carries any guarantee of continued employment. Because the client doesn't have to go through any rigmarole to fire you (no paper trail, no Human Resources call, no hearing or evalua-tions), it's easy to dump you: just stop calling. This means that once you're a freelancer, you're constantly being put to the test.

To be a success as a freelancer, you have to know your stuff. Approach every job with the attitude that you'll do the best possible job. Freelancing has no room for time-servers, people who are putting in their hours until the senior citizen discount kicks in and the *AARP Bulletin* arrives in the mail.

People Who Need People

Mind Your Own Business

To make it as a freelancer, treat every job as though it's your first job. Pretend that your reputation depends on it—because it does.

Let's suppose you've been on the same job for a few years. Your supervisor knows and trusts you, respects your work, and appreciates your sense of initiative. You're a well-rated employee, presumably highly valued, too. You get along with all your co-workers. You've played nice and shared your toys, and people think well of you—and with good cause. You're a valuable worker, admired colleague, and all-around nice person. Now is the time to mine the good will you've built up.

A solid relationship with your soon-to-be former boss and your colleagues can be a resource even more valuable than a savvy stockbroker, reliable baby-sitter, or faithful plumber. Your former employer and co-workers can be extremely valuable sources for freelance assignments in the future. Here are a handful of proven ways to work the system. Each one has been tested in the field, by me and my fellow freelance friends.

1. As soon as your plans are firm, tell your supervisor.

2. Ask your supervisor's advice about your career change; carefully consider what he or she has to say. Odds are, your boss has been around the block a few more times than you have.

3. Ask your supervisor for the names of other people in your business who have become freelancers. These people can become valuable sources of work as well as information about the field.

4. Give plenty of notice. No matter how desperate you are to go freelance, *never* leave your supervisor and co-workers in the lurch. Tie up all the loose ends at the office. You can always wait another few weeks to make the break.

5. As soon as your plans are firm and everything is worked out with the boss, tell your co-workers about your new career as a freelancer.

6. Describe your plans in detail so people know what type of freelance work you will be doing.

7. Don't be shy! Ask your supervisor for assignments you could do as a freelancer.

8. Solicit everyone's advice and ask them for potential leads. Take careful notes so you get the names and addresses right.

9. Be sure that everyone has your telephone number and e-mail address so you can stay in touch. Get their addresses and telephone numbers, too.

10. Once you leave, call your former supervisor and colleagues often to keep up with the business and to snag potential leads.

11. Don't forget to take your Rolodex with you! It's a gold mine of possible contacts.

12. Finally, have new business cards printed up before you leave your staff job. Hand out cards to everyone before you clean out your desk.

Home Alone
An increasing number of freelancers get their start by first *telecommuting*, working at home while remaining on the company payroll. Currently, about 11 million people are telecommuting, usually tethered to the company via computer. This arrangement allows you to stick a foot in the water before jumping off the diving board.

Mind Your Own Business
Always tell your boss you're leaving before you tell your co-workers. Never let your boss hear your plans from someone else— even if you hate the boss.

Home Alone
Your former employer and co-workers can be a great source for freelance jobs even if you're going into an entirely different field. You never know who someone knows.

Bet You Didn't Know

In general, call established contacts about every ten days to two weeks. More often and you'll look like you can't get a date for the prom. Less often, and people might think you're only calling for work. (Which is largely the truth, but you *do* want to maintain the illusion of personal concern.)

You know that your former supervisor and colleagues can be valuable sources for potential customers. But what if you're leaving your job on a less-than-cheerful note? First and foremost, don't burn your bridges. You'll make enough necessary enemies in life. Don't make any extra ones.

Okay, so you hate the job. Is that any reason to bail without saying *sayonara*? I know you're tired of stagnating wages, inflexible schedules, and obsolete promises about job security. I know you need to strike a blow for personal and professional freedom—but don't go postal. Never. It's as dangerous as getting between Dagwood and his sandwich or Arnie and a barbell. Remember, you need those contacts more than ever once you're on your own.

The Thrill of the Hunt

What happens if you don't have any good contacts from a previous job? Or you've tapped them all and the phone still isn't ringing? Here are some other places to look for work:

1. It's the latest, it's the greatest, it's the library! Check the vocational indices, the business newspapers, and the want ads.

2. Your local Chamber of Commerce. Find out who's looking to hire freelancers who do that thing you do.

3. Colleges and universities. They frequently hire freelancers to write, index, and manage financial affairs. They're also a great place to find freelance work in public relations. Colleges are also a source of information, through alumni associations and classes.

4. City and government agencies, especially the Small Business Administration, are another potential source of freelance work and useful information.

5. Small-business development agencies are a good place to network. More on this in Chapter 17.

6. The World Wide Web. Keep reading.

Working the Web

The *Internet* is a vast computer network of computer networks. It's composed of people, hardware, and software. With the proper equipment, you can sit at your computer and communicate with someone at any place in the world as long as that person also has the proper equipment. Did you know that...

Home Alone
"Working from Home," a forum offered on CompuServe Information Service, is an electronic network of several thousand home-based freelancers. It includes a library of newsletters and articles on an array of business and marketing issues.

➤ The Internet is accessible in more than 100 countries—and the number is increasing every day.

➤ More than 30 million computer users populate the so-called "global village."

➤ The number of participants increases by 15 percent a month.

➤ In five years, several hundred million people are expected to be online.

➤ There are currently about 50 million Web pages.

➤ By the magical year 2000, online advertising will exceed $2.6 billion. (*Time*)

By "surfin' the Web," you can peruse databases at the Library of Congress, book airline tickets, balance your checkbook, view masterpieces from the Louvre, dissect a virtual frog, receive electronic newsletters, send e-mail, and chat with others online. Most important for our purposes here, you can check online databases for jobs.

Take My Word For It
Electronic mail (e-mail) involves the transmission of messages over a communications network.

It's plain as Donald Trump's ego that e-mail and other electronic methods of communication are an increasingly important method of getting work. Some freelancers argue that being online isn't an option, it's a necessity. Be there or be square. Also, e-mail is a big money-saver; it cuts way down on phone bills and courier charges.

Here's what you'll find in these information networks:

➤ Job directories

➤ Job listings

➤ "Bulletin boards" for specific industries

➤ Resumes

➤ Web pages for professional associations

➤ Web pages for specific industries

Home Alone

Many public libraries now offer free access to the Internet, from on-site computers or from home on your own PC. Just dial into a special phone number and your modem can link to the Net.

Some companies recruit freelancers heavily through the Internet, especially those focused on technology. But even those industries that have traditionally shunned technology like a vampire shuns garlic are getting into the act. For example, I've seen job offers for computer mavens to write ancillary textbook products, such as CD-ROMs, Web sites, and animated "books."

Even if you're technophobic, you can surf the Net with confidence. Hey, if all those three-year-olds who can't even tie their shoelaces can do it, so can you. You can drive on the Information Superhighway (as the Internet is often called) any number of different ways, many for less than it costs to take a spin down the New Jersey Turnpike. But if you're just getting into computer technology, consider signing on with an ISP (Internet service provider) such as America Online, CompuServe, or Prodigy. These services make merging on the Superhighway easier than parallel parking.

Hit the Bull's Eye

With all of these places to look for work, it's important to zero in on the correct market. Your ability to get jobs is largely the result of targeting your clients. Don't waste your time and effort on a scattershot approach. Find the right place to enter the field, pinpoint a list of hot prospects, and go to it.

Time to bare my soul. I didn't have a clue about targeting clients when I started free-lancing in 1981. At the time, I was teaching high school English. Over our egg salad at lunch one day, a fellow teacher said, "You know, what we need is a good review book for the Advanced Placement English exam." Actually, what we needed was an air conditioner in the lunch room, but that's another story. With absolutely no experience, contacts, or background in publishing (well, I *had* read a lot of books), I decided that I was going to write that great review book. I checked the competition, wrote a sample chapter and a table of contents, and sent them to every publisher of review books I could find listed in *Literary Market Place*. Let me tell you, there were a lot of review book publishers in 1981.

Bet You Didn't Know

Literary Market Place is the bible and telephone directory of the publishing business. It lists every publisher in the United States. (There are companion volumes for foreign publishers.)

So who bought the book? The first company on the list: Arco. I shall forever be grateful to the editor who gave me my break, the wonderful Linda Bernbach. She taught me a great deal of what I know—especially the importance of targeting my efforts. Since then, I've saved a lot in postage, aggravation, and embarrassment.

Now, I do a whole lot of research before I send out a single word. I find out which companies are buying what I have to sell, what they pay, and what terms they offer (such as work for hire versus royalties). I check to see if I have any personal contacts in the company, too.

Like a Virgin

Deciding who to target is the easy part. Selling yourself is the really, really hard part, as every freelancer I have ever known agrees. I've never met a single freelancer who is really comfortable hawking it, even if they know they are ideally suited for the job they're going after. Scouting for business is especially scary for novice freelancers, who usually feel tentative about their new work status in any event.

But selling yourself as a freelancer is one of those things you just can't dodge. Remember what Queen Victoria is rumored to have told her daughter to help her endure her wifely duties on her wedding night: "Just close your eyes, dear, and think of England." The same advice applies to trolling for work.

"Until you've been out there selling yourself without the mantle of a large corporation behind you, you can't know how difficult it can be," one freelancer told me. That's true for everyone, including the most affable and sociable among us. Even if you're accustomed to marketing and selling a product or service for someone else, it's an entirely different matter when it's *you* you're selling.

First Contact

Eventually, you'll have to boldly go where many other freelancers have gone before. How can you reach out and make that first contact? There are really only two ways: write or call.

Many staff workers much prefer to be contacted by mail first, because it gives them the option of responding at a time when it's convenient for them. I interviewed Steven Jay Griffel, an executive at PubWorks, about this. "Being contacted by phone is an intrusion in my day," he said. "In many cases, I won't even take the call if I don't already know the freelancer. It puts me on the spot to have to evaluate someone without seeing their resume first."

I recommend that you send your resume and cover letter and wait four to five days. Then call the client and ask politely if he or she has received your material. If so, say, "When would it be convenient for us to talk about my doing some work for you?" You can set up

Home Alone
Most freelancers report getting their best jobs from personal contacts, but don't rule out snagging some work from advertisements. Don't wait for a bolt from the blue: Study the ads every day, as you would *TV Guide*, the Weather Channel, and the cutie who dishes the slurpees in the 7-Eleven.

an appointment to talk on the phone or have some face-time in the office. This way, you avoid putting the client on the spot, give the client ample time to review your qualifications, and get the chance to speak with the client when he or she is in a receptive mood. See Chapter 16 for specifics on preparing your resume and cover letter.

Story Hour

So you've set up an appointment for an interview, by phone or in person. Gulp. Now what do you do? Well, for starters, reaching out and touching someone doesn't mean you have to be best friends. It doesn't even mean you have to be friends—and usually you shouldn't be. Making a personal business contact doesn't imply intimacy. No kissy-face, please. Too many freelancers come on like they've been locked in solitary longer than the Birdman of Alcatraz, willing to spill their guts for an extra slice of bread. Read on to find out what to say when you make contact—and what *not* to say.

Bosom Buddies?

Personal matters have no part in a business relationship. Even though there will be days when you'll feel like you've been locked up tighter than Houdini and longer than the Hunchback of Notre Dame, resist the urge to let it all hang out with a client. You're better off dialing 900 numbers than unburdening yourself on your unsuspecting prospective clients.

Here are some guidelines for keeping the client conversation on a professional plane, where it belongs. You might be able to relax your conversation after you have worked with someone for a while, but especially in the beginning, err on the side of caution.

Talk about:

➤ The current job, especially its scope and parameters

➤ Related past assignments you have completed

➤ Your qualifications, especially the experience you've had that suits you for this assignment

➤ The computer system you use, if relevant

➤ Your competence with e-mail and other relevant technology

➤ When the client needs the job: deadlines

➤ Compensation (*if* you are offered the assignment)

➤ The possibility of compensation for expenses (ditto)

➤ Chain of command: To whom do you report?

➤ How the client wants the job: courier services, electronic transmission, fax, and so on

➤ How you came to be offered this job (personal recommendation, advertisement, and so forth)

➤ Whether this job can lead to others

Don't talk about:

Home Alone
Always thank people who recommend you for an assignment—whether you get the assignment or not. For a small job, send a note on your personal stationary. (Be sure to enclose a business card.) For a biggie, spring for a nice thank-you lunch.

➤ Your spouse, as in how he's lost his job and you really, really, really need this assignment

➤ Your children, as in your teenager's new tattoo or latest body piercing

➤ Your pets, as in what Fido did on the rug last night

➤ Your problems getting your dainties whiter than white

➤ How your mother/father/Aunt Venus is driving you crazy

➤ How your eczema/scabies/toe fungus has cleared up since you got that new medicine

➤ How you're using this client's meager little job as a stepping stone to some *real* work

➤ Your cruise through the Greek islands, trek up K2, or foray through the Velt

➤ Why you think the current administration is corrupt

➤ Any litigation you're involved in

➤ Your sex life, or lack thereof

This isn't to say you can't become friends with *some* of your customers. Notice that key word is *some*—meaning two or three. Hey, you might even marry a few of them. But you don't have my permission to invite them all to Thanksgiving dinner. This is business, kiddo.

Talk Soup

Here are some additional guidelines to keep you on track.

1. Set aside a certain time each day or week to make calls. This will help you get motivated. I make business calls in the morning, before my brain has filled up with trivia.

Mind Your Own Business

Clients are always reassured when prospective hires cite past clients. But be very careful not to violate client confidentiality by describing a project you're currently working on. Often, the project is under wraps until it's completed.

2. Write out a script and practice what you're going to say. (Remember when you started dating? Okay, so it was yesterday. The script worked, didn't it?)

3. Be enthusiastic, but not effusive or phony.

4. Don't boast, but be sure to state your qualifications for the assignment.

5. Never lie. Don't even stretch the truth.

Dot the I's and Cross the T's

Be sure to keep track of all the calls you make. (This holds for all the letters you send, too.) I keep all my records on my computer hard drive with back-up disks, but friends of mine who hang with the pen-and-paper crowd prefer using index cards. Whatever method you use, here's what you should record:

➤ The date and time of the call

➤ The name of the person to whom you spoke and his or her position in the company

➤ How you got the lead (former colleague, online source, advertisement)

➤ A summary of the conversation, especially any promises or leads

➤ When you intend to next make contact

Sometimes It's Over *Before* the Fat Lady Sings

Sometimes, a lead just doesn't pan out. Who knows why? Perhaps they don't like your voice; maybe the company is shaky and no one's getting work right now. Whatever the reason, it's important to know when to throw in the towel. There's no sense wasting your time if you're not going to get any work out of it. Here are three hints that you're barking up the wrong tree:

➤ They're never available to take your calls.

➤ They never call back.

➤ When you do make contact, they're rude.

If you don't make the cut, don't despair. There are plenty of other places to find work. Don't waste time beating yourself up for real or perceived wrongs; instead, just move on. Take the hint and close the door behind you.

The Least You Need to Know

➤ Make new friends but keep the old. One is silver and the other gold—and they can both give you work.

➤ In addition to personal contacts, work the Web and use other resources.

➤ Target your market. You'll save time, money, and embarrassment.

➤ Once you've got some leads, get out there and make contact. Be professional and keep good records.

➤ Want work? Go after it. Hustle, hustle, hustle.

Part 3
Setting Up Shop

In 1992, one-person offices constituted a $7.5 billion segment of the computer-equipment and office-equipment market. By 1996, the purchasing power of these one-person operations topped $10 billion. According to market researchers, there's hardly a phone, fax, or computer maker who isn't desperate to reach what promises to be one of the fastest-growing markets for such manufacturers.

In addition to computers, software, fax machines, and telecommunications systems, freelancers need furniture, office supplies, and lighting. And let us not forget photocopiers and scanners, business cards, and stationery. The following section teaches you how to be a smart shopper when it comes to equipping your home office—so you don't have to shop 'til you drop!

Chapter 9

Space: The Final Frontier

In This Chapter

➤ Get the inside skinny on zoning laws

➤ Choose the best place for your new office

➤ Figure out the best way to make some space for yourself

➤ Furnish your home office

Carving out a niche for your home office may be more difficult than it first appears. After all, you have to contend with the well-established "Law of Diminishing Space." I'll bet that you've had firsthand experience with the two parts of this law:

1. Your possessions expand relative to the amount of available space, until they fill all of it.

2. You always need just *a little* more space than you have.

In this chapter, I'll help you find the space you need to set up a home office. Then you'll explore what equipment you need for your freelance career. Along the way, I'll share a few words on zoning laws, to make sure that your office is legal in the first place.

Zoned Out

Everyone loves Sara Lee; unfortunately, the same cannot be said of home offices. More than one solid citizen has tried to crumble *that* cookie by babbling to the authorities about a neighbor's illegal home office. For the most part, municipalities worry that home offices will translate into increased traffic, deliveries, and parking problems that jeopardize the residential flavor of the neighborhood. And sometimes, they do.

Mind Your Own Business
There are free-lancers who really don't need an office. If you are a consultant who works outside your home, you may not need a home office per se. A file cabinet and shelf may do the trick nicely. Consider your needs carefully before you shop.

How would you like it if your next-door neighbor operated a backyard fireworks company—day and night? What about a recording studio for rock-bottom rock bands? A training ground for performing geese? What about something as common as a doctor's office, a lawyer's office, or even a beauty parlor? Definitely better than the honking of geese, you say, until you realize that these offices bring scores of cars double-parked up and down your otherwise peaceful street. More honking, only this time it's horns rather than beaks.

"But I'm just one itty-bitty person working at home," you yelp. "Tough nougies," your neighbors may reply. "There's plenty of office space out there, and that's where business belongs—in the business district, not in the residential district. If we let *you* in, next come the performing geese."

Fortunately, zoning officials aren't dopey. They recognize the need to restrict noisy, bustling small businesses in residential areas. At the same time, the laws make exceptions for many small home-based businesses.

Boning Up on Zoning

Most communities are divided into zones that limit the types of buildings and activities allowed in each area. Here are the five most common zones:

1. Residential
2. Commercial
3. Institutional
4. Industrial
5. Agricultural

Agricultural zones are generally nonrestrictive. As a result, just about any type of business can be set up within an agricultural zone. That's because the population is sparse and few neighbors would be annoyed by a home office. In fact, the most common home business in an agricultural zone is the family farm.

The same cannot be said for the other zones, however. Most of us live in residential zones. Houses line the streets; the only business is an occasional ice-cream truck. Local town zoning laws generally focus on limiting the size of the office and the number of employees you can hire, especially in residential areas. An estimated nine out of ten towns have some restrictions on the type of home employment allowed. For example:

Mind Your Own Business
There can be zones within zones, further restricting the types of activities that can take place in a certain area.

IS THAT CLEAR?

➤ In one Long Island town, "professionals" are allowed to have a home office that measures no more than 400 square feet and have no more than one employee.

➤ In a certain midwestern town, home offices cannot take up more than one-third of the first floor of the residence.

➤ One town forbids home offices to display business signs.

➤ In another instance, employees must be members of the owner's immediate family (no third-cousins-twice-removed-on-my-mother's-side need apply).

➤ Commonly, a display of goods or services relating to the home office must not be visible from the outside of the residence.

➤ Zoning laws often restrict the number customers at a time, usually to no more than three.

➤ In another area, home offices are completely forbidden in any area designated as "Residential Zone A." Even an unobtrusive freelance writer (much less an obtrusive one) cannot work from a house located in Zone A.

However, regulations vary from town to town, so any freelancer contemplating setting up a home office should check with the local authorities first. More on this later.

Tattle Tale, Ginger Ale

Most building officials don't obsess about ferreting out illegal home offices. In part, that's because they rarely have the personnel to go from community to community peeking behind doors. Besides, they usually don't have to bother. Why not? Their work is often done for them: A freelancer's neighbors often spill the beans about a home office. The neighbors are usually disgruntled over increased mail deliveries or jealous about what they perceive as the freelancer's colossal earnings.

Home Alone
If your business cannot function if bound by local zoning regulations, you may be able to get a special use permit to do business. Commonly, this is handled by your local zoning board and requires a public hearing.

How do zoning officials follow up leads? Here are two clues they use to determine whether a freelancer is indeed running a home office:

1. A sign in the window
2. An ad in the Yellow Pages

Bet You Didn't Know

Fines for an illegal home office usually range from $250 to $1,000. The larger fines are levied against freelancers who deliberately violate the law, especially after they have been warned.

Twilight Zone

Before I set up my home office on the ground floor of my modest Cape Cod–style home, I trotted down to the local zoning board. To the local officials, it didn't much matter if I was a true freelancer selling services or a product independently or a telecommuter working solely for one company. What *did* matter to the members of the zoning commission was the possible disruption my working at home might cause to my neighbors. They questioned me about toxic odors, loud noises, and excessive visitors.

As a writer, I tend not to emit many toxic fumes, I rarely play the radio over a hum, and the only regular visitors I get are the Federal Express delivery man and an occasional Jehovah's Witness. Aside from that, most of my neighbors didn't seem to know that I was *working* at home; they assumed I was spending my days lounging on the sofa eating bonbons and reading romance novels. (Hey, I have to keep up my strength and do research, don't I?) Since I was neither noxious nor noisy, my papers went through smoothly.

Home Alone
In addition to contacting the local zoning board, you can call your local Chamber of Commerce or the planning commission to get the scoop on zoning laws in your area.

The moral of the story: Before you start working at home, get the inside skinny on the local zoning laws. Here are three guidelines to follow:

➤ Find out if your home office is in compliance with the local zoning laws.

➤ If it isn't, take whatever steps are necessary to obey the laws.

➤ File all relevant documents.

A Room of One's Own

There are people who could work quite well propped up on a pile of bricks smack in the middle of Route 66. There are also people who appear in public wearing pink curlers and rubber thongs, but I won't go *there*.

You can't set up your office on Route 66, but you *could* work in the shed next to the barracuda Uncle Albert bagged in Bermuda—but would you want to? Do you *really* want to sizzle in the summer, shiver in the winter, and stare at a stuffed barracuda's razor-sharp incisors throughout? You'll be spending many hours every day sitting in your office. Why make work harder than it has to be? Here are some suggestions that can help you size up your space.

And in This Corner...

Physically, your work space should be separate from everything else. Your office has to be a place for work, not pleasure (even though work *can* be pleasure, of course). Your office should be relatively quiet, private, and allow you easy access to your business supplies, especially necessities such as a telephone, paper, and chocolate-chip cookies.

It's also important for tax purposes that your home office be a "defined work space used exclusively for your business" (as the IRS tax code reads). If your office is a corner of your den or family room where the tykes frolic, for example, the IRS could bounce your home office deduction. See Chapter 21 for more details, and remember to consult with your tax expert before you select a location.

The following worksheet can help you narrow your preferences and requirements for a home office. Write your answer to each question on the lines provided.

Up Close and Personal

1. How much space do I need?

   _____

2. What kind of space do I need?

   _____

3. Do I have any special restrictions on the type of space I need for my office? (For example, do I need ground-floor space for handicap accessibility?)

   _____

4. Will clients visit my home? What special needs does that present, such as an outside entrance?

   _____

---

5. Will I have an assistant? How will this impact my family?

_____

6. What are my personal preferences? (For example, do I want to be within earshot of the squabbling kids or as far away as possible? Must I have a window or will a basement be okay?)

_____

IS THAT CLEAR?

Mind Your Own Business
Regarding home offices, size matters. You'll *always* need more space than you think.

Head Space

Even if your home is bursting at the seams, there's usually room for the things you *need* to do—and *have* to do. But not every nook and cranny in your house would make a good spot for a home office, even though it may appear that you have no choice but to locate there. For example, if you choose a busy place in your house, you may run the risk of having your important papers used to wrap fish and your floppy disks used as props for uneven table legs.

Here are some places that make poor home offices and the reasons why:

Place	Potential Problems
Dining room	You'll have to move everything before every meal (assuming you like to eat on a regular basis).
Kitchen	Grape jelly on your papers told a tale on you.
Your bedroom	Do you really want to have clients visit you there?
Bathroom	Oh, pleeze. Has it come to that?

This isn't to say that you can't carve a small space out of one of these areas and make it all your own. It *is* to say that it won't be easy. If at all possible, consider these ten areas as potential locations for a home office instead:

1. Part of a finished basement

2. A *separate* section of the den or family room

3. A large closet that has been gutted and refinished

4. A spare bedroom

5. Part of the laundry room

6. The attic

7. The porch

8. Under the stairs

9. Landings

10. The living room (does anyone *ever* use it?)

Mind Your Own Business
Never put your home office in bad space. Bad space is too cold, too hot, too damp, too bright, too dark.

I know a freelancer who created an office in her mother's house. With the kids grown and flown the coop, there's plenty of room in the old split-level homestead. Mom even makes lunch sometimes.

While we're here, consider setting up your home office outside your home. Commercial rent is usually figured on square feet of space. Below are some of the major advantages and disadvantages of establishing an outside freelance office.

Advantages	Disadvantages
Greater privacy	Higher cost
Feels more professional	Adds a commute
Separates personal and business lives	More rigid hours

Up Against the Wall

How can you find the space that will work best for you? I suggest that you take an inventory of your home. Walk through each possible location (spare bedroom, basement, and so on) and try to imagine how you would use the available space to set up your office. As you do, complete the inventory on the following page. Make additional copies if you are blessed with more than three possible places in which to set up your office.

Mind Your Own Business
Avoid using your freelance office and materials for your personal chores. Mingling life and work will make it impossible for you and your beleaguered accountant to sort out tax deductions at the end of your fiscal year. More on taxes in Chapter 21.

Good, Bad, Ugly?

Room #1: _____

Advantages as an office

    1. _____
    2. _____
    3. _____

Disadvantages as an office

    1. _____
    2. _____
    3. _____

Room #2: _____

Advantages as an office

    1. _____
    2. _____
    3. _____

Disadvantages as an office

    1. _____
    2. _____
    3. _____

Room #3: _____

Advantages as an office

    1. _____
    2. _____
    3. _____

Disadvantages as an office

    1. _____
    2. _____
    3. _____

Possession Is 9/10 of the Law

Remember how you felt when your younger sibling violated your space by reading your comic books, trading your baseball cards, or (worst of all) eating the rest of your Halloween candy? My younger sister borrowed one of my dresses without permission—and then altered it to fit her. I was not happy.

Remember and respect your family's space. Don't appropriate someone else's territory. Maybe that empty room isn't empty after all; perhaps the kids use it for a playroom or a den. The empty workbench area in the basement may be cherished space for your "one day I'll be handy" spouse. This isn't to say that you can't pull rank. After all, work is work. But if you do decide to become a space invader, try to keep the peace. You don't want to start out with everyone on your case. Wait a while for that to happen.

Home Improvements

You've searched high and low and low and high—there's no place at all in your home that can become an office. In this case, you might have to remodel to make the space you need. For instance, you might decide to erect a wall in the middle of one large room to make two smaller rooms. Whenever possible, first try a cheaper and less drastic alternative. For example, perhaps you could use a bookcase as a room divider. This would not only give you the separate office you need, but also provide storage space.

You might decide to go all the way—raise the roof, add a room, and so on. In these cases, I strongly urge you to hire an architect or other building professional to help you plan the renovations. Even if you know your way around a circular saw and can do the work yourself, it's never a bad idea to have a pro take a look. These folks can also advise you on local building and zoning codes, and help you avoid expensive errors. Renovations can cost an arm and a leg—and they might very well be worth it. But spend the money wisely.

Home Alone
Always check local zoning codes before you start slicing and dicing your home. Get all the building permits you need so you don't give the nosy neighbors more ammunition.

Also remember that if your clients never visit, you can get away with a minimal office. But if your clients are going to come to you, you should spiff the place up a little more. Or a lot more.

Before you start tearing down walls, think twice. It's not a good idea to undertake any drastic renovations in your home until you have been established as a freelancer for at least a year. Then you'll have a better idea of your needs.

A Loaf of Bread, a Jug of Wine, and a $1,500 Chair?

To be a happy and comfortable freelancer, you don't need custom-made shelving, an antique oak desk, and a $1,500 chair. On the other hand, we do live in an age of conspicuous consumerism, and *someone* has to keep the economy chugging along. Goodness knows, I have done *my* share.

And hey, you work in your office all day long, so it should be comfortable as well as functional. You're not a monk and your home office shouldn't be a cell. (If you *are* a monk, that's a different story.) Let's start with the five business basics and build from there. Here's a list of the bare necessities you need to get down to business:

1. Something to sit on
2. Something to work on
3. Lights
4. Storage space
5. Special needs (whatever your particular job requires—there's always something)

Within each category, you can spend a lot or a little, depending on your budget and needs. Below is a description of each of these necessities.

Home Alone
Consider buying used office furniture. You can often get just what you need at the price you want. Just be sure to measure everything before you buy (to make sure it will fit in the space you've picked out for it), because making returns may be difficult.

The Best Seat in the House: Something to Sit On

There are times when a cigar is just a cigar, but nowadays, office furniture is rarely just what it appears to be. The key word in office furniture is *ergonomics,* which means achieving the most comfortable relationship between you and your tools. It applies to all furniture, but especially to chairs.

Take My Word For It
Ergonomics is achieving the most comfortable relationship between you and your office furniture.

Here's what to look for when you shop for an office chair:

➤ *Seat height:* The height is correct when your body is properly supported and your feet are flat on the floor. Correct height supports the small of your back.

➤ The *knee tilt* mechanism lets you tilt back while your feet remain flat on the floor. This relieves pressure on your spine and reduces leg muscle strain and fatigue.

➤ *Lumbar support* lets the chair move up and down or in and out to support the small of your back. This minimizes pressure on the base of your spine and reduces fatigue caused by long hours of sitting.

➤ *Adjustable armrests* move up and down to promote proper forearm support. Some armrests also
tilt forward and backward to maintain optimum
skeletal alignment. This helps prevent neck and
shoulder aches.

➤ The *seat and back angle* can be changed by tilting
back in the chair. The angles can be adjusted
independently on some models. Equal distribu-
tion of body weight helps to prevent backaches.

Be prepared to shell out some serious bucks for such a
chair (after all, it does everything but the laundry). On
the low end, figure on spending about $100 to $150. A
high-end office chair can cost you more than $1,500.
For instance, the Aeron chair ($765–$1,125) molds
itself to your contours. Figure it this way—with a boffo
chair, you won't need a personal trainer!

Join the Desk Set: Something to Work On

Back when Father Knew Best and we left things to the
Beaver, freelancers worked on desks. Today, in the
"Nick at Nite" age, we have workstations. These are
multi-level, adjustable surfaces for work events. Think
of them as superdesks. So nix on the dining room
table for work—even if you do add a leaf or two. I
have nothing against the dining room table for
dinner, but it's not the work surface of choice for the
savvy freelancer. Today's office furniture is *adjustable,*
easy to change to suit your changing work needs.

> **Mind Your Own Business**
> Look for a chair that carries a reliable warranty. After all, if you're going to spend as much for an office chair as you did for your first car, you better be able to return it if it doesn't suit your needs. A 15-year limited manufacturer's warranty is standard for a good office chair.
>
> IS THAT CLEAR?

> **Home Alone**
> I recommend that you buy a chairmat. You know, a vinyl slipcover for the floor. They're cheap (less than $15) and provide a smooth, hard surface so you can roll your chair easily without mangling the carpet (or wearing thin the linoleum).

I'm a big fan of adjustable office furniture because it's cheap and can accommodate your
changing needs. It also gives you the choice of different units, such as a computer cabinet, open cart, desk, table, or databoard. Further, commercial office furniture tends to be
too big and bulky for the average home office. Ask yourself these five questions as you
shop for office furniture:

1. How much space do I have for my office furniture?

2. What will I be using my desk space for?

3. What equipment will I need and where will it go?

4. When will I be upgrading my equipment?

5. What is my budget?

You can buy office furniture from any fully stocked office store. Increasingly, warehouse superstores are carrying some decent low-end office furniture as well. If you're looking for a bargain (and who doesn't like a bargain?) consider looking beyond the standard office-supply stores. Check out tag sales, house sales, garage sales, yard sales, and even school surplus sales.

For a quick fix, consider a laptop. You can take your computer with you to the chaise lounge on the back porch or to the picnic table at the park, thus creating a portable work space. Of course, this only relates to freelancers whose work is based mostly on the computer and who want to get a really even tan. You'll still need a workstation for the everyday grind (and for cloudy days!).

Darkness Visible: Lights

Home Alone
If you can't get rid of glare, you can purchase an aptly named *glare screen* for your computer. This handy-dandy little device greatly cuts down on eyestrain.

Give considerable thought to lighting. For example, if you work on a computer all day long (as I do), you'll want soft light to minimize glare. This reduces eyestrain and head-aches. Draw a scale picture of your office, including all windows and noting whether the exposure is north, south, east, or west. Bring this sketch to a lighting center and consult with an expert to select the lighting that's best for your specific work and needs.

If you're starting from scratch or can install new lighting in your office, think in terms of indirect light. I'm a big fan of track lights, because you can aim each individual bullet where you need it. You can adjust the bullets in the after-noon and evening, too, as the natural light shifts. The effect is gentle and soothing, not brassy.

Then there's task lighting, which can be anything from an old-fashioned desk lamp to a custom-designed combination of sophisticated fixtures. I like an architect's lamp, because it can be twisted and turned to illuminate just about any corner.

Here are three more factors to consider when you shop for lighting:

1. A white ceiling and white walls help diffuse the light from indirect light sources.

2. Avoid reflective work surfaces, especially those that are shiny white or black. These create glare.

3. Don't rule out under-the-counter lighting. It can eliminate the shadows that tend to surround equipment.

File It: Storage Space

Some hoity-toity interior designers scoff at the lowly file cabinet as being, well, lowly. Because file cabinets are bulky and ugly, they sneer, you're better off storing your papers in prehistoric beehives or antique Armenian armoires.

Well, I like file cabinets. They do exactly what they were designed to do: store papers. Further, file cabinets are inexpensive, especially if they're second-hand. File cabinets even come in different styles: vertical files (tall and thin, like me), lateral files (drawers pull out sideways), and rolling files (on casters). This makes it easy for you to find exactly the kind of file cabinet you need to fit the space you have.

Home Alone
If you have to prioritize because money is tight, here's the order of purchase: chair, lights, workstation (also known as a desk), and storage.

Special Needs

Tailor your office furniture to meet your special needs. These have to do with the nature of your work, the space you have available, and your personal requirements. Also take into consideration the needs of any clients who will be coming for appointments. Try to make your office as handicap-accessible as possible.

The Least You Need to Know

➤ Check your local zoning laws, so you don't find yourself out of business before you're even in it.

➤ Find yourself a good space—in your home or out of it.

➤ Line up your office basics: a chair, workstation, lights, storage space, and accommodations for special needs.

➤ Invest in a good chair. Your body will thank you.

113

Chapter 10

Hard-Wired for Success

> ## In This Chapter
>
> ➤ Assess the impact of technology on your freelance business
>
> ➤ Learn the basics of buying computer hardware and software
>
> ➤ Find out more about fax machines, photocopiers, and scanners

A man in a Ford Granada pulled up next to a Rolls. He yelled at the guy in the Rolls, "Hey, you got a telephone in there?"

The guy in the Rolls said, "Yes, of course I do."

"I got one too...see?"

"Uh huh, yes, that's very nice."

Then the man in the Granada said, "You got a fax machine?"

"Why, actually, yes, I do."

"I do too! See? It's right here!"

"Uh-huh."

The light was just about to turn green and the guy in the Granada said, "So, do you have a double bed in back there?"

And the guy in the Rolls said, "No! Do you?"

"Yep, got my double bed right in back here. See?"

The light turned and the man in the Granada zoomed off. Well, the guy in the Rolls immediately ordered a double bed for the back of his car. When the job was done, he drove all over town until he found the Granada. The Granada's windows were all fogged up and he felt a little awkward, but he tapped on the foggy window.

The man in the Granada finally opened the window and peeked out. The guy in the Rolls said, "I got a double bed installed in my Rolls."

"You got me out of the shower to tell me *that*?" the man in the Granada replied.

A shower in your car? You mean you don't have one yet? A pasta machine/can opener/ice shaver with a massage attachment in your kitchen? Been there, done that. You name the gadget and you can probably get it, and at an affordable, price, too. This is especially apparent with home office equipment—and vitally important. When it comes to being a freelancer working from a home office, technology can move mountains.

In this chapter you'll learn what computer equipment, fax machines, photocopiers, and other neat-o technology is available to make your job as a freelancer easier and more efficient. Then you can decide which machines are best suited to your specific type of freelance work and lifestyle.

Hello, Dave

New office technology is dramatically changing the way we live and work. In the negative column, technology is taking away jobs by enabling companies to downsize, restructure, and reengineer. With today's computer and telecommunications equipment, more work can be done electronically, and so companies need fewer full-time employees. To our sometimes delight but more frequent frustration, we're served these days by automated tellers, voice mail, and electronic kiosks rather than by real live people. Whole floors of factories operate in the dark, housing only robots, not people.

Home Alone
Entrepreneurial Edge Online Webzine (*www.edgeonline.com*) is filled with how-to articles and links for small businesses.

But in the positive column, new technology is also putting powerful tools once available only to large organizations into the hands of individuals who are using them to become freelancers. For example, a decade or two ago, the computer sitting on my desk would have been larger than the old VW beetle. It also would have cost more than the GNP of a mid-sized banana republic. Not so today. Today's PCs are modest affairs and cost less than my last (used) car—by far.

Computers can help you streamline your freelance business in an astonishing number of ways. They can make you more agile than your larger competitors, help you produce high-quality products, and enable you to establish checks and balances. Most importantly, in many fields such as design, television, animation, publishing, and film, you can't do the work without a computer and all the peripheral equipment.

Here are a few more things that computers can do for your home-based business:

➤ Budget resources

➤ Monitor cash flow

➤ Keep records

➤ Track accounts receivable

So what if a computer can't dice and slice? It *does* do everything short of making julienne fries. And today's programs are so easy to operate that there's no reason to be afraid of Mr. Computer. Nonetheless...

Cyberphobia Strikes!

For every freelancer whose home office is so filled with machinery that it resembles the bridge of the Starship Enterprise, there's another freelancer who does his or her job the old-fashioned way—with a typewriter, pen, and paper. Sometimes these freelancers don't know what's out there; other times, they're afraid of buying the wrong item and getting stuck with a clunker. As a result, they may be taking a lot longer to do their work. Worst-case scenario: They can't accept certain jobs because they don't have the technology to complete them.

 Bet You Didn't Know

According to an article in *Time* magazine, fewer than half of all small businesspeople own computers. And of those who do, an amazing number have never even plugged their machines in! These virgin computers are being used as expensive tables, bookshelves, and plant stands instead. There are no statistics available on the number of freelancers who use computers, but I'd like to think that we're more tuned in to the realities of work today.

A disturbing number of freelancers suffer from *cyberphobia*, an irrational fear of technology. You know that computers are invaluable to your operation, but are you afraid that your computer will eat important documents and burp back little ***'s? You know that computers track inventory and customers' needs, but do you fret that you'll waste your time arm wrestling your computer for the information it has? Then you, too, may suffer from *cyberphobia*. Take the following quiz to see. Put a check next to every item that describes you.

---

1. You type 2,500,000 words per minute blindfolded.

2. You have many fingers. Unfortunately, they are all thumbs.

3. You can assemble a nuclear reactor, intercept messages from Venus on your short-wave radio, and program a VCR.

4. You can sharpen a pencil.

5. You can sit at a workstation and type for so long that your rear end assumes the shape of the chair.

6. You can fill out invoices and tally numbers in a bubble bath until you turn into a prune.

7. Your friends call you a computer nerd.

8. Your friends call you a Luddite.

9. You own an espresso machine the size of a compact car, a car that cost more than the President's annual salary, and a watch that shows the time on Pluto (in binary).

10. You have a rotary phone.

Answers

If you checked 1, 3, 5, 7, and 9: Beam me up, Scottie.

If you checked 2, 4, 6, 8, and 10: Bet you still bake from scratch, too.

Techno Time

What do your answers to this quiz reveal? Are you a technophobe or a technocrat? If you fall into the former category, it may be time to bite the bullet and become a part of the (soon-to-be) 21st century, bunky. Like it or not, the new technology is something your freelance business just can't afford to do without.

A computer isn't magic. It won't transform mediocre work into a contract-winning presentation any more than I can become Michael Jordan by putting on a basketball uniform. But a computer can give you *power,* the power to do your work easier, faster, and more completely. And thanks to technology, your work will very likely be more accurate, too.

Yes, I know that technology becomes obsolete. Like a fresh starlet, new technology gets old fast. A few years ago, I had a lovely 286 IBM clone. We were very close; we understood each other. Unfortunately, my 286 workhorse was a pony when it came to carrying heavy loads: It didn't have the power to get me on the Web or linked to e-mail. As a result, she had to go out to pasture. Many a tear was shed that day, let me tell you.

Further, buying the wrong system can be an expensive boo-boo. You can get stuck with the computer equivalent of the Edsel, which could be one reason why so many computers end up being glorified plant stands. But computer prices have dropped faster than my stomach on a roller coaster ride and software has improved almost as much as Roseanne's face. Today's computers are far more reliable than ever before.

Home Alone
The best thing of all, from my standpoint, is that computers give you access to information, especially through e-mail, the World Wide Web, and CD-ROMs.

Bet You Didn't Know

Unlike cars, computers don't usually trade in well. Instead of selling my old computers, printers, and so on, I always donate my outdated technology to technical schools. Students learn how to repair machines by working on old ones. This gives my life purpose (and a tax break).

The Well-Equipped Freelancer

Successful freelancers who cling to their typewriters rather than get a computer system are about as common as legitimate tax deductions, sweet-natured teenagers, and skinny linebackers. Nonetheless, there was a sighting of a small but hardy band of typewriter aficionados somewhere in the Michigan woods a few years ago. They were having some difficulty finding typewriter ribbons and correct-o-type, but unlike the Donner party, they were not yet reduced to eating each other.

You know that you have to join the rest of us in the 20th century, even if I have to drag you kicking and screaming. So let me teach you the basics of equipping a freelancer's modern electronic office.

Two Sides of the Same Coin: Hardware and Software

➤ *Hardware:* The physical and mechanical components of a computer system— the electronic circuitry, chips, monitors, disk drives, keyboards, and printers.

➤ *Software:* The programs that make the computer operate.

Take My Word For It

Hardware refers to the electronic circuitry, chips, monitors, disk drives, keyboards, and printers. *Software* refers to the programs that make the computer operate.

Mind Your Own Business

Often, *bundled* software doesn't come with disks. If so, copy the software from the computer onto disks or call the manufacturer and get disks. This way, you can reinstall the software if your computer "crashes" and wipes out its contents. Crashes aren't common, but like tornadoes and tidal waves, they *do* occur.

Fortunately for enterprising freelancers, today we have more software programs available than Captain Kirk had Tribbles, which means that your computer can do just about anything you need it to do, from accounting to zoology. At the very least, you'll need a word-processing program and an accounting program. In addition, you can buy the specific software programs you need to run your freelance operation.

Your hardware determines your software. Don't buy software that can't run on your machine. On the other hand, sometimes the software you need will determine the kind of computer you choose—a Macintosh for people in graphic arts, for example, and a PC for people in accounting. Check with people in your industry to see what the standard is.

Make sure the software you buy suits *your* business. The good news is that more and more software companies are moving away from "one-size-fits-all" software to "you-centric" products. This means that it's a safe bet that the software you need for your freelance business is out there; you just may have to do some searching to find it.

Very often, your computer will come *bundled* with some basic software installed. Obviously, this is the least expensive way to get software and have it installed, too—if it's exactly the software you need. Otherwise, it's as useful as those Tribbles.

You may wish to buy a laptop computer rather than or in addition to a desk model. A laptop computer enables you to work anywhere short of the shower (so stay out of that Granada). All you have to do is fire up the laptop (plug it into the wall outlet—or into the cigarette lighter in your car—if you're low on battery power) and go to town.

Some final words of advice: Beware of computer fanatics, people who swear that their brand of computer is the Holy Grail of machines. And stay away from the cutting edge, unless you want to risk getting sliced. It's always smartest to buy software and hardware that have a proven track record.

Bet You Didn't Know

The *Internet* is a vast worldwide network of interconnected computers that you can tap into. To hop on the Infobahn you'll need a computer with at least 4 megabytes (but preferably 16 or more) of random-access memory (RAM) and a few megabytes of storage space on your hard drive. You'll also need a modem that can handle a flow of at least 14.4 kilobytes per second of data. (You'll get some real speed with a 28.8 or faster.) Last, you'll need software that gets you on the Net. You can sign up with a commercial service such as *America Online, CompuServe,* or *Prodigy,* or check out a local Internet Service Provider (ISP).

Just the Fax, Ma'am: Fax Machines

For freelancers, fax machines have become as much a necessity as a telephone. *Faxes,* electronically transmitted facsimiles, let you instantly send a rough copy to a client for comments, get that finished job in under the wire, and even order a pizza from the corner deli. Fax machines can be built into your computer as a fax modem. In addition, freestanding fax machines can serve as photocopiers. I love my fax almost as much as I love my photocopier.

Thanks to an extra car battery, you can keep a fax machine powered up in your car 24 hours a day. This way, you can send and receive business contracts on a job site.

Mind Your Own Business

One of the newest machines is a printer, fax machine, and photocopier combined. (No, I didn't make that up; it's real.) While these are great space savers, I've never been one to put all my eggs in a single basket: If the machine breaks, you're up the creek without a paddle. But each to his own taste, as the lion said to the mouse.

Instant Gratification: Photocopiers

Picture this: The rain is lashing against the window, the lightening is ripping across the sky, and the thunder is tripping all the car alarms. You have to go to the copy shop to make a few crucial copies. As you yank on your boots and bang your head against the wall, you mutter, "If I only had a photocopier." So what are you waiting for? Even though these machines can be costly to operate (the cartridges cost about $100 a pop), the first time you don't have to trek through the rain/snow/sleet/dark of night, you'll bless me.

Home Alone
Check specialized tech magazines such as *Home Office Computing* and *PC World* to get the ratings and reports on new products.

Small desktop copiers start around $300 and go all the way up. Mine cost about $500 a decade ago and has required only one repair (knock on wood). I feel so strongly about my copier I will likely request that it be placed in my tomb, along with a very large chocolate cake and a quart of milk.

Beam Me Up, Scotty: Scanners

A *scanner* is a machine that inputs material into your computer. As such, it's especially useful when you don't want to retype huge chunks of copy or try to figure out a way to redraw pictures. If space is a problem, you can now get a scanner that's built into your keyboard, computer, fax, or telephone. Scanners will set you back from $300 to over $1,000.

The Rules of Acquisition

But before you plunk down your hard-earned clams, follow my four easy rules of acquisition. Here they are.

1. Assess your needs.
2. Do your research.
3. Check your budget.
4. Shop 'til you drop.

Let's take a closer look at each guideline.

1. Assess Your Needs

How will you use the computer system? For example, will you use it simply for bookkeeping or for more sophisticated functions such as online research, animation, or desktop publishing? Rank your needs in order of importance.

Ways I Will Use My Computer System		
Most Important	Important	Least Important

2. Do Your Research

Technology changes faster than the prime-time TV lineup, so you're going to have to talk to computer nerds and read the computer mags to get with the flow. Don't be shy about asking for help; otherwise, how can you learn? On a recent trip to Greece, for example, I asked just about every person in Athens how to get where I needed to go. I may have looked a little silly, but at least I didn't end up in the men's room.

Bet You Didn't Know

You know you can save big bucks buying last year's "new" cars when this year's models come out. Did you know the same principle applies to computers? For example, the price of the 486 models bottomed out when the 586s debuted. This can be a great way to save money—*if* the older model will serve your needs. Be sure to weigh your future techno needs as well as your present ones.

3. Check Your Budget

In the best of all possible worlds, we'd all have an unlimited budget. We'd also have something worth watching on TV, but I dream on. When you contemplate getting your computer system in place, decide how much money you can spend now. Then figure out what pieces of equipment you must have now and what components can wait until you have a healthier bank balance. For example, if you decide you must have a $4,000 computer system now, the photocopier will probably have to wait. Set a budget and follow it so your business stays in the black.

Figure that a good home-business computer will run you $2,000 to $4,000. I picked up my latest computer in a warehouse discount store for about $2,500. An IBM-clone 586 with a Pentium processor, this baby is more muscular than Mr. Universe and does everything short of the Funky Chicken. It has more bells and whistles than the slot machines in Vegas, too. My Pentium and I have grown close, even though I have still saved a place in my heart for that ol' 286.

Be careful not to get too chummy with your computer, though. Fellow freelancer Jeanne's first PC had a 100-MB hard drive, and she thought, "I'll never need more than 100 MB." Guess what? She upgraded that sucker to death. Her second PC had 460 MB, and she thought, "I'll never need more than 460 MB." She ended up upgrading *that* one to 2.1 GB. Her new PC (the third in five years) has 2.1 GB, and is upgradable like mad. As computers evolve, software requires more and more resources. As a rule of thumb, buy as much speed and memory as you can afford, and expect to need more in half the time you figured on (when they come up with some new memory-hungry software you just can't live without).

Mind Your Own Business

On average, figure on upgrading your system every five years. Fortunately, the IRS allows you a break in the form of depreciation for your business equipment. Always check with your tax preparer to see when it's best tax-wise to upgrade. I cover this in depth in Chapter 21.

123

On the other hand, a used computer can be a good deal if you only do fairly straight-forward work such as word processing. If all you need to do on your computer is write letters and create basic invoices, you don't need a brand new top-of-the-line superfast machine—a gently-used 486 will work fine. You can often buy these machines at local computer fairs, from businesses that are upgrading, even from yard sales. They will cost much, much less than a new Pentium—some people have spent as little as $200 for a used 486. Be aware, however, that unless your 486 has a fast modem (14.4 just to get on-line), you'll grow old waiting to get on the Web.

4. Shop 'Til You Drop

There's no shortage of places to buy computer equipment, from small specialty shops to monster warehouses. Each venue has its advantages, depending on your needs. Small computer stores often give fabulous service, while larger warehouses may have slightly better prices. There are also a number of computer companies that sell by mail, chief among them the Texas-based computer firm Dell.

IS THAT CLEAR?

Mind Your Own Business

Hardware alert! Stay away from Mad Mel's $300 computer wannabe and its first cousins (Conte's Computer Haven, Lucky Louie's House of Great Deals, and so on). Stick with the major players, such as IBM and clones from places like Dell.

You also have to decide if you want to buy a name brand or a clone. There's a lot to be said for cloning around: Clones can be much cheaper than name brands and often come with fabulous support packages such as 24-hour help hotlines. Be sure to do serious research before you decide.

And while you're comparison shopping, big spender, don't be afraid to bargain a little. Some people are delighted at the opportunity to shave a little off the top; others recoil in horror at the concept of asking for a better price. Go with your personal style; bargain if you feel comfortable with it. If you decide to try it, you can say, "What's the best you can do on this?" or "Can you take a little off this (fill in name of coveted item)?" You'll do better if the item is a floor model, last of its kind, or grossly overstocked.

Finally, consider leasing computer equipment and related items if you're not sure what specific pieces you want, or if money is an issue.

Captain Hook-Up

No matter what system you acquire, it's worthless if you don't hook it up. I won't lie to you and claim that installing a PC, printer, and software is the same as plugging in a toaster or hair dryer. It's not. If you're a technophobe and proud of it, this is a classic

"Don't try this at home kids" situation. Instead, spend the money and hire a computer maven to get your system up and running. It's money well spent.

Skilled computer technicians get enviable salaries, often more than $100 per hour. If this is a budget breaker, contact your local high school or community college. You may be able to hire a student who can get your system up and running for an affordable price. Then hire the child to give you lessons on using your system (read on) and upgrading it in the future.

Use It or Lose It

Once you've got the system, you've got to learn to use it. "I have too much work to do right now," you say. "I'll get around to it right after this project," comes up often. Today's the day, bunky. Here are three hints to get you started:

➤ Read the instruction manual.

➤ Hire someone to teach you in your home.

➤ Take a computer course in adult ed or at a local college.

While we're at it, here are the five cardinal rules for working on a computer:

1. *Save your work to the hard drive often.* I recommend every ten to 15 minutes. Many programs have automatic save features. The person who invented this feature deserves a medal for saving my you-know-what more times than I'll admit.

2. *Save your work to a floppy.* Here's your new mantra: "Copy to the floppy." Repeat after me: "Copy to the floppy." Never assume that your work is safe because it is on your hard drive.

3. *Protect your disks.* Never place a disk near any magnetic source. Place a disk next to a magnetic source and your work is deader than yesterday's news.

4. *Print out your work often.* Hard drives crash. Floppy disks vanish faster than that chocolate bar you hid from the kids. That's why you should print out your work often. Make a hard copy at least once a day and keep it in a safe place. With a printout, you'll have a copy of your work even if your hard drive crashes or your floppy ends up in the bottom of someone's cereal bowl.

5. *Know what you're doing.* If you don't know what a button does, don't press it when you've got an important document on the screen. This is just like making that new dish, ham balls in brown-sugar gravy à la mode, when your in-laws are coming to dinner. Save the experimenting for another time.

> IS THAT CLEAR?
>
> **Mind Your Own Business**
> Make sure you have the electrical wiring to support your equipment. Have an electrician check the wiring; you might very well need an upgrade. In addition, invest in a surge protector (about $20) to prevent disaster in case of a power surge.

Love 'em or hate 'em, computers are an essential part of the freelance workplace. And they have a lot to recommend them. Here's what freelance writer Paula Hartz says about a freelancer's mobility, thanks to technology: "I like being able to throw my computer in the car, plug it in at my cottage on a lake, work from wherever I happen to be, e-mail manuscript back to my editor, have a nice swim, and still get credit for working! It's the life."

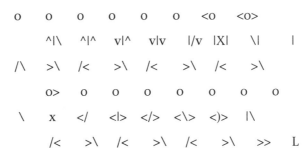

Bet You Didn't Know

Here's reason #173 to fear technology:

```
o     o     o     o     o     o    <o    <o>

      ^|\   ^|^   v|^   v|v   |/v  |X|   \|     |

/\    >\    /<    >\    /<    >\   /<    >\

      o>    o     o     o     o     o    o     o

\     x     </    <|>   </>   <\>  <)>   |\

/<    >\    /<    >\    /<    >\   >>    L
```

Mr. E-mail does the Macarena.

The Least You Need to Know

➤ Assess your needs, do your research, check your budget, and comparison shop when you're buying the technology you need.

➤ Know how to operate all your equipment before you start using it for business.

➤ Get wired; everybody who's anybody is on the Net.

➤ When you're all wired up, you're no longer the little twerp down the block—because you're running your business with the same technology as the big kids.

Chapter 11

Don't Stay Home Without It: Tools of the Trade

In This Chapter

➤ Find out about telecommunications systems for freelancers

➤ Learn to create professional stationery and business cards

➤ Find out how to buy the office supplies you need

➤ Discover the joys of courier services

➤ See what type of office security is right for you

How Freelancers Use Technology	
Telephone answering device	77%
Phone card	68%
Personal computer	55%
Call waiting	54%
Modem	47%
Cellular phone	26%
Computerized pocket organizer	24%
Fax	23%
Voice mail/voice messaging	7%

(Source: Newsweek, *1996)*

As you can see, many freelancers know their technology—and use it. State-of-the-art techno stuff like computers and fax machines can make a freelancer's life much easier. So can telecommunications systems, professional-looking business cards and stationery, the right office supplies, courier services, and security systems. In this chapter, find out about more tools of the freelancer's trade that can make your work easier, more professional, and more secure.

Reach Out and Touch Someone

Few aspects of your home office technology are as important as your telecommunications system. That's right; we're long past plain old telephones, kiddo. Even a bare-bones telecommunications system can do everything short of make your morning coffee…and that service is probably not far off.

When you worked in an office, you most likely had a receptionist, voice mail, and perhaps even an assistant to filter and field your calls. Now, it's up to you to provide your customers with this level of professional service. Today, telecommunications systems have become more sophisticated than Cary Grant. In fact, we're fast approaching the time when your telecommunications system will be part of your computer.

You Say Hello, and I Say Good Buy

Today's telecommunication systems have a variety of options that can help you run your freelance business much more smoothly and profitably. Here are a few of the most important ones:

1. Call forwarding
2. Call waiting
3. Caller ID
4. Call answering
5. Voice mail

Let's look at voice mail a little more closely. Your voice-mail system can be just like the ones the big kids have. As a result, potential clients who call you up don't know if they've reached a sole freelancer in her bathrobe and bunny slippers sitting in a basement office or an administrative assistant at a multinational firm sitting in a chrome-and-glass monolith.

I recommend voice mail over answering machines or call waiting: Even if you're on the line or online, voice mail answers, and you're not doing that "Oops" (click)—"I'll be right back" stuff that seems really unprofessional and annoying to clients. It can take awhile to get your phone set up right with a fax, modem, home phone, and business phone all juggled on two phone lines. Although it's tricky, it can be very important to getting work and keeping clients happy. Be aware, however, that some people don't like voice mail. They find it cold, lacking that human touch. Each to his/her own taste, I always say.

And while we're at it, if you decide to go with an answering machine, make sure that your message is crisp, audible, and professional. Please, no themes to "Star Wars" or heavy breathing from your two-year-old. Also, get an answering machine that you can check remotely and that lets callers blather on as long as they want. Because they are the clients, they're entitled to leave messages as long as a bad movie, if they so wish.

Bet You Didn't Know

Voice mail just keeps getting better and better. Recent innovations include "Personal Ring," a double ring on the house line when people use a special phone number.

It's crucial to have at least one completely separate telephone line for business. First of all, this prevents clients from getting busy signals because your teenager-in-love is glued to the phone or you're doing some online research. In addition, the IRS frowns on sharing telephone lines for business and family use. Also, with separate lines, it's much easier to see what you've spent where.

Here's where more *is* better. With two business lines, you can have one line for call waiting and call forwarding and the second line for fax and modem use. Yep, it's more expensive, but it can make the difference between being a pro and an amateur.

Price, you ask? The cost of telecommunications systems varies enormously depending on what options you select. You can purchase a basic phone machine for well under $100 in a phone store or warehouse, while a sophisticated soup-to-nuts machine can run into the four figures. Assess your needs carefully, but here I recommend that you s-t-r-e-t-c-h your budget if need be and get the very best system that you can afford.

Here's a free tip: If your business is conducted mostly on the phone, get a headset. A headset can help you avoid neck and shoulder problems. It also frees your hands so you can shuffle paper, scratch yourself, or hang wallpaper while you're talking. Nothing like a little multi-tasking to make you more efficient.

ET, Phone Home

Another great innovation for freelancers is the cellular phone, because a cell phone can make you much more accessible to clients. The gimmick here is service. A cell phone itself is very reasonably priced (some companies are even giving the phones away!)—but the service is costly. With the wrong set of options, using a cell phone can be as expensive as getting a new nose. To avoid getting chopped by the phone company, be sure to shop around for the best deal and read the fine print on any and all contracts.

Mind Your Own Business

With a cell phone, they have you coming and going: You get billed for incoming as well as outgoing calls. Ouch.

The prices for cell phone service vary widely, depending on where you live and what billing package you select. For example, an introductory package might offer 30 minutes of free calls per month for only $29.99—-but then charge $1.00 a minute for every additional call. If you make more than 30 minutes of calls a month, you're looking at a bill that could float a small boat. At the very least, figure on spending $50 a month for basic service on a cell phone.

Beepers can also make it easier for you to keep in touch with your clients. Beepers are much cheaper than cell phones, sometimes running as little as $10 a month. For that price, who can resist? (Besides, they come in cute colors that coordinate with my outfits!)

Front Men: Stationery and Business Cards

Few things help create a professional image like your business stationery and business cards. Because they serve as an unofficial "front man," stationery and cards often make that crucial first impression on a prospective client. I'm a big fan of elegant paper and cards, since the impression created is worth far more than the cost incurred. Good paper gives you a lot of bang for the buck.

Like vacations, vans, and victories, stationery and business cards come in all levels of quality and price, depending on the frills you select. Variations include:

➤ *Color.* Expect to pay more for each color you add.

➤ *Paper quality.* The more cloth (or "rag") in the paper, the greater the cost.

➤ *Size.* Any unusual size—very large cards or letter paper that isn't the standard 8 1/2" × 11"—will cost more, because it has to be cut to order.

➤ *Fancy typefaces.*

➤ *Die-cuts.* These are designs cut into the cards.

➤ *Photographs.*

➤ *Folds.* Business cards with two and three folds will cost more than non-folded cards.

➤ *Elaborate designs.*

➤ *Quantity.* The more you have printed, the less each piece will cost, because the initial setup is where the cost is incurred. But don't be tempted to have 1,000,001 cards printed unless you're sure you'll use them before you move, get a new e-mail address, or change your name or gender.

Bet You Didn't Know

Use your letterhead for invoices. In my experience, this increases your likelihood of getting paid on time, since your invoice is less apt to get misdirected or used as a coaster.

Many copy shops now have machines that make business cards for astonishingly reasonable prices. You can choose from several standard formats and get 50 cards for about $5—in just a few minutes.

While you're at it, have extra matching envelopes printed up. Envelopes tend to disappear, like socks in the dryer. And don't forget to order second sheets (without the letterhead) for longer letters.

Card-Carrying Freelancer

What should you include on your stationery and business cards? Here are the six basics:

1. Name
2. Address
3. Telephone number
4. Fax number
5. E-mail address
6. Occupation

Here's a sample freelance business card that I think is elegant as well as functional.

Fredericka F. Freelancer
101 Main Street
Glassy Point, Iowa 72168

phone: (615) 555-1234
fax: (615) 555-4321
e-mail: *Freelancer@AOL.com*

Freelance Computer Consultant

Card Me

When you visit the printer, ask to look through a book of business stationery and cards. The printer is apt to have piles of these books, which makes it easy for you to see the wide selection available.

Then select a *typeface*, a style of letter. Here are several standard typefaces, drawn from Microsoft Word:

➤ Courier New

➤ Times

➤ **Britannic Bold**

➤ **Arial**

➤ Clarendon Condensed

➤ Century Gothic

They are all the same size, 12 point, but notice the difference in apparent size. Ask yourself these questions as you make your choice:

➤ Which typeface do I find easiest to read?

➤ Which typeface best represents the image I wish to convey?

 oH!

Bet You Didn't Know

It will cost about $30 to $200 for the printer to set the type. This is a one-time cost; you can reuse the type to reprint identical cards and stationery.

You're not done yet. There are three more steps to make sure you get the look you want:

1. *Check and double-check.* Be sure to proofread the type carefully before the printer starts churning out your letterhead and cards. Don't skip this step! Errors occur all the time, especially if your name or address is spelled in an unusual way. Check phone numbers carefully, too; numbers often get transposed or even dropped.

2. *Paper chase.* Select the paper stock, the type of paper that your stationery and cards will be printed on. In general, err on the side of stuffiness, unless you're in a very creative business. White, cream, buff, tan, and gray are all appropriate colors. Use 20- to 24-pound bond paper to give your stationery the heft it needs. Don't cheap out on cards, either. You want them standard weight to convey your solidity in your field.

3. *Ink stained.* Now comes ink. As with paper, go conservative: black on white, gray, or cream; brown on tan, and so on. Save the purple for eye shadow.

The Medium Is the Message

I'm all for tarting up a dessert (can't heap that whipped cream too high for me), but the same principle doesn't hold for business stationery. With letter paper and cards, simple is better. For example, if your stationery is too big to fit into a standard file folder, you're apt to annoy the client. Who wants to take the time to fold and cut your resume to fit? Likewise, if you've selected an elaborate typeface that's hard to read, your card might just get tossed. Ditto with your business.

This brings up the issue of *logos*, a design that represents your individual business. Apple Computers has its little apple logo; Nike has its trademark swoosh logo. NBC uses a peacock; Mickey D has golden arches. If you decide to use a logo, keep it simple. Printers often have a stock of ready-made logos that you can use.

Cards more ornate than Carmen Miranda's fruit basket headgear are largely the result of computer software and color printers. It's become so easy to add another piece of clip art or another color that some freelancers end up designing cards that look like the ceiling of the Sistine Chapel done by someone on hallucinogenic substances. Fight the urge to create eccentric cards.

Take My Word For It
A *logo* is a design that graphically represents your company.

Mind Your Own Business
I know you can create gorgeous business stationery and cards with your home computer. I also know I'm going to get letters on this one, but I still prefer professionally printed stationery and cards. I think they look richer.

Supply-Side Economics

Don't forget the rest of your supplies. Here are some home office essentials that are often overlooked—until you go looking for them and they aren't there!

Use the checklist on the following page as you shop for the basics. At the end of the list, I've left you a few lines to fill in any additional items you need.

Smart Shopper

_____ Art

_____ Clock

_____ Coffeepot

_____ Fan or air conditioner

_____ Floppy disk and CD-ROM storage

_____ Notepads

_____ Paper clips

_____ Paper

_____ Pens and pencils

_____ Rolodex (crucial!)

_____ Rubber bands

_____ Scissors

_____ Stamps

_____ Stapler, staples

_____ Tape

_____ Tissues

_____ Wastebasket

_____ _____

_____ _____

_____ _____

_____ _____

_____ _____

Fortunately for busy freelancers, just about anything you can purchase in person you can order by phone or computer. Unfortunately, there may be a stiff freight charge, so check the fine print before you order. At least one office superstore offers free delivery for any order over $50. For free, I should schlep my own reams of paper? Read on for more shopping tips.

Hey, Big Spender...Shopping Like an Expert

Office supplies can set you back a bundle. So take it from a varsity shopper, there's more to spending money than just flashing the plastic. Let me show you how to be a smart shopper when it comes to business supplies. (Now, *shoes*, that's a real challenge!) Just follow these nine hints:

1. See if you can get a discount for using cash. (You remember cash, don't you? It's that green stuff we see so rarely.)

2. Wait for sales, if possible, and then stock up on the supplies you need.

3. Use coupons. I just saved $30 on a printer cartridge with a coupon clipped from the front of the latest office-supply catalog. Hey, $30 is $30!

4. Comparison shop. Don't spend the whole day schlepping from store to store. Instead, call to see who has the best price on what you need.

5. Consider buying in bulk. You can save 10 to 15 percent on many items this way.

6. Reuse and recycle. Fold manila files the other way to reuse them for personal files (never for clients!); don't be so quick to throw out paper clips attached to old projects.

7. Check for special programs. My #1 office supplier (this year) gives "frequent buyer" points for each purchase. I redeem these for free merchandise and discounts on future purchases.

8. Look for ways to save time. Since you're self-employed, time is money. Often, having something delivered can save you money, despite the delivery cost, since you can use that time to generate more income.

9. Try mail order. Many mail order office-supply firms offer outstanding prices, very fast service, and no freight charges. Best of all, ordering by mail is fast and easy. Just dial their toll-free number, read off the items from the catalog, flash the plastic, and voilà! Office supplies will arrive on your doorstep! (I love living in the 20th century. I would have been a very cranky cave chick.)

Mind Your Own Business
Buying in bulk is only a savings if you're going to use the items. I go through printer/copier paper like Sherman tore through Georgia, but my pens last as long as the Civil War.

135

Home Alone
Check out *business1.com*, an online source that features business suppliers, government resources, and related links.

As a home-based worker, it's easy to become a little less vigilant about personal grooming. Perhaps you've given up shaving for the winter; maybe you've taken to wearing your high school sweater—you know, the one that's three sizes too small and missing the left sleeve. Hey, that's okay by me; I don't have to work with you. But I *do* have to see you when you leave the house. That brings up the issue of such "office supplies" as a good briefcase or portfolio. Quality leather goods add that finishing touch, the extra polish that gives you confidence as well as a look of professionalism.

You don't have to invest a decade's salary in a Louis Vuitton portfolio, but a nice-looking briefcase makes an appropriately professional impression when you do venture past your front steps. You can find good briefcases in many office supply houses, department stores, leather shops, or other shopping arenas. I bought two beautiful leather briefcases in the local flea market, and they cost well under $50 each. Shop and ye shall find.

In the Nick of Time

Nothing can save a freelancer's toast from the fire like a reliable courier service. When you're up against a deadline tighter than the Dallas Cowboys' defensive line, you need that extra hour to work—rather than driving to the client's office to drop off the package. A courier service can help you snatch victory from the jaws of defeat. Here are the big four couriers:

IS THAT CLEAR?

Mind Your Own Business
Always weigh what your time is worth. If you spend $10 to have a package delivered and save a hour—in which you earn $50—you're $40 ahead. And the $10 is tax deductible!

➤ The U.S. Post Office

➤ Federal Express

➤ Airborne Express

➤ United Parcel Service (UPS)

Each service has its specific advantages and disadvantages, which is why savvy freelancers (like you) use all four, depending on the nature of your job and your deadlines.

Use the following checklist to decide which courier works best for you in each situation:

1. Will the courier service pick up at my home?

2. What is the last pickup time in my area?

3. How close is the nearest drop box or depot if I miss my pickup? How late can I drop off the package for next-day delivery? In my area, for example, the last Federal Express home pickup is 6:00 PM, but the depot is open until 7:00 PM.

4. Is there an extra charge for home pickup?

5. What is the earliest delivery time? Federal Express guarantees delivery by 10:30 AM. When a client uses FedEx, I know I won't lose the morning waiting for the mail or the courier.

6. Is there an extra charge for Saturday pickup? For Saturday delivery?

7. Does the service deliver on Sunday? Of the big four, only the U.S. Post Office does at this time.

8. Does the courier deliver to a Post Office box? Federal Express and Airborne Express won't.

9. What is the charge for comparable packages?

10. Can I get a discount for volume?

Bet You Didn't Know

Establish accounts with your favorite courier services. For no charge, most of them will give you a pack of preprinted airbills, complete with your very own name and address. This looks professional and can save you a lot of time filling out forms. Sometimes that extra ten minutes is all you need to make your deadline!

Better Safe Than Sorry

There's one last thing you have to deal with when you set up your home office—security. You must protect yourself from both fire and theft. In Chapter 22, you'll inventory your possessions to see what you own. This will help you pinpoint how much insurance you need.

In the meantime, take the following simple steps to secure your office contents—and yourself.

➤ Install a good door. Too many doors are flimsy and very easy to kick in.

➤ Secure the door with a solid lock, such as a deadbolt.

➤ Install locks on all windows, too.

➤ Vary your habits so you don't follow a predictable pattern of coming and going. Thieves often track patterns so they can be sure an office will be empty when they break in.

➤ Have friends or associates keep an eye on the office when you're out of town on a business trip or vacation.

Lock Down

Mind Your Own Business

Be sure to lock up when you leave. Let's not make it any easier than we have to for the nasty little robbers.

There are other ways to secure your office and peace of mind, too. On the simple end is a burglar alarm. There are several different kinds of office security systems; the most secure alarms ring in the police station or protection agency. Such systems are costly, however, usually starting at around $2,000. In my area, though, many utility companies offer burglar alarms and security systems for free when you sign a five-year heating oil/burner maintenance contract. If you are interested in an office alarm system, you may wish to investigate similar special offers in your own region.

Then we have the '90s version of Big Brother: observation systems. A wireless observation system starts at about $300 and includes a portable camera and monitor that attach to a VCR to record all on-screen activity. A simple system can accommodate up to two cameras and unlimited monitors for viewing more than one location.

You might also want to purchase an office safe. A high-quality fireproof office safe starts at around $300; a fireproof four-drawer file cabinet runs about $900. Here's where it pays to spend the extra money. A cheap safe is like an oral contract: not worth the paper it's written on!

Here are a few other guidelines to follow when you buy an office safe:

➤ Bolt the safe down. A thief in my area tried to carry a huge safe out of an office. The safe stayed safe—but not the now-flat thief.

➤ Secure the combination.

➤ Don't load the safe with goodies. That's why we have bank safe-deposit boxes. Let the bank people do the worrying, not you.

I know, we never have the time to think about security. We're too busy looking for work, learning new skills, and working on current freelance projects. I could load you down with cautionary tales about robberies and worse, but they're all too sad. Take the time to protect what matters. You'll be glad you did.

Little Things Matter a Lot

Here are a few extra goodies that can make your office safer for very little extra moolah:

1. *Fire extinguishers.* A good-quality fire extinguisher will cost you around $30—and it's well worth the bucks. By the by, most fire extinguishers use a powder, and it can sometimes cake up. If it does, your extinguisher won't work, even if the gauge reads full. When you check your extinguisher once a month (like the good person you are), give it a shake. If you can't hear the powder move, get a new one.

2. *Smoke detectors.* Where there's smoke, there's usually fire...but it really doesn't matter, because the smoke can kill you just as fast. Although smoke detectors are required by law, they are overlooked surprisingly often. Buy extra smoke detectors and install them all over the place, including stairs and hallways. And don't forget to check the batteries. A smoke detector is useless unless the batteries are good.

Home Alone
Some smoke detectors come equipped with escape lights. Consider this handy (and potentially life-saving) feature when you buy your next smoke detector.

3. *Motion sensor floodlights.* These outdoor lights can detect motion up to 50 feet away. At $25 each, they're a cheap and effective way to scare off potential intruders.

4. *A good flashlight.* Very handy for power outages and finding that lost earring under the desk. A heavy-duty flashlight runs about $10–$25.

Who has the time to get this stuff? Not you—you're too busy reading this book. That's why you might want to consider hitting up friends and relatives who moan, "I never know what to get you for your birthday/anniversary/ Christmas/Chanukah/Kwanzaa/ Groundhog Day celebration." Why not suggest they get you a good flashlight? Don't sneer; it worked for me.

The Least You Need to Know

➤ Skimp on the groceries if you have to, but not on your telecommunications system.

➤ Create a professional image with the right stationery and business cards.

➤ Shop smart and stock up on the office supplies you need.

➤ Courier services can save your...er, bacon.

➤ There are meanies out there, bunky. Secure your office with a good door, lock, and perhaps even a burglar alarm.

Part 4
Crossing the Road: The Business of Freelancing

Question: Why did the chicken cross the road?

➤ *Freud: The fact that you thought that the chicken crossed the road reveals your underlying sexual insecurity.*

➤ *Grandpa: In my day, we didn't ask why the chicken crossed the road. Someone told us that the chicken had crossed the road, and that was good enough for us.*

➤ *Emily Dickinson: Because it could not stop for death.*

➤ *Ernest Hemingway: To die. In the rain.*

➤ *Saddam Hussein: It is the Mother of All Chickens.*

➤ *Dr. Seuss: Did the chicken cross the road? Did he cross it with a toad? Yes, the chicken crossed the road, but why he crossed it, I've not been told!*

➤ *Colonel Sanders: I missed one?*

If you're ready, it's time to take a deep breath and cross that road to the business side of freelancing. In this section, you'll learn all about such niceties as setting rates, negotiating fees, dealing with contracts, and keeping good financial records.

Chapter 12

Money Business 1:
Setting Your Rates

In This Chapter

➤ Learn how to deal with money like a pro

➤ Discover how to calculate your rates

➤ Learn how to negotiate fees

From *The Wall Street Journal* comes the report that the manufacturer of sweatshirts that boasted MONEY ISN'T EVERYTHING is no longer in business...

It's been called *moolah, cash, bread, lettuce, clams, fins, ten-spots, C-notes, travelin' money, folding money, bucks,* and *greenbacks.* No matter what we call it, we know what we mean—money. The word "money" comes from the Latin *moneta* (from *moneo,* "to warn"). Since ancient times, money has fascinated people like few other tangibles.

I'll be the first to assert that money *isn't* everything, but then again, I have enough of the delightful folding green stuff to be able to say that without wincing. For the beginning freelancer, it often seems that money *is* everything, or at least the most important thing at the time. Here, I'll first teach you the basic secret to making enough money so economic concerns no longer take center stage. Next, you'll learn how to figure out what to charge for your services. Finally, I'll show you how to negotiate fees.

Gilt Trip

Too many freelancers cheat themselves by undercharging for their product and services. Are you one of them? Take this simple quiz to find out. Put a check next to each item that applies to you.

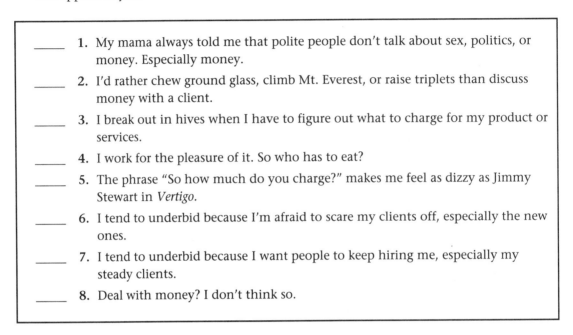

_____ 1. My mama always told me that polite people don't talk about sex, politics, or money. Especially money.

_____ 2. I'd rather chew ground glass, climb Mt. Everest, or raise triplets than discuss money with a client.

_____ 3. I break out in hives when I have to figure out what to charge for my product or services.

_____ 4. I work for the pleasure of it. So who has to eat?

_____ 5. The phrase "So how much do you charge?" makes me feel as dizzy as Jimmy Stewart in *Vertigo*.

_____ 6. I tend to underbid because I'm afraid to scare my clients off, especially the new ones.

_____ 7. I tend to underbid because I want people to keep hiring me, especially my steady clients.

_____ 8. Deal with money? I don't think so.

Score Yourself

7–8 checks	You need me, you *really* need me.
5–6 checks	I'll bet you *always* buy retail, too.
3–4 checks	Repeat after me, "I'm good, real good. I'm worth every penny I charge."
1–2 checks	We're dealing from the same deck.
No checks	Are we related? Maybe separated at birth?

Dollars and Sense

First of all, let's talk about the proper economic mindset for a freelancer. Before you even consider what to charge for your product or services, you have to think like a business person. You may be working out of your house, but your work is no hobby. Besides, you're no schlemiel. You're an independent contractor, a freelancer. You know you're a professional. It only makes sense to set appropriate rates.

Nonetheless, it can be hard to figure out what to charge, since there are so many different fields in which a person can freelance. You may even be engaged in more than one freelance profession at a time!

In addition, freelancers tend to be an independent lot. If the matter of rates wasn't confusing enough, most freelancers have sliding scales. Long-time clients often get a break; so do first-timers. Then there's overtime and an extra fee for rush jobs. Nonetheless, I *can* give you a method for calculating your rates, based on my own experience as a writer and on the experiences of my freelance friends, colleagues, and acquaintances.

> **Take My Word For It**
> *Schlemiel* is a Yiddish word meaning "fool." In a pinch, *schmo, nudnick,* and *putz* will do just as well.

Here are the top five rate rules:

1. Set your rates in advance. "I'll have to get back to you about rates" is not an acceptable answer when a client asks you about your fees.

2. Price fairly, neither too high nor too low. If you charge too little, you won't make enough to live. You might even have trouble getting work because clients will think there's something wrong: "He's so much cheaper than anyone else! Must be desperate!" Conversely, if you charge too much, you'll likely be turned down for work—and clients probably won't tell you why.

3. Always be ready to negotiate.

4. Expect to earn what you are worth nearly all the time.

5. If the client too quickly accepts your initial rate, it's probably too low.

> **Mind Your Own Business**
> You can always lower your first quote, but you can never raise it. Once you quote a price that's too low, you're stuck. But there is some consolation: At least you'll know for the next time.

Penny Wise, Pound Foolish

The first few times I quoted rates to potential clients, they seemed too eager to accept them. While I wanted to believe that they were just delighted to get someone of my caliber so easily, the truth was a little less flattering: I was charging too little. This truth was about as subtle as a rock concert or a mule kick in the side of the head.

Home Alone
Some excellent software is available to make the task of calculating your expenses a snap. Check out your local computer store or a superstore's mail order catalog.

So how can you figure out what to charge? Start by determining your basic costs. You have to take the following factors into account:

➤ Your living expenses

➤ Your taxes

➤ What the market will bear

This is where most freelancers flop. They tend to think in modest terms, such as "Golly, $40 an hour sounds good. That's a lot of money." Whether it is or isn't is beside the point. Here *is* the point: What do you need to make your monthly mortgage payment?

In addition, you're going to need a cash cushion of about three month's worth of living expenses to fall back on during lean-and-mean times. That's true even if you're not yet ready to go out on your own as a freelancer. So if you're still employed full-time, start saving now. Look for ways to build up savings and reduce debt before taking that final plunge into independence.

To get the facts, list your expenses. Not too tricky, you say. There's food, clothing, housing, car payments. But freelancers always seem to overlook "incidental" items such as taxes, Social Security, and saving for retirement. So you don't fall into this trap, use the following worksheet to calculate your expenses.

Monthly Expenses

Fixed monthly expenses:

Rent/mortgage _____

Car payment _____

Any other loan payments _____

Insurance _____

Alimony/child-care payments _____

Child care _____

Income taxes _____

Social Security _____

Estimated variable monthly expenses:

Food (at home and out) _____

Electricity _____

Heat _____

Water _____

Phone bill _____

Medical costs _____

Gas/car repairs _____

Clothing _____

Entertainment _____

Gifts _____

Charity _____

Reference materials _____

Vacations _____

Office supplies _____

Business travel _____

Education and retraining _____

Retirement savings _____

Emergency savings fund _____

TOTAL _____

Now that you've got your figures, read on to find out what to do with them. Don't worry; it's not as bad as it looks. I promise.

Figure It Out

Time to get down and dirty, fellow freelancer. Follow me as I show you how to calculate your expenses.

1. First, determine your personal tax bite. Currently, the top federal income tax rate is 39 percent, and it goes down (thank goodness) from there. For the sake of simplicity, let's assume you are taxed at the 24 percent rate, which is about average. That means you should put aside at least 24 percent of every check to pay the IRS. (See Chapter 21 for all the gory details on taxes.)

> **IS THAT CLEAR?**
>
> **Mind Your Own Business**
> Don't forget that insurance costs include home-owner's, car, life, and health. See Chapter 21 for a detailed discussion of insurance.

2. To the Feds' 24 percent, add Social Security. The employee's portion of FICA is 7.65 percent, but since you are now the boss, you also have to kick in the employer's 7.65 percent, for a total of 15.3 percent.

3. Then there's state and local taxes. These taxes vary from state to state (some states don't even have taxes!), so consult your tax preparer or state revenue department. Your total chunk for all of this will likely be around 50 percent. Yes, you read that number right.

Mind Your Own Business
Never touch the money you've set aside for retirement. Take a staff job, work like a lunatic, or sell your blood instead.

4. Next comes retirement savings. Five percent is okay, but 10 percent is even better. Believe it or not, once you get used to slicing 10 percent or so off the top of every check for your retirement account, it's fairly painless. By now, assuming a prudent 10 percent for retirement, around 60 percent of your check is gone before you've even cashed it.

5. Now it's time to see how the remaining 40 percent of your income will be spent. Look at the budget you just prepared. Always plan on the worst—use your highest utility costs, the most caviar you ever ate in one month, and the business trip to Guam. No cheating allowed.

6. Multiply this by 12 to get your yearly expenses.

7. Now you know what you have to set aside for taxes and expenses. Who needs *Nightmare on Elm Street* or Freddy Kruger? You have yearly expenses!

8. Now calculate your work year. Assume that you work eight hours a day, five days a week, 50 weeks a year. (Hey, you deserve a two-week vacation.) Based on this calculation, you work 2,000 hours a year.

9. Divide your yearly expenses by 2,000. This figure will be the basic hourly rate you have to charge to make all your expenses.

Profit from My Advice

Now, this hourly rate gives you the amount of money you need to make your expenses. What about *profit*? That's the amount you have to add in once you decide how much extra money you want to make. Warning: This is the step that freelancers often omit. But why work if all you're going to make are basic expenses? Where's the fun in *that*?

Besides, profit is necessary to keep your business afloat. It's the money you use for expansion when times are good, and the money you use as a cushion when times are tough. Figure a minimum of 15 percent. Beyond that, go for whatever the market will bear.

Comparison Shopping

Now it's time to compare your final rate to the going rate in your area to see how you stack up against the competition. Often, other freelancers are unwilling to reveal their rates. This is an "I'll show you mine if you'll show me yours" situation. You can't get any information without giving some of your own. Remember, we're all in this together.

In addition, you can call the kind of client you will work for and ask about the going rate. Just asking, "What's your budget for this type of job?" often works surprisingly well. Cold calling takes nerves of steel, however, so you might want to consider these options:

➤ Check with professional organizations. The Editorial Freelancers Association, for example, publishes a biannual survey that includes the going rate for various kinds of work.

➤ Do library research in trade journals.

➤ Contact newsgroups on the Internet.

What happens if your final rate is way out of whack with the going rate in your area? If you've followed the formula I've outlined here, I can't assume that your ego is as big as the Goodyear blimp. Perhaps your expenses are too high. In this case, you've got to give up cable TV, the VISA card, or at least one meal a day. Or perhaps everyone in your area has underbid to get the work; in that case, you will have to look further afield to get jobs that pay a fair rate.

The Long and Short of It

Okay, so you know how much you're charging per hour. You're not quite done with your math yet, since you never know when you will be offered a long-term job. As a result, in addition to being able to quote an hourly rate, you should be able to reel off daily, weekly, and even monthly rates.

When you calculate these rates, know that it's common to give a discount for long-term projects because the job is locked in. Here's how to do the math. (Not to worry; this one's a breeze.)

➤ *Daily rate.* Multiply your hourly rate by 8 and deduct 10 percent. (The 10 percent is the discount you give for steady work.)

➤ *Weekly rate.* Multiply the daily rate by 5 and deduct 10 percent. (The 10 percent is the discount you give for steady work.)

➤ *Monthly rate.* Multiply the daily rate by 20 and deduct 10 percent (or sometimes even a bit more because the work is longer term).

What about charging a *flat fee* or a *package price*, one set price for the entire job? If this fee arrangement is mutually agreeable to you and the client, figure out how many hours you would need to complete the job, add 10 to 20 percent to make sure you're covered for

Home Alone
Be sure to tell the client if you are giving a discount, because that break can often help you land the job.

extras, and use that figure as your base quote. Don't forget to factor in time that might be needed for rushing the job or making last-minute changes.

Also consider the issue of expenses. If the project will involve a lot of couriers, long-distance phone calls, and heavy photocopying, factor in these expenses as well, or ask to be paid separately for them. I find that itemizing the costs and getting reimbursed works best for me because I'm never sure how much to allow for.

If you are working for a flat fee, be aware that sometimes clients ask for changes that are not in the contract. I call these clients the "I don't know what I want, but I'll know it when I see it" folks. I love these clients—*if* they pay extra for all their diddling. My feelings are not quite the same if they expect me to keep noodling with the job for free until they're as happy as Yogi Bear with a picnic basket. Be sure to ask about changes up front, and calculate your fee accordingly. (See Chapter 14 for more on contracts.)

Cash on the Barrelhead

Mind Your Own Business
Don't try to make up a low rate one client paid by overcharging another client. Treat everyone fairly. They may not return the favor, but you'll get the freelancer's most valuable possession: a good reputation.

Setting your rate isn't the hard part; sticking to it is. Do the very best you can to make sure that your income for any given project stays at or near your hourly rate.

Does it bother you to figure out your rates in such a cold, businesslike way? After all, you love your job and your lifestyle. But as a freelancer, you're not very different from the people who own the corner deli, flower shop, or tattoo parlor. We're all business people, no matter what we sell. You have to set rules and follow them—or you won't be in business very long.

The name of the game is making what you need to live (and having some left over) without working yourself to a frazzle. Often, this means that you will have to balance less lucrative jobs with those that pay like oil gushers. For example, let's assume that a certain publisher pays me $100 a page. Measuring that against my $65 hourly rate, that means I can afford to spend only 1.53 hours per page. I like the publisher, there's a ton of this work, but can I do a good job in the time I've allotted to get it done? Should I take this job—or not? Hmmm…

Use the checklist on the next page to help you evaluate the advantages and disadvantages of jobs that don't meet your regular rate.

Sitting on the Fence

_____ 1. Will this job lead to other, more profitable work?

_____ 2. Will this job be enjoyable—or a real drag?

_____ 3. Do I owe this client a favor that I can make up this way?

_____ 4. Can I use this job to build good will and cement a business relationship?

_____ 5. Can I make enough money on volume to make up for the low rate?

_____ 6. Do I have more profitable work waiting in the wings? Is the promised assignment definite or iffy?

_____ 7. Do I have many outstanding accounts and know that this client will pay promptly?

_____ 8. Can I do a good job while devoting fewer hours than usual to the work?

Score Yourself

If you answered yes to more than three questions, taking the less lucrative job may not be a bad idea for you at this point.

To the Virgins, Make Much of Time

Don't make the mistake of taking extra time on your current project because you don't have any other assignments. This is a very common freelancer's error. "I have the time," they think, "so why not use it on my job?" Wrong. Use the time you set aside for the job on the job. Then use your extra time drumming up more business. The time you'd otherwise be investing in this lower-paying job can be put to better use in these ways:

➤ Come up with new ideas.

➤ Do basic research.

➤ Network to find more work.

➤ Pitch ideas.

Home Alone
I have one client who pays about two-thirds of my regular rate. However, the client pays within one week, while other clients have kept me waiting as long as six months for a check. When I need quick cash, I always give this delightful fellow a jingle.

If you've done all you can on work and you still have some time, don't alphabetize your soup cans or clean the bathroom grout. Instead, catch up on your reading. It's legitimate research that can pay off big.

Bet You Didn't Know

Sticking to your rate can make it easier for you to avoid interruptions. If you're contemplating dashing out to have your shoes resoled during your normal work time, ask yourself, "Would I pay someone $65 to run this errand?" If the answer is no, go back to work. You can always run the errand when you have free time or after your set workday.

Reality Check

Even if you can stick to your hourly rate, you might not work enough to make the money you need. This can happen when you just don't get enough hours to work. Take a look back at your figure of 2,000 hours of work a year. What happens if you only work 1,000 hours a year, even if you stick to your rate? Your hourly rate is slashed in half. If you're charging $65 an hour, for example, this means you're making $32.50. Work just 500 hours a year and you're making $16.25. See where I'm going here? The best hourly rate won't make up for insufficient work. That's why freelancers have to keep beating the bushes for work, work, work.

Home Alone
Try to combine personal running around with work-related errands to save time and money. For example, drop off your library books when you go to complete work-related research.

For instance, yesterday I went to a bookstore to arrange for a seminar/signing I'm doing in a month to promote four other *Complete Idiot's Guides* that I've written. After I met with the manager, I spent about an hour checking the shelves to see what was new. I spoke with the clerks to see what was moving; I asked browsers what they were looking for. Then I came home, wrote up my findings, and pitched six new ideas to various editors. Even though I'm still in the middle of *this* book, waiting until I'm finished to line up my next job could mean a month or two without work.

What else can you do to make more money? You can try to move into a more lucrative aspect of your field. Another approach is to work more billable hours. The more you work, the more you earn.

Talk the Talk and Walk the Walk

In the Old Country, my grandfather was a horse trader—a successful one, too. If biology is indeed destiny, I can use my lineage to explain my ability to stand up for myself and negotiate fees. Now it's your turn to learn how to negotiate, even if you're not born to it.

Always figure that you're going to have to negotiate. You may not have to, but if you go in with this concept, you'll be much less likely to be blown out of the water. Here are my Top Ten suggestions for negotiating fair fees.

1. If possible, always try to have the client name a figure first. That relieves you of the danger of bidding too low.

2. Never name a figure off the top of your head. Always do your homework. Know what the job entails and what it's worth. If possible, also try to find out who else is bidding on the job and what other numbers have been placed on the table.

3. Don't be afraid to ask for time to consider a counter offer. As long as you've carefully calculated and presented your figures, you'll come across as competent.

4. Don't fear bringing in other considerations. For example, it might be worth it to you to take a little less money in exchange for extending the deadline. Or take a lower fee if there is a firm promise of more work.

5. Be confident. If you're meeting in person, dress well; you'll feel more in control.

6. Appreciate what your time and product are worth. Don't be afraid to convince clients of your worth by citing successful projects you have completed in the past.

7. Learn your personal style and then go with it. I use humor to relieve tension during a negotiation; you may use facts and statistics. Working with your own style will help you be much more successful in the long run.

8. Never, never, never lose your cool. Don't recoil in mock horror, act mortally wounded, or use inappropriate language.

9. Stick with it. Clients admire perseverance. It suggests that you'll apply the same tenacity to getting their job done well.

10. Whatever happens, try not to take it personally. Unless you're doing a job for your mother-in-law, it isn't personal; it's business.

Mind Your Own Business

Under no circumstances use pity ("I really need this job to pay for my brain transplant") or stupidity ("I can't believe I was dopey enough to quote that price"). Remember, you're a pro, not a basketcase.

One final word. Never mention fees until you're sure you have the job. Jumping the gun this way could cost you the assignment.

Pass the Bucks

What can you do if you really can't negotiate? What if you become as animated as a deer caught in the headlights when you have to talk about money? If this is the problem, you can hire an agent, lawyer, business manager, or associate to do your negotiating for you. This is a common practice in many freelance fields, such as acting, modeling, and writing.

Just be aware that such services don't come cheaply. Most agents take between 10 and 15 percent of your profit. In addition, most agents function as exclusive marketing representatives. This means that your hands may be tied if you want to cut your own deal in a certain situation. Therefore, assess your situation carefully before you decide if you really need a front man (or woman).

The Least You Need to Know

➤ Calculate your expenses to know how much to charge.

➤ Don't forget to include profit!

➤ Learn to negotiate for a fair fee, or hire someone to do it for you.

➤ Remember this song lyric when you think your rates are too high: "They're only puttin' in a nickel, but they want a dollar song."

GREAT! THAT'S GOOD TO HEAR...

Chapter 13

Money Business 2: Getting Your Rates

In This Chapter

➤ Learn about some different ways to get paid: speculation and consignment

➤ Find out what to do if you don't get paid: dealing with deadbeats

➤ Get paid more: Give yourself a raise

There was an Orioles fan with really lousy seats at Camden Yards for the playoffs. Looking through his binoculars, he spotted an empty seat right behind the Orioles' dugout. "What a waste," he thought to himself, and decided to sneak into the empty seat.

When he arrived at the seat, he asked the man sitting next to it, "Is this seat taken?" The man replied, "This was my wife's seat. She passed away. She was a big Orioles fan."

The other man replied, "I am so sorry to hear of your loss. May I ask why you didn't give the ticket to a friend or a relative?"

The man replied, "They're all at the funeral."

So we all have our priorities. For some, it's getting good seats at a baseball game; for others, it's making—and collecting—money. After all, money can buy a lot of nice things, including great seats at the baseball stadium! In this chapter, let's chat a little more about money and the freelancer's life.

Life on the Edge: Working on Spec

The first time you work for a new client, you might be asked to work on *speculation* or *spec.* When you work on *spec,* you produce something without any guarantee of payment. You may have gotten a flicker of interest in the assignment, but there's no contract or even an agreement. The results can be spectacular...or stinky.

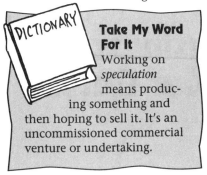

Take My Word For It

Working on *speculation* means producing something and then hoping to sell it. It's an uncommissioned commercial venture or undertaking.

According to the dictionary, speculation is "engagement in business transactions involving considerable risk for the chance of large gains." Now, one person's "considerable risk" is another person's stroll in the park. Pogo, the comic strip character, once said, "The certainty of misery is better than the misery of uncertainty." If you subscribe to this philosophy, working on spec probably isn't for you. In general, most people (especially freelancers) like an assurance of payment, so think carefully before you accept a spec job.

The Good...

That's not to say working on spec is totally without advantages. There *are* instances when it can be to your advantage. Here are three examples:

1. This may be the only way you can get your foot in the door, especially when you're just starting out.

2. Your work will usually be seen by a wider range of potential clients than if you were just dealing with one buyer.

3. You may make more money, especially if your work proves impressive or hits the client just right.

As you've probably guessed, I consider working on spec the same as getting stuck between a rock and a hard place: There are times when you have absolutely no choice—like getting a tooth filled. You're in that chair, and they've got you by the short hairs. You're stuck. Now, don't you wish you'd flossed more?

The same applies to selling your work. If at all possible, hustle a little harder to avoid working on spec. Once you're fairly well established in your freelance career, you should be able to avoid it entirely. Remember: You can find more hotel workers who like Leona Helmsley than freelancers who like spec jobs.

...The Bad and the Ugly

The downside of spec jobs is bigger than Michael Jackson's plastic surgery bill. Here are the most notable disadvantages:

➤ The client has no pressure to buy your work.

➤ You're working without a net—you have no guarantee of a present or future sale.

➤ It's not professional. The client is pushing the envelope and taking advantage of your status as a freelancer.

➤ You're spending time that might be better used looking for guaranteed work, researching new assignments, or making contacts.

➤ If you get a good (i.e., paying) job in the middle of a spec assignment, you're in a bind. Should you drop the spec work and risk alienating a possible client or keep on working on spec with no guarantee of a sale?

➤ Whatever you spend on doing the spec job is tied up until you sell the work…which may never happen.

➤ You don't get any money until the job sells.

➤ You are rarely paid quickly for spec work, even if the work sells fast.

➤ You're apt to get stuck with a lot of changes for which you may not get paid. The client knows you're anxious to sell your work (otherwise, you'd have a contract), so unscrupulous clients tend to take advantage of you.

> **IS THAT CLEAR?**
>
> **Mind Your Own Business**
> Clients sometimes use the gambit of working on spec as a ruse to gauge your level of desperation. If you refuse a spec assignment, you may be offered a firm commitment, for you have proven yourself to be a serious professional. Or, you may have bupkus (which is Yiddish for "nothing").

If you *have* to work on spec, try these two suggestions to make it more likely that you'll sell your work:

1. See if the client will make a firm commitment based on *part* of the product rather than a complete job. For example, if you're trying to sell a novel on spec, work up the table of contents and a sample chapter or two rather than the entire book.

2. Do thorough research to see where else you might sell the product if the initial client doesn't snap it up. Here are some research possibilities:

   ➤ Networking

   ➤ Professional organizations

   ➤ Professional journals and reference books.

See Chapter 17 for a detailed discussion of making business contacts and networking.

Taking the Wind Out of Your Sales

So you thought setting up your freelance business was the hard part? Naw, selling is! Actually, deciding *how* to sell can be tricky. Besides straight-out "I-do-the-work-and-you-give-me-the money" deals and working on spec, there are two more ways to make money in the freelancer's bag of tricks: selling on consignment and bartering. Let's look at each one of these sales methods now. Get to know all about them so you have smooth "sale-ing"! (Sorry; that was bad, wasn't it?)

How Much Is That Doggy in the Window?

Take My Word For It
Working on *consignment* means producing a product and then offering it for sale with an intermediary. You get paid only when the product sells.

When you sell your product on *consignment* you place the product with a seller and get paid when—or if—it sells. The seller may be an art gallery owner, an agent, or a broker.

"Pish tosh!" you say? You may not have an option. Some freelancers, such as weavers, painters, sculptors, and other designers, have no choice but to sell on consignment, at least in the beginning of their careers. Most freelancers try to avoid working on consignment, since the risks of not selling are great.

Even Steven: Trading

The barter system is alive and well; just ask freelancers! Now, the IRS frowns on this method of payment because it's impossible to figure out how to assess taxes on deals where products and services were exchanged but money wasn't. As a result, please read this section in bed under the covers. You can use a flashlight.

It's not uncommon for freelancers to barter services. For example, a freelance writer may create a performer's resume in exchange for the performer donating the entertainment at a children's birthday party. Or, a freelance accountant may prepare a freelance baker's tax return in exchange for a tray of fresh-baked cookies. If you decide to go this route, just be sure that both participants are content with the agreement. And don't say you read about bartering here.

Show Me the Money: Dealing With Deadbeats

In the best of all possible worlds, every job would pay fairly and promptly. As you've probably figured out by now (no doubt the hard way), we don't live in the best of all possible worlds. This world is filled with skinflints, deadbeats, and misers. No doubt some of them will be your clients. I've worked for a few losers myself, so let me advise you on how to survive this particular minefield.

First of all, you're not the First National Bank. Your job is not to extend credit to your clients. Even if you cried when you found out that Peter Pan was flying on strings and you've adopted enough stray cats to start your own animal shelter, this is no time to get soft on me. You did the work; you earned the money. It's yours now, not theirs.

This means never having to say "I'm sorry" for demanding prompt and full payment. Don't grovel, sniffle, or whine. Be upfront, professional, and assertive. There's no need to give excuses, as in "I need the money to pay my vet bill or they're going to repossess my iguana" or "I wouldn't press you for payment except I'm running out of Prozac." Nope.

Instead, follow these guidelines:

Ready...

➤ Submit a bill with every job, even if you have a contract that does not require you to bill separately. This helps jog overworked staffers into getting your payment processed.

➤ Always set a deadline for payment. If at all possible, get the deadline in writing. This helps prevent misunderstandings, as in "We thought you didn't expect a check until Haley's comet reappeared" (a variation on the standard "You expect to get paid in this lifetime?").

➤ On the bill, clearly mark when the job was done and when you expect payment. If not, companies will often delay payment as long as possible. They're not fools: Why should they pay you before they have to?

➤ Be sure to include your name, address, and social security number or tax identification number on every invoice. For some clients, you may also have to include a reference number for each particular job. This is used for tracking. Complete and accurate information helps ensure prompt payment.

Mind Your Own Business
Never assume that size matters. Bigger firms are sometimes the worst when it comes to prompt payment; smaller firms can be the best. But then again, it might be just the opposite for you.

Mind Your Own Business
Set reasonable time limits for payment, depending on industry standards. In publishing, standard pay schedules are between 30 days and 90 days. Almost no one is going to pay you within a week, unless you hit the pay period at just the right point on the curve. After 90 days, the client is usually pushing the limit.

➤ Number each invoice so you can track payment more easily. I learned this trick from a great accountant named Edith. (That's a thank you, Edith!) Some computer programs will do this automatically for you.

➤ Familiarize yourself with the payment schedules of your various clients. One of my best clients, for example, processes invoices on the last day of every month and pays within 45 days. If I miss the deadline, I have to wait 90 days—but that's my own tough luck.

➤ Keep very accurate records to know when payment is due. Don't let payment slide. Some computer programs can help you track this.

Aim...

➤ Start by assuming the best: Your invoice was misplaced or the check was lost in the mail.

➤ Nonetheless, take action. A few days after the payment is overdue, call the client to check on the status of the check.

➤ Remember that the squeaky wheel gets the oil. Don't be afraid to request the money you're due. There's no need to be nasty, just firm.

➤ Stay within the chain of command by dealing with your direct in-house contact. Some people advise violating the chain of command by calling accounting or someone higher up the ladder. I strongly suggest that you avoid leaving tire tracks on someone's forehead. Seek satisfaction higher up only if you don't get paid within a reasonable time or your contact tells you to move up the ladder.

➤ If you're really shy about hounding deadbeat clients, try this. Instead of calling when the initial payment is late, send out a copy of the original invoice, marked "SECOND INVOICE." If this doesn't result in prompt payment or a call from the client, you're going to have to bite the bullet, call the client, and discuss the matter.

 **Bet You Didn't Know**

Knowing the industry scuttlebutt is especially important when it comes to getting paid. Keeping your ear to the ground can help you know why the check is late: Your in-house contact is a scatterbrain, the project was canceled, or the company is in serious financial hot water, for example.

Fire!

➤ If your phone calls and second invoice don't do the trick, write a formal business letter summarizing the situation and demanding payment.

➤ Allow a reasonable time for payment to appear in your mailbox.

➤ If no cash appears, you can take the matter to Small Claims Court if the payment is less than a set amount, usually between a few hundred dollars and about $2,000. The amount varies from state to state. It costs a nominal fee to file in Small Claims Court, and you don't need a lawyer.

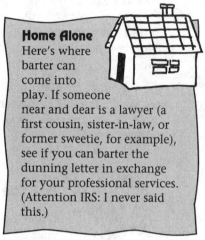

Home Alone
Here's where barter can come into play. If someone near and dear is a lawyer (a first cousin, sister-in-law, or former sweetie, for example), see if you can barter the dunning letter in exchange for your professional services. (Attention IRS: I never said this.)

➤ For larger jobs, you might hire a lawyer to send a follow-up letter. Lawyer's letters tend to get results because they have that "official fright factor." Always try to find a lawyer who specializes in cases of your type.

➤ If you can't afford a lawyer or can't find one who will do the job for free, check out the professional organizations for your freelance specialty. Many such organizations offer free or very inexpensive legal services.

➤ Some freelancers charge interest for late payment; others give a discount for early payment. I have never cottoned to either method; it's too much bookkeeping. I just want to be paid the amount I earned. If you decide to charge interest or give a discount, be sure to check the standard practices in your freelance business to make sure this is an accepted alternative.

Just When You Thought It Was Safe to Go Back in the Water...

➤ When you do finally get paid, make a careful note of the payment. You don't want to goof and hound a client who has already paid you.

➤ Before you cash the check, study it carefully. Make sure that the name, date, and amount are correct. Unscrupulous vendors have been known to scam by issuing faulty checks.

➤ Look carefully for disclaimers and waivers of rights. By endorsing the check, you may be signing away all future rights to your work—no matter what your contract says. This practice resulted in a major (and ultimately successful) lawsuit on behalf of the artist and writer who created Superman.

➤ What about rubber checks? If the check bounces for insufficient funds, go right to the lawyer or Small Claims Court. And make a note never to work for this client again.

One final note: Keep careful records of which clients paid and which ones didn't. Also jot down the excuses you were given for late payment: Some may be valid, like your in-house contact was fired and your invoice was never properly filed, or the company was undergoing a reorganization. You may think you'll never forget a client who stiffed you, but memory slips. With careful records, you won't get trapped working for the same deadbeat twice.

You will make money, I promise, and you'll even collect nearly all of it. As a matter of fact, only a handful of freelancers I know have gotten stiffed. I've had two bad experiences. In one instance, I was out $200; in another, $300. Not bad for 15 years in the business.

 **Bet You Didn't Know**

It may not be a total loss if you can't collect on a job. Check with your tax preparer to see if you can write off non-payment as bad debt. To that end, always keep meticulous records to help document your claim.

We're in the Money: Give Yourself a Raise

As you journey through life as a freelancer, the day will come when you've established a solid reputation. You'll have steady work and a stable of loyal clients. And then it will be time for you to raise your rates. How will you know when this happy day has arrived?

First of all, always keep an eye on what your competitors are charging. My friends and I have arranged an informal network of freelance writers. Most of us specialize in education publishing, focusing on text books, trade books, and reference books. A few times a year we meet, have lunch, and talk frankly about work. As we swap war stories, we're not shy about asking what different clients pay.

Here are some other suggestions for gauging what the market will bear:

1. See how quickly your clients agree to your rates. If they snap them up like hungry piranha, it's time to up the ante.

2. Check your expenses, especially any increases in the Consumer Price Index and inflation rates. As prices increase across the board, so should your salary. Otherwise, you're eating into your profit.

3. See what employees in general are getting as a Cost of Living (COLA) increase. At present, it's between 2–3 percent. If you give yourself a COLA raise, you're just keeping up with standard living costs. This is necessary unless you live on rice cakes and marshmallow fluff. If you don't get at least COLA, you'll fall behind fast.

4. You don't have to raise your rates across the board. Instead, keep your rates flexible. This will give you more play with new and old clients, the amenable ones and the cranky ones.

5. Keep increases within logical bounds. Rather than doubling your rates from $60 per hour to $120, increase by 5 percent or 10 percent —the types of raises you'd get in a standard corporation. The only exception is raising rates sharply to meet industry standards if you're grossly underpriced (which of course you won't be, since you read Chapter 12).

6. Raise your rates at a logical time, such as January 1. Sticking to a standard fiscal calendar makes you seem more professional, which in turn makes it easier for clients to accept the change.

7. Raise your rates at least once a year. People who work for large corporations get raises. You deserve the same rewards.

8. Finally, be prepared to lose some clients. Even a small raise—2 to 3 percent—can freak some vendors. Only you can decide how valuable these clients are to you and how much you're willing to sacrifice to keep them.

Mind Your Own Business
It's tempting to jack up your rates to pay for your new yacht, jewels, or alimony payment. Track the market trends before you pass all your expenses on to clients. Be fair, not piggy.

Home Alone
Some free-lancers raise their rates for troublesome or annoying clients. This way, at least they're getting paid extra for the aggravation factor. Worst-case scenario, they'll go away and bother someone else. (Actually, this might be the best-case scenario!)

Mind Your Own Business
Never raise your rates without first telling your clients.

The Least You Need to Know

➤ Freelancers can go out on limbs more often than cats. If you work on *spec*, you produce something without guarantee of payment.

➤ Working on *consignment* means producing a product and then offering it for sale with an intermediary. Guarantees of payment are better.

➤ Don't be afraid to collect money that's owed to you. It's yours; you earned it.

➤ Give yourself a raise at least once a year. (And while you're at it, change the oil in your car, turn the mattress, and call your mother.)

AND THIS CLAUSE WILL GUARANTEE PAYMENT.

Chapter 14

Legal Beagles: Business Structure and Contracts

In This Chapter

➤ Discover the three ways to structure your business

➤ Select the legal structure that's right for you

➤ Learn about contracts and letters of agreement

A certain truck driver amused himself by running over lawyers he saw walking down the road. One day the truck driver saw a priest hitchhiking. He pulled over and asked, "Where are you going, Father?"

"I'm going to the church down the road," replied the priest.

"No problem, Father! I'll give you a lift. Climb in," the truck driver replied. The priest climbed into the passenger seat and the truck driver continued down the road.

Suddenly, the truck driver saw a lawyer walking down the road and swerved to hit him. Remembering there was a priest in the truck, he swerved away, narrowly missing the lawyer. However, he still heard a loud THUD.

Not understanding where the noise came from, he glanced in his mirrors. When he didn't see anything, he turned to the priest and said, "I'm sorry, Father. I almost hit that lawyer."

"That's okay," replied the priest. "I got him with the door."

It's almost too easy to find a good lawyer joke: They're more common than lawyers at the scene of an accident. But all joking aside, a lawyer can be a freelancer's best friend when it comes to helping a business run smoothly. In this chapter, you'll learn your rights and responsibilities with respect to legal business structures, contracts, and letters of agreement. Then you'll know when you *do* need a lawyer and when you *don't.*

Legal Aid

There may be 10,000 maniacs, but there are only three ways to structure your freelance business. The envelope, please:

➤ Sole proprietorship

➤ Partnership

➤ Corporation

In a nutshell, the legal structure you select affects how much of your hard-earned money you fork over to the government and the degree of liability you face. Since you've already made the choice between chunky peanut butter and smooth, red or white wine, and a staff job or a freelance career, it's now time to decide which type of organizational structure is best for your business. Read on to learn the advantages and disadvantages of each structure.

O Solo Mio! (Sole Proprietorship)

A *sole proprietorship* is a business owned and operated by one person. More than three-quarters of the freelancers operating in America are sole proprietors, which makes this the most common type of business structure, the tuna-on-white-bread of businesses. In part, it's because a sole proprietorship is the easiest type of business structure to establish and close down. Legally, all you have to do to set up sole proprietorship is get to work; to stop, just stop working. (Legal concerns aside, you know you also have to set up an office, create a business plan, work out your finances and all the rest of the rigmarole you've already learned. Just hanging out a shingle doesn't protect your hindquarters.)

Take My Word For It
A *sole proprietorship* is a business that is owned and operated by one person.

Why is a sole proprietorship as popular as Pop Tarts, Pez, and Playtex? 'Cause it has more advantages than the Wonderbra. Here are some of its main benefits:

➤ It's easy to create; there are no legal papers to file.

➤ The profits aren't shared.

➤ You're the boss: There are no co-owners or partners to cramp your style.

➤ There's no one looking over your shoulder.

➤ Decisions can be made quickly.

➤ The outlook is flexible and nimble because only one person is involved.

➤ There's little governmental control.

➤ There's no special taxation.

A further word on taxes: With a sole proprietorship, taxes are as straight as U.S. 50 going through Nevada. You pay taxes on the profits as an individual; there are no business taxes as such. Fortunately, with a sole proprietorship you are allowed a generous number of business deductions, such as a portion of your own Social Security payments, all explained in detail in Chapter 21.

There's always a downside; what would life be without calories, cavities, and constriction? Here are some of the primary disadvantages of a sole proprietorship:

> **Home Alone**
> The overwhelming majority of freelancers start as sole proprietors. They know they can always change their status as their business needs change.

➤ The owner (that's *you*) assumes all business debts.

➤ Ditto for lawsuits that might be filed against the business. That means that people sue *you* personally, not a business entity.

➤ There's a limited viewpoint, since only one person is contributing ideas.

➤ Less capital is available, because there is only one owner earning money.

➤ You're not allowed certain juicy tax deductions, such as your own salary.

➤ You're the head weenie at this roast. You get all the reproach as well as the rewards. Remember what New York Ranger Barry Beck said about the person who started a brawl during NHL's Stanley Cup playoffs: "We have only one person to blame, and that's each other."

> IS THAT CLEAR?
>
> **Mind Your Own Business**
> If you decide to adopt a business name, you will most likely be required to file a *Doing Business As* form or *DBA*. This way the state knows who actually owns the business.

Pas de Deux (Partnership)

Legally, a *partnership* is a business owned by two or more people. A partner's contribution can be financial, material, or managerial—or any combination of the three. Partners can be as cooperative as a sleeping baby or as obnoxious as a hormonally challenged teenager.

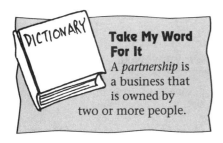

Take My Word For It
A *partnership* is a business that is owned by two or more people.

Mind Your Own Business
If you decide to form a partnership for your freelance business, be sure to maintain at least 51 percent interest—or you may find yourself working for someone else. Also be sure that you and your partner clearly understand the financial agreement and division of labor.

It's not difficult to form a partnership, and the government pretty well keeps its nose out of it. However, there are some potential drawbacks. First of all, you have to share any profits with your partner(s); second, there is less wiggle room because decisions are shared. Another big problem is *liability*. Like sole proprietors, partners may be left holding the bag if things go sour. There's also the matter of clashing personalities. Finally, what happens to the business if one partner loses interest, moves far away, or, God forbid, bites the big one?

Freelancers rarely form partnerships because we tend to be an independent lot—which is usually one of the main reasons we became freelancers in the first place. Besides, with people bailing out of marriages faster than lemmings pole-vaulting over a sea wall, who wants to get saddled with a business partner? (They don't even have to take out the garbage, empty the dishwasher, or fold the socks. All *they* have to do is work.)

Here are some points to consider as you ponder whether or not to partner:

1. Why do I need a business partner?
2. How might having a partner *help* my business?
3. How might having a partner *harm* my business?
4. Do many people have business partners in my field? Why or why not?
5. If I do want to form a partnership, which kind will be best for me and my business? (This is where you need a lawyer. You can throw in an accountant for good measure.)

It's very common for freelancers to form temporary partnerships to take on big projects. Since forming a partnership isn't as easy as making toast, I strongly recommend that you get some legal advice if you decide to go this route.

You, Inc. (Incorporation)

Then there's a *corporation*, the final type of organizational structure for your freelance business. I put incorporation last because forming and running a corporation are usually more complex than planning a family vacation, having both sides of the family over at the same time, or renewing your driver's license. That's because a corporation is a legal entity, separate from the individuals or the personal finances of the people who own it. Corporations are identified by using *Inc.*, *Co.*, or *Ltd.* after their names.

Corporations must have a board of directors. In some states, one person can function as the board of directors; it's usually three or more people, however. And that's just the beginning.

Here's where you need a lawyer, preferably one who specializes in incorporation for freelancers or small businesses. Because you are forming a legal structure, it's important to color within the lines.

Let's take a look at the pros and cons of freelancers forming corporations. Here are some of the most important advantages:

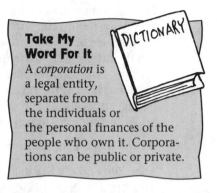

Take My Word For It
A *corporation* is a legal entity, separate from the individuals or the personal finances of the people who own it. Corporations can be public or private.

➤ As a corporation, it's much easier to secure capital, usually through the sale of stock or bonds in the corporation. ("Sale of stock!" you moan. "I haven't even gotten to the chapter where I learn about *buying* stock!")

➤ As a corporation, it's easier to obtain financing.

➤ Members of the corporation are shielded from personal liability. Your personal assets cannot be touched in case your business goes bankrupt. This is important if you are entering a speculative business or have significant personal assets. (If you do have significant personal assets, please call. You're someone I'd like to get to know better…)

➤ In a corporation, authority is delegated.

➤ Ownership is easily transferred.

➤ Corporations are the most stable and permanent of the three types of legal entities. (After all, you've spent too much time and money to split.)

The disadvantages? Here are the Big Three:

➤ Corporations face major in-your-face government regulation.

➤ It's expensive to form a corporation.

➤ Your earnings are taxed twice: The business profit is taxed, and your personal salary and dividends are taxed.

oH! **Bet You Didn't Know**

In an S corporation, shareholders can offset business losses incurred by the corporation. This dodges the double taxation rap. Freelancers who do incorporate often form S corporations. Get a lawyer.

Should you or shouldn't you? Unlike hair dye, when it comes to incorporation, you can't trust your hairdresser (unless she's a lawyer on the side). If you think your freelance business is going to grow very large, you might want to learn more about incorporation. On the other hand, if you're a one-person freelance operation, the probability of liability is slight, and you don't see yourself growing into the Very Big Business ("We Care Big"), then you have little to gain by incorporating. You'd probably stand to lose a fair piece of change in legal fees and the tax bite, too. In general, most freelancers incorporate only when the corporate taxes are much lower than their personal income taxes.

As you make your decision, consider these points as well:

➤ You can file the incorporation papers yourself to save money, but this is a lot trickier than making Jell-O, so consider biting the bullet and paying an attorney to do this for you.

➤ Because a corporate tax structure is complex, get an accountant on board, too. Find one who specializes in small businesses.

Help Me, Rhonda: Deciding on a Legal Structure

Deciding on a legal structure can be as hard as getting a pair of well-fitting jeans (a feat I still have not mastered). To help you make the best possible choice, you may wish to check out these sources:

Mind Your Own Business
Review your business structure at least once a year to make sure it still meets your needs.

1. Contact the county, city, and state in which you will be doing business to get the specific rules for operating a business in that location.

2. Obtain a packet of information from the IRS on operating a small business. It's free!

3. Solicit input from your lawyer and accountant as you decide which business structure to adopt.

In addition, you may wish to use the following worksheet to help you decide on a legal structure. Answer each question in the space provided.

Decisions, Decisions

1. How much risk is involved in my business? For example, what liabilities do I think I'll face? Am I likely to get sued?

_____

2. Do I need additional expertise to run my business?

_____

3. Do I need additional capital to run my business?

_____

4. Which legal structure is most adaptable to my needs as a freelancer?

_____

5. What is my ultimate goal? Which legal structure can best serve that purpose?

_____

6. What is the start-up cost for this legal structure?

_____

7. What are the tax ramifications of the structure I am considering?

_____

8. How complex are the start-up procedures?

_____

9. How much legal help will I need to set up this structure?

_____

10. How will the applicable laws affect me?

_____

Home Alone
For more information, write to the Small Business Administration for its pamphlet "Selecting the Legal Structure for Your Firm." The address is Small Business Administration, P.O. Box 15434, Fort Worth, Texas, 76119. And it's free!

Now that you've surveyed the different business structures that freelancers can form, it's time to look at another key way to protect your interests. We'd all like to think the best of people, but we're big kids now. As a result, we've learned that not everyone is looking out for our best interests. Freelancers can be especially easy to rip off, because we're out there on our own. This next section can help you make sure that you get paid for your work.

Clause and Effect

One size may fit all with T-shirts and spandex pants, but not when it comes to selling your product or services as a freelancer. Some clients work only by a handshake agreement, while others have contracts as thick as the phone book. Contracts and letters of agreement vary considerably from client to client. A *contract* is a formal business agreement; a *letter of agreement* is simply a less formal contract. I have always been a fan of getting it in writing. Here are some of my reasons why:

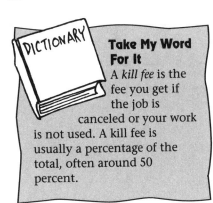

Take My Word For It
A *contract* is a formal business agreement; a *letter of agreement* is simply a less formal contract.

Take My Word For It
A *kill fee* is the fee you get if the job is canceled or your work is not used. A kill fee is usually a percentage of the total, often around 50 percent.

Contracts are good things because…

➤ They help avoid misunderstandings, as in "You wanted the job *this* Tuesday?"

➤ They save you unnecessary work, as in, "The job calls for six pieces, not 60."

➤ They save you money, as in "Since these changes are not required by contract, how much will I get paid for them?"

➤ They help ensure payment if the assignment is canceled, as in "My kill fee specifies that I receive 50 percent of the total."

➤ They help you collect your money, as in, "The contract specifies my invoice will be paid within 60 days of satisfactory completion of the assignment."

Remember: The more detailed the contract, the more protection you have against dilemmas and deadbeats.

Terms of Endearment

As I mentioned earlier, contracts or letters of agreement can be as fat as a sumo wrestler or as skinny as a socialite. Nonetheless, they must all contain the following elements:

1. Name and address of both parties
2. The date the agreement was made
3. Your social security number
4. A complete description of the work
5. All agreed-upon fees (including a kill fee if the project is yanked)
6. The payment schedule
7. All deadlines
8. The form in which the work is to be delivered (on disk, in hard copy, on film, and so on)
9. Who owns the work you produce (you or the client)
10. Lines for signatures

Remember, effective contracts and letters of agreement try to cover every possible contingency, such as money, responsibility, and deadlines. Keep this in mind whether you or your client is framing the document.

Warning: Contents Under Pressure

Some things in life are inflexible, like two-year-olds, teenagers, and stale toothpaste. Other things have a little elasticity, like politics and waistbands.

Mind Your Own Business
Have the contract witnessed if it's a big money job or you suspect the client is cranky and there's apt to be a problem down the road.

Fortunately for savvy freelancers, contracts and letters of agreement are rarely take-it-or-leave-it deals. If you suspect that a specific contract is carved in granite, never fear: Your in-house contact will let you know up front. At that point, you have the choice of deciding how much you want the assignment and what you are willing to compromise to get it. But nearly all companies are open to some negotiation. Learn to stand up for what you think is important, but be willing to bend when it's necessary to make a sale. You may lose a skirmish but you'll win the war.

Always talk to your client and read your contract carefully to see which rights you are keeping and which rights you are signing away. "Why should I bother reading the contract that carefully?" you might ask. "After all, there's not much I can do about it. I want to sell my work and these guys are paying me real money." True to a point. There are some clauses that you can't do a thing about. In other cases, however, there are clauses that you can—and should—consider modifying. Here are some possibilities:

➤ *How the money will be paid.* For example, you may wish to get one-third on sign-up, one-third upon half completion, and one-third upon completion, rather than 100 percent upon completion.

➤ *Delivery date for the job.* Consider negotiating a bonus for early completion, for instance.

➤ *Reimbursement for expenses.* If the expenses are heavy, consider asking for reimbursement. Why should you have to eat all the telephone bills, photocopying expenses, and fax charges?

➤ *Whether your name will be listed in the credits, if there are credits.* This could be a great way to generate more work!

Don't be afraid to stand up for your rights. You'd be surprised at how often people will be perfectly happy to give you exactly what you almost didn't dare ask for.

Here are some additional points to focus on:

1. Make sure all points are resolved. Don't leave anything hanging.

2. Be sure the contract or letter of agreement contains the terms you agreed to orally. Errors occur in the best of firms; shady companies, in contrast, have been known to pull a fast one and ignore your terms.

3. Check the fine print. Things do get slipped in there—and they are rarely in your favor.

4. Be sure all changes are legible. Initial small changes; have major changes retyped.

5. Be sure you understand every, and I mean *every,* term of the contract. If you don't, check with someone who does.

6. Finally, proofread the document. Pay special attention to non-standard parts (the items that are specific to this particular contract), such as the spelling of your name and your Social Security number.

7. If there's a lot of money involved, you may wish to have a lawyer look at the contract. No doubt a freelancer who got burned by a devious contract coined the cliché "Better safe than sorry."

8. Be sure to keep a copy of the contract or letter of agreement.

No Uncertain Terms

Here is a sample contract for a writing assignment. This is called a *work for hire* agreement because you're a hired hand. As such, you get a flat fee, a one-shot payment. Under this type of contract, you have no claim to what you produce; everything belongs to the client. The minute you sign the work for hire agreement, you are signing away all future rights to the work.

Notice that the contract gives virtually all the protection to the client and very little to the freelancer. For example, the contract doesn't specify a payment deadline. This clearly works in favor of the client, not the freelancer. Unfortunately for us freelancers, this is a standard contract in the field.

Mind Your Own Business

Some freelancers use their invoices as contracts. I am not a fan of this practice. I prefer a formal letter of agreement or a contract. All an invoice must state is how much you are to be paid; it does not describe the terms of the agreement.

Read the contract carefully to see what protection it does and does not offer to the writer.

This agreement between <u>Big Brother Publishing Company, Inc.,</u> and <u>I. M. Writer,</u> an independently established business person, is entered into with respect to <u>Job #000.</u>

I agree to the following:

1. Any and all materials submitted by me to Big Brother Publishing Company, Inc., is my original work and no materials submitted by me contain libelous or slanderous material. No material submitted by me infringe on any copyright or other person. I further agree to hold Big Brother Publishing Company, Inc., harmless for any infringements or violation of any rights of any other persons arising out of the use and publication of materials submitted by me for publication.

2. I understand that any materials I submit to Big Brother Publishing Company, Inc., are intended for publication. I understand that the copyright in any such materials shall be claimed by Even Bigger Brother Publishing Company, Inc. Accordingly, I agree to assign any title, right, interest in any materials submitted by me which are accepted by Big Brother Publishing Company, Inc., to Even Bigger Brother Publishing Company, Inc., including any rights to renewal of copyrights. I further agree that this assignment shall be binding upon my successors, heirs, and assigns, and that my only right in any of these materials shall be limited to my right to payment as set out in Paragraph 4.

3. I understand that materials I submit to Big Brother Publishing Company, Inc., must be acceptable for publication by both Big Brother Publishing Company,

continues

---

continued

Inc., and Even Bigger Brother Publishing Company, Inc. Final acceptance within the meaning of this agreement shall be evidenced by payment pursuant of Paragraph 4. Big Brother Publishing Company, Inc., may cancel this agreement if work is not deemed acceptable by the company.

4. In consideration of the above agreement, Big Brother Publishing Company, Inc., agrees to pay <u>writer</u> the amount of <u>$$$$</u> upon completion of the following assignment: <u>description of writing assignment.</u>

5. I understand that I will receive from Big Brother Publishing Company, Inc., various instructions and other information to be used by me in the preparation of materials for publication. I understand that these materials were designed for Big Brother Publishing Company, Inc., for projects of a confidential nature. As a result, I agree not to disclose to any other persons any information about these materials and agree not to copy these materials. I agree to return such materials to Big Brother Publishing Company, Inc. I further agree to hold Big Brother Publishing Company, Inc., harmless from any damage caused by any breach of this provision by me.

6. I understand and agree that I am retained by Big Brother Publishing Company, Inc., for the purposes and to the extent set forth in this Agreement, and my relation to Big Brother Publishing Company, Inc., is to be that of Independent Contractor. I shall be free to dispose of such portion of my time, energy, and skill as it is not obligated under this Agreement and may do so in such a manner as I see fit and to such persons, firms, and corporations as I deem advisable. I shall not be considered as having employee status or as being entitled to participate in any plans, arrangements, or distributions by Big Brother Publishing Company, Inc., pertaining to or in connection with profit-sharing, or similar benefits for their regular employees. I further understand that as an Independent Contractor I shall be paid in full with no taxes withheld and I am therefore responsible for any federal, state, and local taxes that I may owe.

AGREED   APPROVED

_____   _____

Signature   for Big Brother Publishing Co., Inc.

_____   _____

Social Security #   Date

_____

Address

_____

_____

Freelance writers can also get contracts that pay an *advance* (money paid up front, upon signing the contract) and a *royalty,* a percentage of earnings. The amount of the advance depends on a writer's fame. Big-name writers and creative types usually nail down six-figure advances; the peons get $2,000 and up. The royalties are calculated on a sliding scale, based on the number of books sold. The more books sold, the higher the royalty that is paid. All advances are just that: money deducted from the royalties. Graphic artists and other creative types get similar contracts.

Mind Your Own Business
Remember: An oral contract isn't worth the paper it's printed on. Always try to get the agreement in writing.

Regardless of the type of contract you and your client negotiate, the key is making sure that you understand what you are signing. If not, you might find yourself signing away potentially lucrative rights or chaining yourself to endless revisions. Remember, if you don't understand it, don't sign it. Have a lawyer take a look at it. It's likely to be money well spent. Agents can also help with contracts. See Chapter 18 for details.

The Least You Need to Know

➤ There are three ways to organize your freelance business: as a sole proprietorship, partnership, or corporation.

➤ One size doesn't fit all. Get the partnership size that fits you.

➤ Use a contract or letter of agreement to avoid misunderstandings and protect your interests.

➤ Read your contracts. Then read them again until you understand them. And don't sign them until you really do understand them!

➤ Consider having a lawyer look over any contract you write or receive. In this case, the lawyer's fee is money well spent.

Chapter 15

In the Groove: Bookkeeping

> **In This Chapter**
>
> ➤ Discover why it's vital to keep good financial records
>
> ➤ Learn how to organize your records
>
> ➤ Find out how to prepare a simple business budget

Wouldn't know a ledger book if it stood up in your soup?

Rather face a ravenous shark than sort a pile of receipts?

Quake uncontrollably at the thought of creating (much less keeping) a budget?

Not to worry, snookie. "No pain, no gain" only applies to building washboard abs and bulging pecs, not to keeping good financial records. In this chapter, you'll get "No pain—lots of gain" and learn how to keep well-organized and logical financial records.

I doubt that you became a freelancer so you could practice your bookkeeping skills (unless you're a freelance bookkeeper or accountant, of course!), but keeping accurate records is a *very* important part of running a small business—and that's what you're doing as a freelancer. That's what I'm going to teach you first in this chapter. Next, you'll learn all about creating a clear and useful record-keeping system. We'll round off the chapter with a section on budgets for a freelance business.

Fear of Finances

Unless you're an obsessive-compulsive, record-keeping can be a major drag, right up there with cleaning the lint out of the dryer or your navel. But nit-picking has its place, especially when it comes to running a business. In fact, an unwillingness to tend to the business side of business is a major factor in the high attrition rate for freelancers.

Mind Your Own Business

More than half of all new businesses—including freelance businesses—fail within a year.

Freelancers tend to be a free-spirited lot, which is why they fly solo. While flying by the seat of your pants can be an asset to many creative people, when it comes to being a success as a freelancer, laissez-faire is a disaster. Unfortunately, I was a case in point.

True Confessions

When I first started out as a freelance writer, I kept my records on the back of an old envelope. Because the envelope was large and only reasonably grungy, I thought I was being very efficient. I carefully threw out all receipts, contracts, letters of agreement, royalty statements, canceled checks, and related pieces of paper. Hey, who needs all that clutter?

When my husband the accountant-turned-publishing executive saw this, he recoiled in real horror. (The last time he was so appalled he saw me opening a bottle with my just-capped front teeth, but that's another issue.) To placate him, I decided to keep all my financial records in a little book (and use a bottle opener to open bottles). I also threw all the receipts in a drawer.

I recorded everything I billed, collected, and spent. Well, *almost* everything. I saved every receipt, contract, letter of agreement, royalty statement, canceled check, and related piece of paper. Well, *almost* all of them. Despite my sloppiness, this system worked reasonably well. Later, I went to a date book and computer spreadsheets. More on that later in this chapter.

Bet You Didn't Know

According to the Small Business Administration, shoddy record-keeping is a major reason so many small businesses go bust.

Now, every time I buy something related to my freelance writing career—from a train ticket to meet with a publisher in New York City to a plane ticket to attend a business conference across the continent—I record it on my spreadsheet. I note the date the expense was incurred, how much I spent, and why. That last column is crucial, for it determines whether or not the IRS will allow your deduction. There's more on tax deductions in Chapter 21.

If I did it, so can you. Despite my present adherence to a solid record-keeping system, I'm not a whit less creative. Keeping good financial records hasn't caused my hair to turn gray, my bicycle to rust, or my tomato plants to wilt. (All these things happened anyway, but I can't blame them on good bookkeeping, much as I try.)

> **Mind Your Own Business**
> If you're seriously math-phobic, you can hire someone to do the adding and subtracting for you. But even if you hire a bookkeeper, accountant, or business manager, you'll have to oversee their work. And you'll still have to track your expenses and earnings yourself.

Money Maven

What keeping good financial records *has* done is let me sleep a little better because I know that if one of Uncle Sam's geek squad tax minions decides to audit my tax returns, I can justify each and every one of my deductions. I can even back everything up with the appropriate receipt. I can check my contracts so I know when something is due and how much I will earn on royalties. So what if it took me more than a (gulp) decade to get to this point? Thanks to my mistakes, I can get *you* a spot in the Land of Good Financial Record-Keeping in a lot less time!

Here are a handful of additional reasons why you need to keep good financial records:

Good financial records let you...

➤ Track and measure your success...or lack thereof. Based on your financial records, you can decide if your prices are too high or too low, for example, and whether you need to take on some extra help or drop the help you have.

➤ Know what tax deductions you have.

➤ Increase your chances of staying in business.

➤ Earn larger profits.

➤ Get bank loans.

➤ Document ownership of expensive office equipment.

> **Mind Your Own Business**
> Even if you're cavalier about your money, make sure that you have a firm grasp of what's going on with your bucks.

➤ Make insurance claims and back them up with solid proof.

➤ Resolve any litigation involving money.

➤ Avoid embarrassing mistakes (like billing a client who has already paid you).

➤ Know your contractual rights.

Now, before you start beating yourself up about the sorry state of your financial records, take a moment to indulge in a little justified self-pity. Unlike other small business owners, freelancers rarely get the help they need setting up their record-keeping system. Most institutions dealing with money, such as banks and the Small Business Administration, are geared for larger small businesses, not lone eagles. Likewise, college courses and seminars on business finances are usually aimed at bigger concerns.

Okay, wallow over. Now it's time to roll up your sleeves and get to work creating a financial record-keeping system that works for you and Uncle Sam. That way, you won't ever have to make the mistakes that I did in straightening out the mess I called my financial records.

Spring Cleaning, Financial Style

There are two things you need to organize the financial part of your freelance life: a *record-keeping system* and a *budget*.

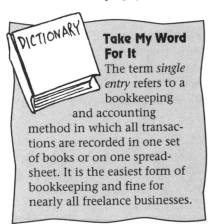

Take My Word For It
The term *single entry* refers to a bookkeeping and accounting method in which all transactions are recorded in one set of books or on one spreadsheet. It is the easiest form of bookkeeping and fine for nearly all freelance businesses.

Home Alone
Try job sharing: Do some work for a freelance accountant or bookkeeper in exchange for tax assistance and record-keeping expertise.

➤ Your *record-keeping system* tracks daily, weekly, and monthly cash flow.

➤ Your *budget* helps you analyze your cash flow so you can see what's going on in your business.

As you can see, both plans help you track your money. Otherwise, it's too easy to find that the bucks have slipped through the cracks—along with your business.

Fortunately, neither system has to be as elaborate as the Macy's Thanksgiving Parade or even the local Zucchini Festival. They *do* have to be complete enough to let you and the IRS see what is happening with your business money. You should be able to see at a glance where the money is coming from and where it is going—supplies, taxes, and so on.

Whatever systems you ultimately decide to adopt must be:

➤ Simple to use, like a fork.

➤ Easy to understand—no Rosetta stones, please.

➤ Consistent, like me.

➤ Kept up-to-date, unlike your closet (ditch the Nehru jacket and love beads, already).

Let's boogie.

Book It, Danno: Setting Up a Record-Keeping System

You can set up your own record-keeping system, or you can have an accountant do it for you. My friend Meish Goldish, one of the most creative and successful freelance writers I know, tracks his money with an easy system: paper and pencil. In contrast, I use a date book and spreadsheet from Microsoft Excel. He's a Luddite; I'm a technobrat. Each to his own taste.

Some fellow freelancers I interviewed have nifty systems set up by their accountants. A few others have set up what I consider somewhat eccentric systems, hybrids of various notebooks, shoe boxes, accordion file folders, and spreadsheets. But each system works equally well for its user.

Bet You Didn't Know

Microsoft Excel is part of Microsoft Office (you can also buy it as a separate application). It's a cinch to use, but any spreadsheet that winds your clock can usually be adapted to a freelancer's financial record-keeping needs.

In and Out

At its simplest level, your record-keeping system must show how much money you earned and how much you spent. Here are some possible sources of money:

➤ Payment for services

➤ Interest on savings and investments

➤ Insurance reimbursements

➤ Royalties

➤ Licensing fees

Here are some ways you spend your bucks:

➤ Office supplies

➤ Equipment

➤ Travel

➤ Business entertainment

➤ Postage

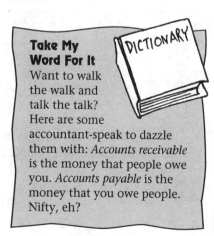

Take My Word For It
Want to walk the walk and talk the talk? Here are some accountant-speak to dazzle them with: *Accounts receivable* is the money that people owe you. *Accounts payable* is the money that you owe people. Nifty, eh?

Spread 'Em

As I mentioned earlier, there are many different ways to set up your financial record-keeping system. You can use two notebooks, one to record what you earned, the other to record what you spent. Or, you can do the same on spreadsheets. Then you can use a series of file folders to store invoices and receipts. Or, you can glue every receipt in a date book. Hey, you can even create a combo system that works for you, using one from column A and one from column B. Here's how I do it:

1. I record everything I *earn* on one spreadsheet. It looks like this:

Track every penny you earn as a freelancer!

			1997 Freelance			
TOTALS		BILLED:	$7,163.00	PAID:		$5,150.00
DATE BILLED	COMPANY	CONTACT	JOB DESCRIPTION	AMOUNT BILLED	DATE PAID	AMOUNT PAID
10/10/97	Big Publishing Co	Joe Smith	travel book-signing fee	$1,000.00	10/31/97	$1,000.00
1/1/97	Big Publishing Co	Joe Smith	travel book-half complete	$2,000.00	3/18/97	$2,000.00
3/15/97	Big Publishing Co	Joe Smith	travel book-final sign-off	$2,000.00	5/28/97	$2,000.00
4/8/97	Scribners	J.T. Capella	Truman Capote biography	$150.00	6/29/97	$150.00
5/12/97	Poem Magazine	Lucia Lewis	Poem:"Me and My Harley"	$25.00		
6/30/97	Small Publishers, Inc	Steven Karvitz	royalties on workbook	$1,238.00		
7/1/97	Macmillan	Carol Mann	3 novel study guides	$750.00		

2. At the same time, I record everything I *spend* on another spreadsheet. It looks like this:

Track every penny you spend on business!

DATE		ITEM		PLACE		AMOUNT		PURPOSE
10/8/96		FedEx		————		12.55		mail Macmillan manuscript
1/7/97		paper		Staples		22.87		office supplies
3/13/97		train		NYC		11.14		meeting at Macmillan
4/8/97		cabs		NYC		8.62		meeting at Macmillan
5/16/97		lunch		Geo's		35.12		w/Sam Harris, editor
6/23/97		cards		B&N		2.55		thank-you note
7/1/97		books		B&N		88.00		research/FL book

3. I glue all my receipts in a date book, matching the date of the expense to the date on the page. A sample is shown on the following page:

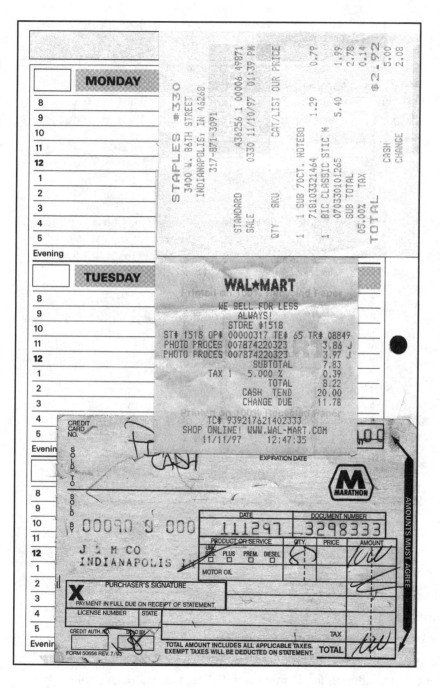

Gluing receipts in a date book makes them easy to find if you need to check an expense or justify it to the IRS.

Bet You Didn't Know

Operating on the same principle as medical records, the IRS likes freelancers to handwrite financial records. This makes them think that you're not fabricating your numbers. If you want to use pen and paper, simply take my two spreadsheets and fill in each one by hand in a notebook.

Fork It Over

A note about receipts: Which ones should you save? Remember: Any expense you incur in running your freelance business is an income tax deduction if your work sells (and under specific circumstances even if it doesn't). Here's a list of receipts you should glue into your date book, sort in file folders, or squirrel away in shoe boxes:

Mind Your Own Business

The IRS has never really straightened out its position regarding freelancers. As a result, you should never throw out any business-related receipt, even if it's over seven years old. Be especially careful to save all your canceled checks. No matter what they say, keep them all.

➤ Business stationery
➤ Office machinery: computers, telephones, copy machines, scanners, fax machines, printers, and so on
➤ Computer disks
➤ Business postage
➤ Business telephone charges
➤ Books, CDs, tapes, and records needed for research
➤ Business entertainment
➤ Pencils, paper, pens, paper clips, etc.
➤ Business travel
➤ Business-related gifts

If you want to save your receipts in folders or envelopes rather than gluing them in a date book, sort them this way:

➤ Postage and courier services
➤ Supplies (paper, cartridges, cards)
➤ Permanent fixtures (computers, printers, lamps)
➤ Transportation (trains, planes, automobiles, cabs, buses, trolleys, etc.)
➤ Entertainment (lunch, dinner, food, movie and theater tickets, for example)
➤ Gifts

➤ Research materials (books, magazines, newspapers, computer programs, etc.)

➤ Services (subcontracting)

Why? Because that's the way the deductions are arranged on your income tax form. Your accountant or tax preparer will give you a big juicy kiss of thanks (or maybe a look of utter astonishment at your keen organizational skills).

While you're at it, think about checking with your accountant *before* you set up your books to get some advice. Some accountants also have their own tax worksheets. Things will be much easier if everyone's reading from the same page.

Another way to get organized is by using financial software like Quicken or Quickbooks. Many freelancers do all their record-keeping in one of these programs because it lets them categorize every transaction as they record it in their bank and credit card accounts. The programs also sort the figures on demand at tax time. Very easy to use and so nice on April 14th.

> **Home Alone**
> Keep a copy of all invoices you send—even after you have been paid. I save mine on a disk; some other freelancers keep one file folder of paid invoices and another of unpaid ones.

Compulsion

Whatever method you adopt, be a good kid—record everything you spend and everything you earn. Ideally, you should update your financial records every day, but I can live with once a week. If you wait any longer than that to record your expenses and earnings, you're apt to forget many of the small expenses that add up to big deductions at tax time.

Budgets

Budgets, like baseball bats, bananas, and belly buttons, are very useful things. They help you track what's happening with your business now and make more accurate plans. Unlike the Emerald City, budgets aren't make-believe. To be useful, a budget has to be based in reality.

There are more types of budgets than Baskin and Robbins has ice cream flavors. Fortunately, most freelancers can manage quite well with a plain vanilla budget. The table on the following page shows an example of a simple six-month budget that will help you track your business earnings and expenses very nicely.

Six-Month Budget

	Jan.	Feb.	March	April	May	June
Income						
Fixed expenses						
Variable expenses						
Balance						

Fill in the blanks for each month, and subtract your expenses from your income. If the bottom-line figure is positive, you've made a profit. If it's negative, you're running on fumes. Then you have two choices:

➤ Increase your earnings

➤ Decrease your expenses

If you can't get your bottom line back in the black without resorting to snacking on Milk Bones, there may be factors beyond your control, such as a downturn in the economy. In that case, you may wish to consider taking on some temp work or a part-time staff job until things pick up.

Singing the Blues

If all else fails, you may wish to consider some outside financing. Here some sources to tap:

Home Alone
Schmooze the banker or loan officer a little while before you put the squeeze on them. This is especially important if your credit is shaky or near the max.

➤ A home equity loan

➤ A revolving line of credit

➤ Loans from family and friends (look for rich, generous kith and kin)

➤ Bank loans

➤ Credit cards

Bear in mind, however, that credit-card debt is the leading cause of personal bankruptcy. As a result, it's a good idea to save your credit until you really need it. Better yet, establish your credit in advance and then try not to abuse it.

Help Is on the Way

Wishing there was somebody to hold your hand through all of this? I've got good news for you, kiddo. Even though Lily Tomlin claims that "we're all in this alone," there are plenty of places to get good, reasonably priced financial advice. Some is so reasonably priced that it's free. For example, for more help with bookkeeping, budgeting, and financial balancing, try scoring with SCORE, an acronym for "Service Corps of Retired Executives." The group is composed of retired business executives who share their expertise with beginning and struggling small business owners. They can be reached through the Small Business Administration.

If you decide to hire a financial expert, be sure to check his or her references and experience carefully. "Like I have the time for this?" you moan. Make the time. It will pay off richly in the long run. You'll be able to track your money, understand your finances, and avoid expensive blunders. Don't wimp out on me now, snookums.

The Least You Need to Know

➤ Keep good financial records.

➤ Save your receipts, too. Forever.

➤ Prepare a budget. You worked too hard for your money to let it slip between your fingers.

➤ Hire expert financial help if you need it.

➤ And while you're at it, wash behind your ears and put on clean underwear.

Part 5
Take It on Home: Survival Skills

Chartreuse stilettos. Pop Tarts and Pez. The Wolfman. What do these items have in common? They all have style, that elusive je ne sais quoi, the "I know it when I see it." The Wicked Witch of the West had it; Good Witch Glenda didn't. Cary Grant, Fred Astaire, and Audrey Hepburn oozed style; pity poor Prince. Even with a symbol rather than a name, he has no style. Velcro doesn't have style; Beemers, Batman, and boxers do.

In this section, you'll learn how to give your freelance business your own distinctive style. Here are some elements we'll cover:

- ➤ *Selecting a name for your business*
- ➤ *Advertising yourself*
- ➤ *Working the Web*
- ➤ *Networking and referrals*
- ➤ *Coping with procrastination and overwork*

- ➤ *Projecting a professional image*
- ➤ *Dealing with clients and agents*
- ➤ *Balancing work and family*
- ➤ *Building a reputation*

Chapter 16

Alert the Media

In This Chapter

➤ Find the right name for your business

➤ Create a great resume

➤ Learn to develop a marketing plan

➤ Discover how to advertise and market yourself

Robert Benchley, the American humorist and critic, took a course in international law while he was a student at Harvard University. On the final exam, Benchley was asked to discuss the arbitration of an international fishing dispute between the United States and Great Britain. He was supposed to pay special attention to hatcheries, protocol, and dragnet and trawl procedures. Benchley, who was not prepared for the exam, began his essay by announcing that he knew absolutely nothing about the point of view of the United States with respect to any international fishing controversy; he also confessed that he did not know where Great Britain stood on the issue. "Therefore," Benchley asserted in the introduction to his essay, "I shall discuss the question from the point of view of the fish."

Like Benchley (himself a freelancer), today's successful freelancers are a nimble lot, able to see the same issue from different points of view. This ability enables them to make the most of their experience and expertise, especially when it comes to marketing and advertising their business.

In this chapter, you'll first learn how to select a name for your business. This will help you create the image you want. Then I'll show you how to write a killer resume and create a marketing plan. Finally, you'll learn about various ways to advertise and market your product or service. In the next chapter, you'll learn additional methods of marketing yourself, including public relations and networking.

What's in a Name?

Sad but true: A girl named Jessica is apt to do better than one named Hortense or Fishface—even if they have the same abilities. Mike, Bob, and Steve are usually more successful than Bubba, Poindexter, and Wee Willie. We even like puppies named Spot better than those named Sid Vicious. Why? People respond better to certain names.

The image you project can make or break your career as a freelancer. A significant part of that image is the name you select for your freelance business. When you're just starting out as a freelancer, you're not going to have a history of proven sales and satisfied customers. As a result, you're going to have to become a magician and create an illusion of success and reliability. The name you select for your business is one of the most important props in that illusion.

When it comes to business names, a rose by any other name doesn't smell as sweet. It's crucial to select a name that best conveys the business image you want to establish. You can be feisty or staid, fiery or traditional, but the name you pick must fit. Take me, for example.

Mind Your Own Business

If possible, don't start your name with an article: "a," "an," or "the." It might make it difficult for especially dopey clients to locate your name in a directory.

As a freelance writer, I wanted to convey the image of scholarly dependability. In addition, I decided to clearly link myself to my business. After all, as a writer, I'm selling my training, accomplishments, and reputation. Since there's nothing frivolous about what I do, I wanted to stay away from anything cute (such as Write Now, Write Away, or Write On!). After a great deal of thought, I decided to use my name and my degree, a doctorate in philosophy. As a result, I call my freelance business "Laurie Rozakis, Ph.D." Simple, but elegant.

The Name Game

Here are some guidelines to follow as you pick a name for your business:

➤ The name should be somewhat general to allow for possible changes in direction. You can't tell from the name of my business whether I write text books, trade books, or fiction, for example.

➤ The name should suggest stability and inspire trust and confidence. I think my "Ph.D." does just that.

➤ The name should convey a positive image. I don't think I would have used my name if it was something like Willa Wacca, Chanda Leer, or Marsha Mellow.

➤ If you sell a product, select a name that suggests or describes the positive aspects of your business. "Green and Growing," for example, works better than "Smith's Flowers."

➤ Select a name that's easy to pronounce. Include enough vowels and consonants to give your customers a break.

➤ Be clever but not klever. Avoid pretentious names like Ye Olde Sweete Shoppe.

➤ Try to keep it short. Avoid Denali-sized names, monikers that seem to go on longer than a meal with your prospective in-laws.

oH!

Bet You Didn't Know

You might wish to use your family name for your freelance business if your family is well known and well respected in town. The celebrity status can rub off on you. "Rockefeller Investments" works well, but "Jack the Ripper Acupuncture" is probably not the way to go. Beware, however, that a far more famous cousin could challenge your right to the name. This could result in a nasty court battle. And even though you have equal rights to the name, they have the money to sue your pants off.

Going Global

Do you intend to do business in other countries? Increasingly, freelancers are branching out to foreign markets, thanks to the Internet, improved telephone service, and reliable couriers. If you intend to do business internationally, be especially careful that you select a business name that translates well.

Remember the car called "Nova"? Among English speakers, it was a moderate success, having the connotation of a heavenly body. The car wasn't quite a hit among Spanish-speakers, however, because "Nova" translates in Spanish as "no go." Ouch.

Here are a few other famous gaffes:

➤ Coca-Cola originally translated into Chinese as "Bite the wax tadpole."

➤ The ad slogan "Coke adds life" literally translated into Chinese as "Coke brings your ancestors back from the grave."

➤ The Perdue chicken ad "It takes a tough man to make a tender chicken" translated into "It takes a virile man to make a chicken pregnant."

Be sure that the name you have selected doesn't translate into anything that could embarrass you in any way. Check for sexual, religious, and cultural misunderstandings.

> oH!
>
> ### Bet You Didn't Know
>
> Here's another trick that will polish up your image: Don't start numbering your purchase orders and invoices with the tell-tale Number 1. To give the illusion that you've been around a while, start numbering your purchase orders and invoices with a high number, such as 2387. And make sure the paint is dry on the walls before any clients come to call.

The Doublemint Twins

IS THAT CLEAR?

Mind Your Own Business

It's tacky to slide a ride on someone else's coattails. If your name is Neuman, for example, don't go for "Neuman's Own," thinking that someone will confuse your freelance business with the dreamy blue-eyed movie star-cum-salad dressing/spaghetti sauce mogul.

Once you decide on a name for your freelance business, do a name search to make sure you're not stealing another business's name. This can have serious legal ramifications. In addition, you might get some interesting wrong numbers if you and a funeral home or a member of the world's oldest profession have the same business name. At the very least, you don't want to start doing business, establish a good reputation, and then have to yank your name and replace it if someone proves prior ownership.

To do a name search, you can simply look in the telephone books for your general area to see if the name you've chosen has already been grabbed by a similar business. I recommend that you go one step further, however, and contact the office of your Secretary of State in your state capital for a name search. The appropriate overworked assistant can punch the name you have selected into the computer to find out if it's already being used. Only incorporated businesses will be listed, but at least you'll know if an incorporated business is already using the name you want.

If the name you selected clears, you might want to register it with the city or county clerk. This can help protect you against someone else swiping your name—and your reputation.

Foot in the Door

You're in business to sell your product or service to make money. Sounds obvious, huh? Right. You know by now that things that sound obvious are usually a lot harder than they seem. Not to worry. You can do this, cabbage. You have a good head on you. Besides, that's why you have *me*.

In Chapter 8, you learned how important it is to get yourself oriented to the new realities of living life as a freelancer. You explored different ways to target the correct market, tap former colleagues from your staff jobs, and contact prospective clients in person. Now, let's look at advertising and promotion.

Advertising means informing the public of the features and benefits of your product or service. *Promotion* is a way of stimulating an immediate sale, such as offering a discount coupon. When some freelancers start out, they spend about 15 to 20 percent of their gross receipts in advertising, depending on the type of freelance business they operate. In most cases, that figure should drop to about 5 to 10 percent of your gross receipts once your customer base is firmly established.

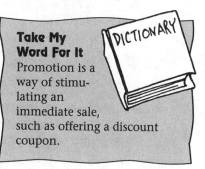

Take My Word For It
Advertising means informing the public of the features and benefits of your product or service.

Card-Carrying Freelancer

For many freelancers, the most basic way to advertise is through business cards. As you learned in Chapter 11, it's both easy and inexpensive to have some business cards printed. Many freelancers (including yours truly and my skilled editor, Mary Russell) often hand out business cards at conferences, meetings, and even social gatherings. This form of networking is both effective and inexpensive.

What happens when you get a nibble? Then it's time to move on to stage two: the resume.

Take My Word For It
Promotion is a way of stimulating an immediate sale, such as offering a discount coupon.

Resumes

A *resume* is a summary (one page if possible) of your relevant skills, education, achievements, honors, and awards. A powerful resume emphasizes the things you've done that are most relevant to the freelance work you are seeking and shows your superiority to other candidates for the job.

There are two basic kinds of resume: the *chronological resume* and the *skills resume*. A chronological resume summarizes what you have done in time order (starting with the most recent events and going back in reverse chronological order). Use a chronological resume if your education and experience are logical preparation for the freelance work you're seeking.

A skills resume, in contrast, emphasizes the skills that you have used rather than the jobs in which you used them. Use a skills resume when your education and experience are not the usual route to the freelance work you seek or if you lack impressive job titles. A skills resume is also more impressive if your recent work history may create the wrong impression. This is particularly true if you have done some job hopping or are moving into a different field.

Mind Your Own Business
Never include your marital status, number of children, height, weight, health, or religion on your resume.

What should you include in a resume?

➤ Name, address, telephone number, e-mail address, fax number

➤ Education

➤ Experience

➤ Honors

➤ Professional memberships

➤ References (optional)

Here are some key points to keep in mind as you write your resume:

1. Be realistic and honest. Present your skills truthfully; never fake it or (God forbid) lie.

2. Use the page layout and typeface to emphasize key points.

3. Be sure to relate your experience to the job you want.

4. Without sacrificing content, be as concise as possible.

5. Don't include personal details like marital status or your current weight on your resume. It's also okay to omit dates that might give away your age, such as the year you finally got that master's degree.

Whatever style you choose for your resume, be sure it relates to the job you want. Study the sample resume for a job as a freelance writer that follows. Since this applicant (who could it be?) has a great deal of experience in the field, she chose to use a variation on the chronological resume format, with later clients arranged in alphabetical order.

A professional resume is a must for any freelancer. Use good paper (see the rules for letterhead in Chapter 11) and don't forget to proofread. Keep your resume updated; you never know when something interesting will come along. And don't forget to send a cover letter along with your resume. That's the place for those professional details that don't fit anyplace else—but make you the perfect fit for the job you're after.

To Market, to Market

As you'll shortly learn, there are scores and scores of ways to market your business. You can't do it all—nor should you. Control your destiny. Develop a simple and solid marketing strategy and promotion plan. Use the following worksheet to focus your thoughts. Answer each of the questions to develop a marketing plan.

1. What customers do I want to reach?

   _____

2. What are my customers' needs and wants?

   _____

3. What makes my business desirable to my customers?

   _____

4. What makes my business different from the competition?

   _____

5. Should I have a slogan? If so, what will it be?

   _____

6. Which methods will best motivate my customers to purchase my product or service?

   _____

7. What aspects of my business should I emphasize in my advertising?

   _____

8. What is my advertising and promotion budget?

   _____

9. What media will best reach and motivate my customers?

   _____

10. How can I make all my efforts consistent to reinforce my message?

   _____

	Name	Telephone number
	Street Address	Fax number
	City, Town, Zip Code	e-mail address

Simon & Schuster:

The Complete Idiot's Guide to Making Money in Freelancing	1998
The Complete Idiot's Guide to Buying and Selling Collectibles	1997
The Complete Idiot's Guide to Creative Writing	1997
The Complete Idiot's Guide to Grammar and Style	1997
50 Ways to Meet Your Lover/50 Ways to Drop Your Lover	1997
The Complete Idiot's Guide to Speaking in Public with Confidence	1996
The A.P. Exam in English '86, '88, '93 *Verbal Workbook for the ACT*	1989
The College Writing Placement and Proficiency Examination	1989

Glenco/McGraw Hill: *Effective Speech*   1993   *World Literature*   1990

Gramercy Book Services:

Prentice Hall Literature	1994	*HBJ Literature*	1992
Macmillan Writing, Spelling	1991	*Scribner Literature*	1991

IBM: *Writing to Write* (Computer Project)   1990

McClanahan and Company:

Glencoe *Literature*	1997	Addison-Wesley *Mathematics*	1997
Scholastic *Spelling*	1996	Kaplan *Advanced Writing Texts*	1996
Regents Prentice-Hall ESL	1994	Scholastic *Literacy Place*	1994
Southwestern *GED Lit and Math*	1994	Addison-Wesley *Quest 2000*	1994
Addison-Wesley *Science*	1994	Prentice Hall *Writer's Companion*	1994
Harcourt Reading	1993	Scholastic *Social Studies*	1993
Silver, Burdett Social Studies	1992	Scholastic *Many Voices*	1992
MCP Multicultural series	1991	*Read It, Write It, Love It!*	1991

Merriam-Webster: *The Merriam-Webster Guide to Parliamentary Procedure*   1994

Byron Preiss:	*Everyday Spelling* 1997	*Everyday Vocabulary*	1997
	Instant British Lit 1993	*Instant American Lit*	1994
Prentice Hall:	*Prentice Hall Literature* 1989	*GED Literature*	1992
Random House:	*The Random House Guide to Grammar and Usage*	1991
	Word Power	1991
Scholastic, Inc.:	*NBA Hot Shot Reading* 1996	*Literacy Place*	1994
	Laura Ingalls Wilder 1992	*Critical Thinking* (2 volumes)	1991

Education

SUNY Stony Brook	Ph.D.	1984	American and British Literature; awarded with distinction
Hofstra University	MA	1975	American and British Literature
Hofstra University	BA	1973	English/Secondary Education

Teaching Experience

SUNY Farmingdale	1986–present	Associate Professor of English; Chancellor's Award for Excellence
Commack Schools	1973–1984	English teacher

A good resume emphasizes the things you have done that relate to the job you are seeking.

How much marketing is too much? How little is too little? In general, look to your competition for parameters. If your competition is active, it's probably not a good idea to sit back and wait for customers to come pouring in. At least meet your competition's efforts, if not exceed them. At all times, focus on your customers. Your volume of sales tells whether or not your marketing plan is working.

Mind Your Own Business
Be sincere. If you don't believe what you're saying in your advertising, no one else will.

IS THAT CLEAR?

Give your plan time to work. With a small budget, it can take about six months to a year for your advertising and promotion plan to show results. Think of your marketing plan as a snowball, gaining size and momentum at each turn. Be consistent with your marketing strategy, but don't be afraid to adjust your plan within three to six months if you're not seeing results.

Advertisements for Myself

You want to attract attention to your business to create an image and encourage sales. There are many ways to promote your freelance business and bring it to the attention of the public. Best of all, some of these methods are cheap as well as effective. Let's look at ten advertising and promotion methods especially well suited to freelancers.

1. Classified Ads

Classified ads are not just for yard sales and used cars! Many special-interest publications offer classified ad space for products and services provided by freelance businesses. By selecting the right publications, you can carefully target your ads to potential customers.

Read the classified sections of the publications you are considering to determine which ones best fit your product and/or services. You can start by copying a style that gets your attention, but make your ad reflect your image and stand out from others in the same category. Develop several ads and pick the two or three that you think will best attract customers.

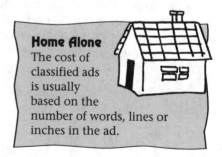

Home Alone
The cost of classified ads is usually based on the number of words, lines or inches in the ad.

Rotate the ads in the same publication or place the same ad in several publications to determine which evokes the better response. Run the ad several times to determine the effectiveness of this advertising method for your freelance business.

2. Display Ads

Display ads are the ones that appear in the body of a publication. They can range from a few inches to a full-page spread. Because there are hundreds of specialty and trade magazines, you can target your display ads directly to your audience, sending your message to your most likely customers. Magazines have a longer shelf life than many other advertising media, so your ad may be viewed several times by the same reader.

Always have your ads initially designed by a graphic artist, the best you can afford. No matter what the salesperson says, the graphics departments in most magazines and newspapers can't cut the mustard when it comes to creating snazzy designs. It's worth the investment to get your ad designed right the first time.

You can run a successful ad over and over because the odds are good that only you will get sick of it. If you're on a small budget, you probably won't be able to afford to run the ad enough to saturate the market. You can also reprint the ad and run it on flyers, handouts, mailers, and so on.

If you use a prestigious local, regional, or national magazine, mention this in your other advertising vehicles, as in "As seen in [title of] magazine."

Bet You Didn't Know

Want to save big? At the last minute, buy unsold ad space. You may have to wait several editions, but you'll save some serious money. (This is even better than the Early Bird special at the local diner or the half-price-before-noon special at the movie theater.)

3. Program and Yearbook Ads

Advertisements in programs for local sporting and performing events and in high school yearbooks can be an effective and easy way to promote your goods and services. It doesn't take a rocket scientist to realize that these ads will be effective only if you are in business to sell something that will be of interest to students, patrons, or sports fans.

However, this method will win you a lot of good will in your community. It's less fattening than buying cookies from the Girl Scouts (and can also be cheaper, considering what those Thin Mints run per box).

4. Yellow Pages

Before you let someone else's fingers do the walking, consider whether or not most of your prospective clients would consult the Yellow Pages to find the services you are offering. My customers, for example, would never look in the Yellow Pages to hire me, but that's not to say the Yellow Pages aren't right for *your* business.

Further, keep in mind that an ad in the Yellow Pages does not create an incentive to buy. Rather, the Yellow Pages simply direct the customer—who is already eager to buy—to the seller. And there's more bad news.

When a potential customer goes to the Yellow Pages to find your freelance business, he or she will also be confronted with ads from your competitors. This makes shopping for price and services all too easy, so your customer may decide on the competition rather than you.

5. Radio

To decide if radio will work for you, ask your current customers if they listen to the radio. (If you don't have any actual paying-real-money customers yet, ask some prospective ones. They'll be flattered to be consulted.) If they say yes, ask them which stations they listen to and when. This will help you target specific stations and times to run the ads.

Home Alone
Some radio stations will trade air time for your products and services. Never turn down a freebie. (Don't tell the IRS.)

6. Television

Now, I'm a real fan of the boob tube at the end of the day when my brains are fried from a day of writing, but I'm also the first to admit that if you're not careful, you can spend a lot of money on television ads with very little to show for it. TV ads are usually not a wise choice for freelancers, because they don't give you much bang for your buck. TV is a powerful medium and can really spread your message, but your ad must be carefully targeted at a specific audience—or it can be a very pricey boo-boo.

There are some sweet bargains to be had on local cable shows, however. Even better, you might be able to plug your freelance business on TV for free. That's right, F-R-E-E. Many cable shows will invite freelancers to plug their products in exchange for a demonstration or chat. This year, for example, I appeared on the Discovery Channel's *Home Matters* show. I got a 20-minute segment to demo the information in my book *The Complete Idiot's Guide to Buying and Selling Collectibles*. The segment will be shown at least twice.

Even some national shows are eager for respectable guests to lend credibility to their programs. In this capacity, I appeared on the Maury Povich show, again to tell a brief story about antique shopping and to plug my *Complete Idiot's Guide to Buying and Selling Collectibles*. Total cost? Zero. (Maury even sent a limo to bring me to New York City!)

Not famous yet? Not to worry! Your local cable company must provide community access channels. Anyone can appear on these channels—and they usually do. The cable company provides the studio and some basic assistance for free.

7. Brochures and Pamphlets

Since brochures can be expensive to lay out and print (especially if color is involved), plan your ad campaign carefully before you go this route. Too many brochures end up fluttering away in parking lots because their purpose wasn't carefully focused.

I also recommend that you have your brochures professionally produced. I have received too many misspelled Chinese take-out menus, shoddy lawn service brochures, and impossible-to-read home improvement leaflets. You can hire a local public relations or advertising firm to design your brochure. In the long run, you'll save money because you'll get a better return on your outlay.

8. Direct Mail

Start by gathering a pile of direct mail that you've received. Which pieces did you save and why? Show the ones you like the best to your customers and solicit their reactions. Test a few approaches with a limited mailing to see the response rate, then select the strongest package and send out a mass mailing.

The right mailing list is paramount to success with a direct mail advertising campaign. It's crucial that you get the most current list possible. Call several companies that provide mailing lists; you may find that even though they all charge about the same, some lists are far more up-to-date than others.

Mind Your Own Business
Direct mail works well with mail order products.

The best return on a general mass mailing is 1 to 2 percent. (Yes, you read that correctly.) If you can't make money with this response rate, direct mail isn't direct enough for you. In that case, go with one or more of the other methods described in this chapter and the next one. However, your response rate will be significantly higher if you direct your mailing at customers already familiar with your company and the services it offers.

9. Postcards

Postcards are an easy and inexpensive way to announce your freelance business, advertise a sale, or serve as a reminder notice. You can also use postcards to thank customers for a referral or their initial business.

Why not print your newspaper or magazine ads on postcards and mail them to customers? This gives you double-duty from your advertising art.

10. Balloons, Billboards, Bumper Stickers, Buttons, Blimps, and Other Bizarros

A two-person freelance publishing company once sent me a cheesecake as a thank you for the marvelous work I had done for them. Now, I am exceedingly fond of cheesecake, and this happened to be an exceedingly good cheesecake. Thanks to a cheesecake that probably cost no more than $15, I would jump over the moon for these people. (Okay, so I'm easy, but when was the last time *you* got a cheesecake as a thank you?)

There are many different ways you can advertise your freelance business and build good will. Some, like balloons and bumper stickers, are almost ridiculously inexpensive. Others, like blimps and billboards, will set you back some bucks. Pick the methods that best suit your image and audience.

In addition to the um, *creative* methods mentioned above, here are some more advertising ideas:

➤ Bus bench/shelter signs

➤ Calendars

➤ Decals

➤ Place mats (big in diners)

➤ Refrigerator magnets

➤ T-shirts

➤ Skywriting

As you can see, there's no shortage of ways to plug yourself and your freelance service or product. But different kinds of freelancing require different approaches. For example, skywriting would clearly be the method of choice to promote your freelance helicopter service. However, a business card tacked up in the local market would be a better bet to advertise your personal shopping business. So give it some careful thought before you plunge right in, buckaroo.

The Least You Need to Know

➤ You wouldn't name your dog something half-witted, so why give your business a dog of a name?

➤ Create a great resume. It can be one of your best, and cheapest, forms of advertising.

➤ It pays to advertise your freelance business, but be sure to make a detailed marketing plan before you start shelling out any money for ads.

➤ Consider your image, customers, and budget when you undertake an ad campaign.

➤ Sell yourself. No one else will.

Chapter 17

Still Spreading the Word

In This Chapter

➤ Use public relations to promote your business

➤ Try incentives to bring in customers

➤ Learn to make networking work for you

➤ Check out advertising on the Internet

A mangy-looking guy goes into a bar and orders a drink. The bartender says: "No way. I don't think you can pay for it."

The guy says, "You're right. I don't have any money, but if I show you something you haven't seen before, will you give me a drink?"

The bartender says "Deal!" and the guy pulls out a hamster. The hamster runs to the piano and starts playing Gershwin songs. The bartender says, "You're right. I've never seen anything like that before. That hamster is truly good on the piano." The guy downs the drink and asks the bartender for another.

"Money or another miracle or no drink," says the bartender. The guy pulls out a frog. He puts the frog on the bar, and the frog starts to sing. He has a marvelous voice and great pitch. A fine singer.

Another man in the bar offers $300 for the frog. The guy says, "It's a deal." He takes the three hundred and gives the stranger the frog. The stranger runs out of the bar.

The bartender says, "Are you nuts? You sold a singing frog for $300? It must have been worth millions. You must be crazy."

"Not so," says the guy. "The hamster is also a ventriloquist."

Unfortunately, freelancers can't get hamsters to front for them. In this business, you have to be willing to speak up for yourself. In this chapter, you'll learn other effective ways to advertise your freelance business so you can get the customers you need to *have* a business.

Toot Your Own Horn: Public Relations and Publicity

Public relations drums up business through means other than paid advertising. These methods include news releases, media events, newsletters, thank-you notes, greeting cards, and other activities. Don't think you're getting off scot-free, however, because it often costs money to prepare publicity.

Effective public relations can increase general awareness and help sales, especially for freelancers just starting out. A solid public relations campaign can help you:

➤ Enhance your business image.

➤ Create good will.

➤ Influence buyers.

➤ Become a welcome part of the community.

➤ Build a loyal following.

Mind Your Own Business
Make sure you have ample supplies of your product or services on hand when you undertake a public relations campaign. It's no fun to be signing books and realize that the store didn't order enough.

Target your message to potential customers by carefully selecting the media outlet that's best for your business. For example, I often use the local newspaper to announce the publication of a new book. A week after my press release is published, I hold a book signing in a local bookstore. To build further good will, I often serve wine and cheese or cookies and punch. People are mellow when they're munching on free eats.

Let's look at six ways you can be your own public relations maven. Remember, if you're not going to toot your own horn, who will?

1. What's the Buzz? News Stories and Press Releases

Planting a story in your local newspaper can be a great way to advertise your freelance business without spending a cent. I should know; I do it at least three times a year!

Now, don't be a piggy. Your news story should be no more than a page long; a single-column is even better. Your press release can announce the opening of your freelance business, the release of a new product or service, or other business milestones. I send out a press release every two books or so.

I hit the jackpot with my press releases when the *New York Times* did a story on my freelance career and the *Complete Idiot's Guide* series (see the following page).

Seize every opportunity to keep your name in front of the public through the media. This can also help establish your credibility and authority in the field. I often get calls to do seminars (for money!) after I've submitted a news story to the local gazette.

Home Alone
Some free-lancers write their own press releases under assumed names, to make it appear that they have public-ity departments or agents.

2. Take a Letter, Maria: Newsletters

In addition to keeping you in touch with your clients, newsletters can give you credibility faster than you can get a burger at the drive-through. Newsletters also:

➤ Pass along useful information about your business.

➤ Establish you as an authority.

➤ Build trust and confidence.

➤ Establish and maintain a client base.

Newsletters are especially effective for freelancing professionals such as accountants, attorneys, health care providers, and financial consultants.

Home Alone
Your newslet-ter can be on-line as well as in print. Online newsletters are perfect for computer-geek freelancers.

3. Bread and Butter: Thank-You Notes

Mother was right on this one: *Always* find a way to thank people who have done you a favor. And who else does you more favors than your clients, the people who support you? Always send a thank-you note to a customer who makes a major purchase, many small purchases, or gives you a referral (even if it doesn't pan out).

The Ubiquitous 'Idiot Guides' Are

By MARJORIE KAUFMAN

"AT the heads first — they shouldn't suffer," Laurie Rozakis said, placing a plate of low-fat animal crackers next to the freshly baked chocolate chip cookies. Just then the mailman approached the front stoop of her Farmingdale home and, the day being hot, she met him at the door with a glass of iced tea.

"My mother made sure I could cook, sew and type," she said in a recent interview. "I even won the Betty Crocker Homemaker of the Year contest in high school." That contest was in 1970 and it was won along with a full academic scholar-

Offering assistance to simplify issues that are difficult for most people.

ship to Hofstra University, where she earned her degree in English and secondary education in three years.

Organizational skills, delegation of power and a sense of humor remain key on her full plate as writer, associate professor of English at the State University at Farmingdale, wife and mother to two teen-agers.

"I live to carpool," she said. She once dressed up as Wonder Woman for a promotion her husband ran as executive director for DC Comics and it wasn't far from the truth.

Equipped with a Ph.D. in literature, a curriculum vitae full of honors, awards and scholarly writing like "How to Interpret Poetry" and "The Dictionary of American Biography," Ms. Rozakis is no cretin, but a writer in the "Complete Idiot Guide" series (Alpha Books/Macmillan).

She has written five books in the

series, with others on the drawing board. At age 45, she has the wit and wisdom of Erma Bombeck, some critics have said. Ms. Rozakis will be on the Discovery Channel's "Home Matters" on Oct. 16 discussing highlights from her book, "The Complete Idiot's Guide to Buying and Selling Collectibles.".

"She's an incredible researcher, an amazing writer," said Gary Krebs, the executive editor of Alpha Books (Macmillan). "She produces quickly and she understands the conversational tone of our series among the best of them, if not the best. She works at such a pace that she can handle two if not three a year, which is remarkable, and she's also funny.". "The Complete Idiot Guide" series began as an instructional guide to computer software.

By 1994, the company expanded the idea into life styles books. By year's end, 100 titles will be on the market "idiotizing" subjects as diverse as "The Idiot's Guide to Choosing, Training and Raising a Dog" to "The Complete Idiot's Guide to Wall Street" (which has sold more than 100,000 copies).

One recent popular title on Elvis Presley commemorated the 20th anniversary of his death. The series continues to gain momentum as readers seek out the titles that offer a "quick fix" of concise and well researched information on topics they may want to relearn or have always sought out but never had the time to investigate themselves.

"All our books have the same format, a conversational witty tone and our writers must understand the formula and write with baby steps through a subject without sounding condescending to the reader," Mr. Krebs said.

"I started out with what I know," Ms. Rozakis said.r "The first was a guide to 'Speaking in Public with Confidence,' next 'Grammar and Style,' one on 'Creative Writing' and one on 'Freelancing.' "

Ms. Rozakis was teaching high school English in Commack in 19886 when advanced placement courses came into vogue. Linda Bernbach, a general reference editor at Arco,/ Prentice Hall Macmillan, received

exams and she successfully published many other study books.

When Ms. Rozakis pitched an idea Ms. Rozakis's first proposal for a test prep book for Advanced Placement English. Her book started a series of similar guides for other for a humorous Valentine's Day book that could be flipped to be read again, she came up with "50 Ways to Meet Your Lover; 50 Ways to Drop Your Lover."

"I have always been looked to for advice on relationships, maybe because of my own long marriage," she said. The small book sold out of the first printing.

Ms. Bernbach recommended Ms. Rozakis for the Idiot Guide series based on her skill and "wonderful light touch."

"The study series were straightforward, Laurie has a lighter side, which made her ideal for the new series," Ms. Bernbach said.

"The Complete Idiot's Guide to Buying and Selling Collectibles" is the first book not directly related to her background in language arts, test prep, writing, but one close to her heart.

Her mother, she said, is "queen of garage sales, a collector without peer." From a very early age, she was introduced by her mother to the world of china, silver, crystal and "tchotckes" of every stripe, Ms. Rozakis said. Antique jewelry has been a collection since childhood.

"The family story goes that when I was 3, I asked my grandmother for her engagement ring," she said. "There are savers and hoarders and there are non-savers. I think it is innate. I am inclined to think it runs in the family. There may not be a gene for it, but it is more a passion than environmental. Generally more women than men collect."

The book is aimed at the generalist who wants to know how to become a savvy collector and how not to get taken.

"You are looking for things of beauty and value," Ms. Rozakis wrote. "You are also seeking a piece of the past. Beautiful objects from

SEPTEMBER 21, 1997

Not Being Written by Idiots

Laurie Rozakis, the writer of several "Complete Idiot's Guide" books.

the past provide evocative memories of the rosy world of family memories and historic events. They connect us to our heritage and our world."

To prepare for the guide, including the care, display, and resale of collectibles, Ms. Rozakis said she combined her collectible background with resources from the Internet, library research and a well-planned weeklong trek upstate with her husband.

They travelled intensely from flea market to antique shop to barn, talking to dealers and collectors about marketing techniques, tips and advice on refinishing, restoration and unusual collections.

Ms. Rozakis defines a collectible as an item that was originally made to serve a utilitarian purpose but has since transcended its original function through intense collector interest. An antique on the other hand must be at least 100 years old. Age does not always equal value.

Traditional collectibles, like stamps and coins, are still the most popular because they are relatively risk free, have easy access and are easy to authenticate. But "pop" culture collectibles, and ephemera like baseball cards and comics, are gaining in popularity.

"We are a celebrity-crazed society," Ms. Rozakis said. "Unfortunately, even if that celebrity has a negative influence on the culture."

To forecast the next "hot" collectible, Ms. Rozakis said, look toward anything linked to the past but evolving. "Di and Chuck related items are hot, anything related to the former royal family," she said. "Anything related to the tobacco industry, match books, advertising like 'Joe Camel.' Halloween costumes, space-related paraphernalia, computer-related items, McDonald's toys, and AIDS-related material. And always save the wrappers," she added.

Since the Industrial Revolution, and particularly since there is more disposable income, Ms. Rozakis said collecting had experienced a resurgence. "With two-income families, there is a new set of values," she said. "The work hard and save ethic has been replaced with the lottery concept of a dollar and a dream. Although the majority of people who collect are out to have fun and collect for pleasure, many are out to make money. They cross the line to become investors when the business aspect takes over."

Ms. Rozakis is as idiosyncratic about her collecting, as she points to color-coded book bindings and cellophane wrapped comics, as she is about her writing.

"I'm a compulsive writer," she said. "The first draft comes easily, but it's all smoke and mirrors. I write, rewrite and write again. Words, like people, have rhythms and personalities, tastes and textures. I want more than meaning; I want beat.

"Will you remember this phrase, suck on it like a ripe cherry, play with the pit in your mouth for half an hour? Will it linger on your tongue like the last sweet cold lick of the cherry ice pop you shared with your sister on those sweltering August nights? If so, I've done my job well." ∎

Who could ask for better publicity—and it's free!

Hate to write? Send a postcard with a two-line *personal* message, such as "Dear Dorrie: Thanks for referring the Hudson Publishing job my way. Your continued support is greatly appreciated."

(And while we're on Mom's advice, wear your boots when it rains, change the oil in your car before the next Jurassic period, and eat more vegetables.)

4. When You Care Enough to Send the Very Best: Greeting Cards

Mind Your Own Business
Always send neutral holidays cards, those adorned with messages such as "Best Greetings of the Season." Jolly snowpeople and delicate snowflakes make the grade; religious symbols don't (unless you do business with a religious organization).

The easiest way to build a client base is by sending holiday cards, which is why you no doubt have a pile of cards offering sincere greetings from roofers, aluminum siders, and real estate brokers who are dying to snag your business. Since I personally send about 200 holiday cards a year, I must believe that this method works. Whether it does or doesn't, it's one of those gestures that's expected, like kissing your Aunt Alice hello or smiling at drooling babies.

Since everyone sends holiday cards in December, why not pick another holiday to card, such as Thanksgiving or the Fourth of July? Be sure to pick a neutral holiday that you can be reasonably assured most of your clients celebrate.

If your freelance business provides a personal service, such as hairdressing or flowers, you may wish to send more personal cards, noting birthdays and anniversaries. Stay away from this, however, if your freelance business is more general. I would never send birthday cards to my clients, since our relationship is much more formal.

You can create your own greeting cards with a simple computer program, such as PrintShop Deluxe, and a color printer. Not only will you be able to personalize your cards, but you'll also save a bundle of bucks. Just be sure they look professional.

5. Charitable Events

Charitable events build enormous good will and can help you make valuable business contacts. To get started giving, check your community calendar for a listing of the charitable events in your area. For instance, I have donated copies of my books to be used as door prizes for Rotary's Gift of Life program, a bazaar benefiting the local food pantry, and a festival for a day-care center. I attend charity pancake breakfasts, strawberry festivals, and silent auctions. I draw the line at charity zucchini parades and all-you-can-eat broccoli feasts, however.

But before you reach down and give till it hurts, here are two warnings:

➤ Make sure that the event will indeed attract customers. With careful planning, everyone comes out a winner.

➤ Believe in the charity you're supporting, or your customers could discover that your motives are less than charitable.

6. Press the Flesh: Speaking Engagements

Short talks and presentations before possible business and client groups can be an easy way to sell yourself and your product or service. Positioning yourself as an authority in the field gives you a way to establish credibility and trust. Just before you conclude your talk, give a brief "commercial" about your freelance business and ask for business cards from people who might be interested in receiving more information about your business. Then follow up on every one of these leads.

Home Alone
Service organizations such as Rotary and Lions are always looking for speakers for their weekly meetings. Several times, I've addressed Rotary about my career as a freelance writer. I have often gotten jobs from these contacts.

Something for Nothing? Incentives

Here are three things you can count on: The national debt will never be paid, rock and roll is here to stay, and everyone likes to get something for nothing. *Incentives—something for nothing—*are ways to get prospective customers to try your goods or services.

Of all the different ways you have to market your freelance business, sales incentives are the riskiest and the most costly. As a result, use them wisely. Don't waste them on customers who are perfectly willing (maybe even eager) to pay full price for your product. Likewise, why give it away to people who are not apt to buy your product in the first place?

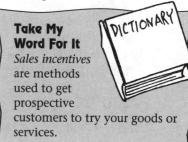

Take My Word For It
Sales incentives are methods used to get prospective customers to try your goods or services.

Marketing experts agree that incentives must accomplish four things to be successful. They must:

1. Support your business image.

2. Create a sense of urgency about your product or service.

3. Motivate the customer to buy your product or service.

4. Inspire the customer to continue buying what you sell.

Here are six sales incentives you may wish to consider to drum up freelance business:

1. You Could Already Be a Winner! Contests

"You could win a 400-carat diamond ring, a car the size of a small banana republic, or 20 zillion dollars a week for life!!!!! In fact, you may *already* be a winner!"

Does anyone really believe this nonsense? The answer must be a resounding *yes,* as shown by the wildfire success of contests around the world.

Contests appeal to everyone's desire to be a winner. While the number one favorite prize is always cash, offering your product as a prize can help you develop a client base. For a contest to succeed in marketing your product or service, it must be fun, exciting, and enticing. People should flock to you.

However, contests can eat up any profit you might make, take a ridiculous amount of time, and leave some sore losers. There might even be some sore winners, as in "You call *this* a prize?" If you decide to go this promotional route, tread carefully.

2. Save Big Bucks: Discount Coupons

Some freelancers have offered discount coupons to entice customers to try their product or service. To maximize your chances for success, distribute coupons at places where you would normally meet customers, such as trade fairs. Here are some coupon facts:

➤ To be effective, a coupon must offer at least 20 percent off the product or service.

➤ Studies show that fewer than 3 percent of all coupons are redeemed.

➤ Further, about 60 percent of all coupons are redeemed by loyal customers who would have bought your product or service anyway.

Therefore, be sure to target your coupons to prospects, not to already existing customers. Obviously, coupons only work for certain types of freelance businesses. A writer, for example, would never use coupons—half off my next *Complete Idiot's Guide?* Carefully consider your image before you decide to offer coupons.

3. Freebies

"Try it, you'll like it." That's the whole idea behind a free offer. If your product or service lends itself to a "free" trial offer, you may wish to consider this incentive. For example, one accountant offers a free hour of consultation for every five paid hours. This method works best with products that are so unusual that they won't attain immediate customer acceptance, or for services that people are reluctant to buy for fear that they'll be unsatisfactory.

4. Free Gifts (Are There Any Other Kind?)

Make sure the items you give away are appropriate and appealing to your customers. For example, a freelance dog trainer once offered a 50-pound sack of dog food free with a three-month dog training course. Customers got well-trained, well-fed pooches. Clever freelancer.

5. Cheaper by the Dozen: Multiple-Purchase Offers

"Buy one, get one free. Buy five, get the sixth one free." You see these offers all the time at the ice-cream store, the donut shop, and the car wash. I often wish I could get a two-fer from a car dealership, orthodontist, or college. Ah, such is life.

Multiple-purchase offers usually *do* get the customer back several times. Rarely, however, do most customers complete the number of purchases necessary to get the one free. Knowing this could save you money.

6. Samples

Depending on your freelance business, you may wish to hand out or mail free samples of your product or service. Be sure to give information about where to purchase the product or service. In addition, you may wish to give your service away free to those who can provide you with strong referrals. I have done this on a few rare occasions when I knew that I would get great paying business as a result.

Finding the Right Strings and Pulling Them: Networking

Networking has been around almost as long as some of the things in the back of my refrigerator. Fortunately, it's a whole lot easier to recognize.

Networking is using personal contacts to help your business and personal life. Networking can make things happen for you. A little judicious networking can help you break into your freelance business, keep it going, and make it grow. For example, I network when I call my high-school friend, now the vice president of a small Manhattan publishing firm, looking for writing assignments. She networks when she calls me asking if I can recommend someone to write a CD-ROM on Shakespeare. Networking is the business version of one hand washing the other.

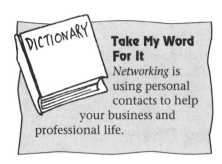

Take My Word For It

Networking is using personal contacts to help your business and professional life.

Here are a few more examples of ways that I have used networking:

➤ A close friend and I are doing freelance jobs for the same company. We compare salaries to see who's getting paid what.

➤ What goes around comes around: I recommend a friend for a job. He recommends me for one.

➤ I call my sister's former boyfriend, who now works for a posh publisher. Fortunately, he dropped her (not the other way around), so I get a job.

Home Alone

You can locate a network association by word of mouth. Just ask other people in your field where they network. You can also find a list of network organizations in trade journals and the "Community News" section of many local newspapers.

In the past, the "old-boy" network allowed preppies to make the key contacts they used not only in business but also in their personal lives. The old-boy network is as important today as it was a hundred years ago, but now it's not the only network in town. About 15 years ago, enterprising business people started network groups to give women and minorities the advantages that wealthy men had always had. These networks soon expanded to include just about any enterprising person who was looking for a job.

Today, networking is a crucial way for all types of freelancers to interact with each other. It's not only a vital marketing tool, but also a way to escape cabin fever and socialize.

Let's Do Lunch

No such thing as a free lunch? Ha! Just the opposite is true. Business lunches often pay for themselves many times over. How? Through networking. While you eat, you schmooze and make valuable contacts. Meals—including the "power breakfast," lunch, brunch, dinner, and a cuppa joe—are another way to network.

If the world was a different place, you wouldn't have to do all this politicking. You could sit home and do your thing and your product or service would sell itself. It ain't so, Sam. Very few people get business by magic; they beat the bushes on their own behalf. Networking is not for the faint of heart, however. Screw up your courage and sally forth.

To help you out, here are other tried-and-true ways to get some face time with people who can help it happen for you.

1. *Become a member of a community group.* Plunge into your community. You'll soon find that a very small group of people run the town...and they can make things happen for you, too. For example, I have been an elected member of the Farmingdale Library Board of Trustees for over a decade. As the president of the board, I helped spearhead a new $8.8 million library, from the passage of the bond issue, through the construction, to the completion. There are over 45,000 people in my community, and many of them got to know my name through my position on the board. This has helped me get writing assignments and sell books.

2. *Join civic groups.* Traditionally, civic groups such as the Chamber of Commerce, Rotary International, Lions, and Kiwanis have been a way to network with the movers and shakers in the business community. Doing lunch and working on special projects allows you to connect with other ambitious business people, many of whom are freelancers, on a personal level. The next time they need a freelance photographer, wedding organizer, or CPA, who do you think they'll turn to?

Home Alone
Business connections are very often made after personal connections are made. People feel comfortable doing business with those they've broken bread with.

For instance, I was a member of Rotary for four years. During that time, I made many good friends, did some important work in the community—and made a handful of business contacts that paid off handsomely.

3. *Link up with your trade association.* Every group has its own trade association. For example, I belong or have belonged to the following professional organizations:

   ➤ International Society of Humor Studies
   ➤ United University Professors
   ➤ Massachusetts Historical Society
   ➤ Laura Ingalls Wilder Memorial Society
   ➤ Modern Language Association
   ➤ National Testing Network in Writing
   ➤ American Association of University Women
   ➤ National Council of Teachers of English

Each one has helped me learn more about being a freelancer. Many have also helped me complete jobs by giving me facts about the specific subject (such as Laura Ingalls Wilder) that I could not get any other way.

Home Alone

Joining a trade association can be a great way to get low-cost insurance and other important benefits. There's more on insurance in Chapter 22.

Before you join any professional group, consider what it can do for you. Finding the right group can take some effort. Here are some criteria to consider.

➤ Look at the number of members: Too many and you might get lost in the shuffle; too few and you might not be able to make any contacts.

➤ Also check out the officers: Are they important in your field? That's always a good sign.

➤ Check the dues, too. If the group charges too much, it might not be worth it. You'll only hate them in the morning.

➤ Also, stay away from the nuts and berries. It won't do your career any good being associated with the oddballs and troublemakers.

Here are two general trade associations you might want to explore:

➤ The National Association for the Self-Employed (800-232-NASE)

➤ The American Association of Home-Based Businesses (800-447-9710)

4. *Don't forget alumni associations.* What about those college chums? What are they doing now? Odds are good that some of your old high school and college buddies are doing something that might help your freelance business. Join your alumni association to find out.

Home Alone

It is also important to read professional trade publications in your field. Their ads can be a great source for contacts, movement in the field, and new product lines. All these things can lead to jobs.

5. *Start your own group.* Can't find a group you like? Why not start your own? I did just that a few years ago with two fellow freelancers, Paula Hartz and Diane Engle. Our group meets for an inexpensive lunch whenever we're in the mood. We trade gossip, compare notes, and celebrate big and small occasions in each other's lives. Between lunches, we keep in touch via snail mail and e-mail. I've faxed our membership list to headhunters eager to fill big freelance jobs; we refer jobs to each other on a regular basis. It's been a wonderful experience on a personal as well as professional level.

6. *Work the Web.* According to an article in *Newsday*, 80 million people will be spending more than $4 billion a year on Internet goods and services by the year 2000. What are you waiting for? More on this later in the chapter.

218

7. *Anti-network.* Yes, you read that right. Remember how you found a great date—perhaps the love of your life—when you had sworn off love? The same can be true of networking. Sometimes you make your best contacts when you aren't even trying. Plunge into community work, a social group, or a trade association. Do the PTA, scouts, or coach a sport. You'll often make valuable freelance contacts through shared interests.

Facts on File

All your networking efforts are useless if your records are sloppy. Keep a Rolodex or card file with up-to-the-minute information on each and every possible contact. There are even some good software programs that accomplish the same thing. Here are some items to record:

➤ *The person's current name.* Hey, with some people trading spouses like we used to trade baseball cards, it's important to keep names straight. And then there's gender switches. Let's not go there.

➤ *Current address, both home and work.* On average, people move every three years. The unsteady job market has many people changing jobs far more often.

➤ *Individual preferences and penchants.* One of my best contacts is a world traveler; another raises show dogs. Recalling little facts about a person can help you make a more personal contact.

> **Home Alone**
> Some business-card software lets you add pictures to the cards. What would *you* like to see when you look up the number of the guy who always asks for revisions and never wants to pay for them?

➤ *Any relevant information about computer programs.* Does your contact use IBM, Macintosh, or is he/she computer-phobic?

➤ *Relevant details about past jobs.* Note anything that might influence present work. For example, does this client reimburse for postage? Pay late?

Play Nice

What goes around comes around, they say. Because much of your work will come from networking and referrals, what is your obligation to return the favor? And what happens if a client asks you to recommend someone for a job? "What!" you yelp. "I'm still trying to get enough work for myself and I'm going to get asked to give referrals? How can this happen?" Here's how:

➤ The client needs more help than you can provide.

➤ The job isn't exactly suited to your abilities.

➤ You are too busy to take the job right now. (It will happen, I promise.)

Are you obligated to recommend someone for a job if he or she has given you a lead? Are you obligated to help a client fill his or her stable? No, you're not. While it's very important as a freelancer to return favors, never recommend someone you cannot vouch for completely. The act will come back and bite you in the butt. This I can promise.

Use this check list when you consider whether or not to recommend someone for a freelance job:

➤ Is the person reliable? I mean *reliable*: Would you let them borrow your Porsche? Date your daughter? Marry your daughter?

➤ Does the person behave in a professional manner? Is this someone who won't embarrass you by throwing a hissy fit or violating chain of command? Will this person become a radioactive desert shrub halfway through the job?

➤ Can the person do the work to your standards? Think about your mother-in-law running her white-gloved finger over your china closet or sneering at your latest attempt to assemble a three-bean casserole.

➤ Have you worked with this person so you know he or she is the very best of the best? (As good as you? Better than you?)

Drums Along the I-Way

A lot of freelancers are said to have vision, but Feeny Lipscomb's All One Tribe mail-order business in Taos, New Mexico, was actually prompted by a vision. A workout on her favorite drum gave Lipscomb the inspiration to tell the rest of the world about the psychic and physical benefits of regular drumming. (I could make this up?)

Home Alone
In 1995, husband-and-wife freelancers Jeff Bezos and MacKenzie Bezos started a Cyberspace bookstore called *Amazon.com*. Two years later, they employ 300 people and boast 2.5 million titles in their catalog.

All One Tribe (*www.allonetribedrum.com*) is Lipscomb's on-line attempt to reach as many potential customers as she can for her freelance drum business. Capturing a specialty market is one thing; expanding that niche is quite another. By tapping into the Internet, Lipscomb has made it globally.

Lipscomb had been advertising through word-of-mouth and local publications with only limited success. Then in mid-1995 she had a Web page set up for her freelance business. Since she didn't know much about setting up and running a Web site, she hired specialists, so called "Webmasters." These online ads have resulted in a few thousand dollars in sales from around the world.

Should *you* consider advertising on the Internet? Yes, if you're in a business that involves technology and you have the budget for it. On a smaller scale, you might want to consider using local electronic bulletin boards. Since they only require a modem, they're ideally suited for nonglobal types on more modest budgets.

Charlotte's Web

Here are some tips to get you started in Cyberspace:

➤ *Vive la difference.* Make use of the Web's graphic nature and interactivity to stay one step ahead of the competition.

➤ *Don't be a cheapskate.* Realize that you'll probably have to spend money to make money. Freelancers tend to underestimate the cost of setting up and maintaining a site. Figure about $100 for the one-time connection to a storage service and a monthly fee of $50–$100 or more.

Further, one of the biggest challenges is making your site visible. It doesn't do any good to have a site if people can't find it.

➤ *Keep your ear to the tracks.* Listen to your clients. Encourage feedback via e-mail and make changes as needed. Client satisfaction can make or break a freelancer.

➤ *Don't be a martyr.* Outsource site creation and maintenance and concentrate on doing what you do best: your freelance business.

➤ *Don't freak 'em out.* Not everyone is wired. Give your clients an option if they're not comfortable doing business on the Net, but make sure you know how to tap this valuable resource so you're all set up when they're finally ready to hop aboard.

Time to boogie. So what are you waiting for?

Home Alone
Many Internet access providers can help you set up your own Web page. For example, CompuServe's Home Page service (*www.compuserve.com*) provides a free Web authoring tool, plus 5 MB of space for your home page. The telephone number is 800-848-8990 for you Cyberphobes.

Bet You Didn't Know

oH!

You don't have to spend a penny and you don't even need your own Web site to advertise on the Internet. You can easily jump on the coattails of another company's advertising efforts. For instance, you can place a free ad for your business on the portion of the American Express Web site geared to small businesses. The address is *http://americanexpress.com*. The businesses are listed by subject matter and geographic area.

Touch Down

There are two kinds of people, those who finish what they start, and... I know *you* are one of those virtuous types, so you'll be sure to follow up on all your marketing efforts. You've spent the money and the time. Don't waste it. In many ways, your follow-up is as important as your marketing campaign itself.

You know what you have to do. Here are some ways to do it:

Mind Your Own Business
Get one and only one datebook to prevent entering appointments all over the place. Use it. Carry it with you all the time. If need be, put Post-its on your forehead to remember key appointments.

➤ Attend the meetings, lunches, and presentations you booked. You'd be astonished at the number of times people forget what they're supposed to do when.

➤ Be prompt. Early is even better.

➤ Write thank-you notes for even the smallest favor.

➤ Return phone calls, even the ones that you don't think will go anywhere. Hey, you never know.

➤ Schedule appointments with prospective clients.

➤ Fulfill the promises you made in your ads.

➤ Ask about customer satisfaction.

➤ Correct any problems as quickly as possible.

➤ Monitor your ad campaign.

➤ Change what's necessary to reach your market.

The Least You Need to Know

➤ Use public relations—news releases, media events, newsletters, thank-you notes, greeting cards—to drum up business.

➤ Consider using sales incentives to get prospective customers to try your goods or services.

➤ Use networking to make the contacts that make things happen for you.

➤ Get wired and work the Web.

➤ Carry the ball to the finish line by following up on all marketing efforts.

Chapter 18

The Professional Edge

In This Chapter

➤ Learn how to build a good reputation—and keep it

➤ Discover how to deal with clients—even cranky ones

➤ Decide if you need an agent, and learn how to find one

1st Person: "Do you know anything about this fax machine?"

2nd Person: "A little. What's wrong?"

1st Person: "Well, I sent a fax, and the recipient called back to say all she received was a cover sheet and a blank page. I tried it again, and the same thing happened."

2nd Person: "How did you load the sheet?"

1st Person: "It's a pretty sensitive memo, and I didn't want anyone else to read it by accident, so I folded it so only the recipient could open it and read it."

Sometimes we get to deal with smart people. Sometimes we don't. As a freelancer, you have to deal with them all. Savvy or silly, nice or nasty, polite or persnickety—you'll have to endure and put on a happy face while you do. That's what you'll learn how to do in this chapter. And for those who want a little bit of a buffer, I'll teach you all you need to know about agents. Read on.

Building a Reputation

➤ "What a loser. I'd never do business with *that* freelancer again."

➤ "A pleasure to deal with, great work and everything on time. I'll recommend this freelancer to all my colleagues."

Which comment would you rather have applied to you and your freelance business? This is a no-brainer. As a freelancer, you may think you're selling insurance, legal services, or widgets, but what you're really selling is your reputation. It's the most valuable commodity you have, and it always will be.

To keep your reputation as shiny as a new penny, try these ideas:

Home Alone

I always try to finish a job just a day or two ahead of schedule. In most cases, that window of opportunity gives my clients the breathing room they need to satisfy *their* clients.

➤ *Be honest.* If you can't do the work, don't take it on. It's as simple as that. You may not have the time or the expertise, the equipment or the inclination. Even if the wolf is at the door, if you can't do the work, don't take it on. Every client would rather be told "No" up front than be stung in the end. I've been zapped a few times when I recommended fellow freelancers for jobs and they didn't do the work. Their dishonesty hurt my reputation.

➤ *Be good.* Do the very best work you can. Word will travel that your work is thorough, complete, and commendable. You'll get referrals as news of your high-quality work spreads.

➤ *Deliver on time.* Pending the destruction of the world as we know it, keep to your deadlines. In some cases, even the best work is useless when it passes the deadline.

➤ *Make the effort.* Go the extra mile. This may mean throwing in a little freebie. For example, last week I wrote part of a literature textbook. My client didn't have time to do some research for the pages, so I did the research and wrote the specific feature, saving her half a day down the road. Yes, it took me some extra time, but this client is worth the effort. So is my reputation.

➤ *Get it together.* Answer all your telephone calls promptly. Ditto on correspondence, both e-mail and snail mail. Don't hold people up by playing coy or being disorganized. Be a pro.

Luck of the Draw: Dealing With Clients

As a freelancer, you can be treated better than the ice-cream man in the Sahara Desert. I have been feted and petted, wined and dined. A major New Jersey publisher once bought me a dinner that cost more than my last winter coat; the editors of this series have done everything but send me roses (hint, hint). Of course, these delightful experiences are a direct result of my sparkling personality. Besides, I am an unbelievably easy person to work with. And if you believe all of that, I have some Florida swamp land that has your name written on it.

On the one hand, being a freelancer does indeed offer you the chance to meet some wonderful folks. I have become good friends with some dear people through my work as a freelance writer. Ironically, I have never even met some of these people face-to-face; we have only spoken on the phone or corresponded. Others, like my first (blessed) editor at Macmillan, I've only seen a dozen times in as many years. Nonetheless, I consider her a treasure.

On the other hand, the casual nature of the freelance relationship makes it easy for you to become a doormat. Even if you behave as the consummate professional, it's all too easy in this business to be treated like the hired help. (Which, after all, is what you are.) We all like to feel appreciated, and that's tough to do when you're getting ordered around.

Here are some guidelines that can make it easier for you to have a good relationship with your clients:

➤ *Set limits.* Like the cleaning lady who refused to do windows, politely but firmly decide what is and what is not included in the fee. For example, how will your job be delivered? Will the company pay the postage or are you expected to foot the bill for a courier service? Getting everything worked out in the beginning can help prevent nasty surprises in the end.

➤ *Get it in writing.* "A verbal contract isn't worth the paper it's printed on," a movie mogul once said. He may have had a weak grasp of language, but he was strong on logic. Set it all down, even the itty-bitty stuff. Cover your behind.

> **Mind Your Own Business**
> Even if you're dealing with a long-time client, get everything in writing. I didn't take my own advice on a really big job this year, and I got scorched good.

➤ *Grow up.* Show grace under pressure. Resist the urge to kick the pooch or call the client something X-rated. If need be, chew through your lip or eat an entire carton of Ben and Jerry's Chunky Monkey instead of unleashing that juicy string of imprecations.

➤ *Obey the chain of command.* There's a reason why someone is called a "vice president" and someone else isn't. Don't jump the chain. It's a sure-fire way to make enemies.

➤ *Don't gossip.* Even if it's really yummy news, zip it up. Mum's the word. And while we're on it, don't get involved in office politics. Don't get manipulated into taking sides.

➤ *Don't tattle or whine.* Things happen. Take your lumps and move on. Don't shift the blame to someone else or moan about your sad fate. It's tiresome and very unprofessional.

➤ *Stand up for yourself.* A wise woman once said to me, "Don't start no trouble, won't be no trouble." However, trouble sometimes has a way of starting. If it does, don't wuss out. If you do, you'll get a reputation as a wimp and you'll hate yourself in the morning. You don't have to be a pit bull, but you do have to stand up for yourself.

I once had a contract dispute with a client. I explained my position by pointing out the language in the contract that protected me. Nonetheless, the publisher withheld a portion of my check. When I hired an attorney, the client called me "the Tonya Harding of publishing"—but I got the money that was due to me. Of course, I'll never work with that client again, but I never would have in any event.

➤ *Don't be a piggy.* Sometimes, your clients will have a fat T&E budget (travel and entertainment). This is money the company has allocated to pay for schmoozing up freelancers like you. Even if you're lucky enough to deal with clients on a T&E, don't wolf down too much caviar and champagne at the 21 Club. Follow your client's lead.

When in doubt, pay your own way. Many clients earn less than you do. Besides, travel and entertaining are tax deductions because they are legitimate business expenses.

➤ *Do it right.* Want to get along well with your customers? Give them what they paid for, and then a little bit more. You can never go wrong doing it right.

➤ *Be responsible.* Do you know the Law of Probable Dispersal? Here it is: "Whatever it is that hits the fan will not be evenly distributed." There will be problems, even with the best of clients. It's the nature of freelance life. Specifications change; orders shift. When something goes wrong, you may have to eat your share of the problem, even if it's not your fault. You may have to cover for an incompetent client. Do it gracefully and be done with it.

 **Bet You Didn't Know**

Here's one of the facts of a freelancer's life: Vital papers will demonstrate their vitality by moving from where you left them to where you can't find them.

The Beaver Is Not Happy: Dealing With Difficult Clients

Despite your sweet nature, excellent on-time record, and fabulous work, you will encounter impossible clients. Some are just rotten by nature; others may be experiencing severe personal or work-related problems that are spilling over into your job. Let's start with the dishonest ones, the ones who get you with the sucker punch.

Liar, Liar, Pants on Fire

Ever hear any of the following Six Big Lies?

1. It's not the money, it's the principle of the thing.
2. You get this one, I'll pay next time.
3. I'll call you later.
4. Now, I'm going to tell you the truth.
5. It's supposed to make that noise.
6. Yes, I did.

You'll hear those six and a lot more when you encounter clients who play fast and loose with the concept of "honesty" and "fair play." Here's freelancer Sharon Sorenson's story about one client who refused to honor a contract:

I had a contract with Company X to develop one grade level of a 6–12 literature series for low-reading-level students. Six others had similar contracts. We met in Baltimore, worked out details for the series, went home, cranked out manuscript. I finished the entire job—found all the literature, did all the detective work for gaining copyright permissions, found suitable art work, wrote all the student text matter, and completed the teacher's manual. Then Company X was bought out, and the new company chose not to publish the series. I had a $1,000 advance; the other folks had not negotiated an advance. So that was it— total payment for my work. The new company refused to honor my contract. Nor could I ever get my manuscript back. One book of the series—not mine— actually saw print before the company sold, but I don't know what happened to it. I've not seen it anywhere since.

> **Mind Your Own Business**
> There are times when you just have to fold your tents and move on. In some cases, there is nothing else you can do, because taking a client to court will cost more than you'll ever get back.
>
> IS THAT CLEAR?

Sharon lost thousands and thousands of dollars to these crooks. This doesn't happen often, but if it happens to you, you'll feel angry and betrayed. To prevent such disasters with scoundrels, here are some suggestions:

➤ *Check a client's reputation before you sign on the dotted line.* Talk to other freelancers. See how long the client has been in business and what kind of reputation the person has build up. Here's where networking is so important. You may even wish to call the Better Business Bureau or Consumer Affairs. Check that the client has the proper licenses, registrations, and a solid credit rating.

Stay away from the deadbeats. You may think that you can outsmart them. Trust me, you usually can't. They've been cheating people since long before you were born. The bad boys may make exciting dates, but they make lousy clients.

➤ *Call in often.* Check in with the client on a regular basis, at least once a week. Don't ever complete an entire project without touching base. This isn't to say that you have to be a nudge and smother the client. It is to say that calling in often will help you keep tabs on what's happening in the home office. This lessens the chance that a takeover will leave you out in the cold.

➤ *Structure payments.* Sharon's mistake was only getting an advance. On a project this large, she should have received an advance and regular payments. These are often structured as follows:

1/5 of total	advance on the job
1/5 of total	one-quarter completion
1/5 of total	one-half completion
1/5 of total	three-quarters completion
1/5 of total	completed job

Home Alone
Consider raising your rates for troublesome or annoying clients. At least you'll be getting paid well for the aggravation. At worst, they'll go away and bother someone else.

➤ *Keep a lawyer leashed.* I have a wonderful lawyer, Fred Schneider, who has helped me out several times. Keeping Fred close by makes it easier for me to get legal help if I need it. This way, I don't have to scramble to find a lawyer who specializes in the kind of help I need. A quick call to the lawyer usually gets things right on track very fast. (See Chapter 13 for more advice on dealing with deadbeats.)

Sorry, Wrong Number

Sometimes, clients treat you badly because they are out-and-out louses. They're just plain rotten people who deserve to suffer a bad case of athlete's foot or jock itch. That's all there is to it. Other times, however, you'll get treated badly inadvertently.

Perhaps you were in the wrong place at the wrong time and got caught in the political cross-fire. For example, your in-house contact might have gotten fired, canceling your project. Or the budget went south and your project was yanked mid-stream. Maybe the company went out of business and you got stiffed for all or part of the money you were owed. Perhaps a small, steady client was taken over by a large corporation, leaving you high and dry. Or your work just got lost and you ended up redoing it—for free. Maybe your disk scrambled in-house and you've got to make a copy—for free. Invoices seem to vanish as mysteriously as socks in a dryer.

What can you do if you get mistreated by accident? Here are some ideas:

➤ Don't take it personally.

➤ Don't assume the blame. It's not *your* fault.

➤ Pick up the pieces and start over.

➤ Follow the contact to the new firm.

➤ Try to sell the work you already completed elsewhere, if you own the rights to it. If not, get a release from the client and then try to sell the work.

Up Close and Personal

And then there are the hazards you may have thought you were finally immune from when you left the corporate womb: "Hey! I'm a freelancer. I work out of my home—all by myself. Who's going to sexually harass me? The postal carrier?" Think again. Just because you're working on your own doesn't mean that you've escaped that problem.

Freelance real estate brokers can be harassed by strangers to whom they show empty homes. Personal trainers, therapists, accountants, nurses, attorneys—anyone who makes appointments with strangers on a regular basis—can be in danger. Sexual harassment isn't the only worry; there's also the potential for physical harm.

Short of wearing full body armor and lugging around a killer fish, what can you do to protect yourself? Here are some suggestions:

➤ Recognize the danger. Don't think you're safe because you're built like the Sphinx. Remember: Its nose got shot off.

➤ Always check a client's references before you agree to meet in someone's home, show an empty home or apartment, or have someone to your home.

Mind Your Own Business

Here are two more warning signs of sexual harassment: The client who makes you pick up assignments at his home could be setting you up. Also beware of a client who insists on evening meetings—and then turns them into dates. And remember that men as well as women can be sexually harassed.

➤ Listen to the vibes. If you get the heebie-jeebies, get out. And don't give the client a second chance without having other people present.

➤ Avoid meetings in secluded spots.

➤ Let someone know where you will be at all times. Leave a copy of your schedule with an assistant, a friend, a neighbor. I know you're a big kid now, but even the big kids get hurt.

➤ If you do a lot of traveling, carry a cellular phone.

➤ Learn to recognize what constitutes sexual harassment. Someone who expects sexual favors in exchange for work is sexually harassing you.

Dump any client who physically or sexually threatens you. No one needs the work *that* badly.

Secret Agent Man: Agents

According to legend, a popular writer requested in his will that upon his death, his body be cremated and 10 percent of his ashes thrown in his agent's face.

As this anecdote illustrates, agents tend to spark somewhat ambivalent feelings among their clients. Nonetheless, some freelancers are simply not comfortable selling themselves. If you fit this bill, think of hiring someone to do it for you. There are two instances in which you can use an agent:

Take My Word For It

An *agent* is your representative. Agents sell your services.

➤ When it's customary in your field, as with writers, photographers, actors, musicians, craftspeople, and artists

➤ When you just can't sell yourself

An agent is your front man or woman. But *exactly* what does an agent do? Here are some of an agent's functions.

An agent:

➤ Is your *exclusive* marketing representative.

➤ Finds the right market for your work.

➤ Sets up meetings with clients.

➤ Negotiates contracts.

➤ Recommends you for other similar work.

➤ Shelters you from conflicts with clients.

➤ Tracks your business accounts.

➤ May or may not provide tax information to the IRS.

That's what an agent *will* do for you. Now it's time to see what an agent *won't* do for you:

An agent won't:

➤ Loan you money.

➤ Act as a therapist.

➤ Be your travel agent.

➤ Be your lawyer (unless this is part of the deal).

➤ Do public relations work (again, unless this is part of the deal).

➤ Function as a secretary.

➤ Be available 24 hours a day, 7 days a week.

➤ Be your best friend.

 **Bet You Didn't Know**

Some freelancers use agents for one-shot deals. A freelance writer might hire an agent to represent them for one book, for example. Many agents are willing to consider such arrangements.

First-Night Jitters

Even if you made the initial contact with a client and even reached an agreement, you may wish to have an agent close the deal. That's because a good agent can often help you get better terms than you can get on your own. This paves the way for more lucrative contracts in the future, too.

"Hold the phone!" you say. "I'll have to shell out 10 to 15 percent of my money for the agent's cut. How can I still do better with an agent?" Logic would suggest that you're better off flying solo on this one. But not so fast.

Your first big contract is important, perhaps the most important one you'll ever get. Mistakes at this point can cost you a great deal of time, money, and aggravation. Losing time and money are bad enough, but having to endure aggravation is simply not acceptable. For example, a well-executed contract can help you avoid conflicts later in the project, when substantial changes are suddenly being requested. Agents can also help you get more money for your work by helping you see what to ask for in a contract.

231

Mind Your Own Business

Be wary of agent contracts that don't specify a limit to expenses incurred on your behalf. Some musicians, among others, have been badly burned by that one.

There are some "hidden" agent-generated charges you should be aware of. Your agent should not charge you for normal business expenses, such as domestic telephone calls or bookkeeping. But it's very common for an agent to charge for special expenses, such as overseas calls, photocopying, and book purchases. Carefully negotiate every item on your contract to make sure there are no whopping surprises down the line.

By the by, if you get a hot tip without your agent that leads to a super deal, are you still obligated to fork over 10+ percent of the gross take? Yes. That's how the game works. No matter how you came to get the lead, your agent will still close the deal and negotiate the contract. Your agent still gets the agreed-upon percentage—unless your contract with the agent reads differently.

Work It Out

Only you can decide if and when you need an agent to represent you. To help you make some decisions, I've whipped up a handy-dandy worksheet. Use it now to decide if you should go out shopping for an agent today.

Write *yes* or *no* next to each statement.

_____ 1. I'm tough enough to negotiate with the big kids.

_____ 2. I'm comfortable in business meetings.

_____ 3. I promise to read the contract all the way through.

_____ 4. I understand legal terms, or know how to get their definitions.

_____ 5. I'm not easy to intimidate.

_____ 6. I have a thick skin.

_____ 7. I'm willing to market my work somewhere else if I can't get the deal I want.

_____ 8. I have the time and energy to deal with contract negotiations.

Bonus: Give yourself ten extra points if you:

(a) Have raised teenagers and lived to tell the tale.

(b) Have survived a cab ride in New York City.

(c) Have programmed your VCR, assembled a bicycle, or shopped the day after Thanksgiving.

If you answered *yes* to most of these questions, you're likely best off lighting out for the territory ahead of the rest—alone. This may change later in your freelance career, however. If you answered *no* in most cases, consider hiring an agent.

Hide and Seek: Finding an Agent

So you decided that you need an agent. How do you find one? If you're a writer, you can consult *Literary Market Place*, the writer's reference book. It lists several hundred literary agencies and agents. Here are some other sources to try:

➤ The Society of Authors' Representatives
(P.O. Box 650, New York, NY 10113)

This group offers a list of agents.

➤ Guide to Literary Agents & Art/Photo Reps
(Writer's Digest Books)

This is an annual directory that provides specific information about agencies.

➤ Trade journals for your field

➤ Word-of-mouth

Check with other freelancers in your field. See whom they recommend. I've always been a strong fan of the personal road to finding an agent. This is another good reason to network.

➤ Trade shows

Many agents attend conferences, conventions, seminars, and workshops to find new clients and to represent their existing stable of workhorses. As a result, these events can be great places to shop for an agent. If you decide to go this route, here are some guidelines to follow:

1. Be professional.
2. Try to arrange a private meeting with the agent.
3. Explain the project you're trying to sell.
4. If you decide to use the agent, send a letter reminding the agent where you met and how.
5. If you don't want to use the agent, follow up with a thank-you letter.

Bet You Didn't Know

If you get successful enough, you can hire someone to be your business manager on salary rather than paying a percentage to an agent.

Caveat Emptor

All missions entail a certain risk, and so it is with agent shopping. Here are a few guidelines that can prevent a stay at Heartbreak Hotel.

First, learn how the client-agent relationship is handled in your specific field. In the music field, for example, it's not common to sign with an agent until a third party has offered a contract. In publishing, an author's money is always delivered to the agent. That shows a close agent-client relationship. Learn the rules so you can discover if they fit your lifestyle and personality.

Next, beware of agents who push long-term contracts. Also avoid contracts that can't be broken by either party at any time. This is not to say you should discard agents like Liz Taylor discards husbands. On the contrary; when you find a good agent, stick around. But shun agents who claim that you'll bolt once they've given you the best years of their lives. If the agent is good, of course you'll stay.

Don't make deals without your agent. After all, that's why you hired an agent in the first place. If someone offers you a project, refer the client to your agent. The line is, "You'll have to talk to my agent about that."

Finally, always get a written agreement with your agent. There are some writers who have enjoyed fine relationships with their agents with only a handshake to seal the deal. There are other freelancers, however, who have gotten badly burned on such deals. Agents can sell their businesses, go bankrupt, decide to raise commissions—and where does that leave you? If you have a good contract, that leaves you just fine in most cases.

Home Alone
Today, some agents are also lawyers. This is great because it offers "one-stop shopping": business and legal savvy together!

You'll get the most from your relationship with an agent if you are a savvy client. Learn how contracts are put together and what they mean. Even though you're paying your agent for advice, that doesn't mean that you're the silent partner in this deal. Even if you have an agent, don't stop networking. Keep your ear to the railroad track; you never know when the gravy train is rounding the corner.

Breaking Up Is Hard to Do

Breaking up *is* hard to do. But it happens. Leaving an agent is like dissolving any important relationship, but it doesn't have to be as painful or protracted as a star's divorce. If things aren't going the way you think they should be with your agent, it's time to call him or her and calmly talk about your concerns. If this approach is too confrontational for your style, say it in writing. Sometimes misunderstandings are just that; other times, they signal the beginning of the end.

If you do decide to seek a new agent, here's where your contract becomes crucial. Whether you've been with the agent for ten years or ten minutes, if your contract specifies that either side can end the relationship with a certified letter saying that 30 days from the date of the letter your professional association is severed, you're in the clear. If not, your departure could take much longer and require legal intervention.

The Least You Need to Know

➤ In the final analysis, all you have to sell is your reputation. Make it a good one.

➤ Don't squander that good reputation. Follow the rules and you'll keep it intact.

➤ You will run into all kinds of clients. Be prepared to deal with the cranky ones.

➤ Assess your professional situation carefully to decide if you need an agent. Having no agent is better than having the wrong one.

I CAN EMAIL THAT TO YOU...

Chapter 19

Home on the Range: Running Life as a Freelancer

In This Chapter

➤ Deal with procrastination—now

➤ Learn to recognize your work patterns and use them to your advantage

➤ Discover the dangers of overwork

➤ Learn to protect your work time by saying *no*

A newcomer, intrigued by stories of Coney Island, got up the courage to ask a girlfriend to go there with him. The next day he met a friend.

"So, how was it?" the friend asked.

"A disappointment, really," the newcomer replied. "The Tunnel of Love was so wet we both caught cold."

"Your boat leaked that much?"

The newcomer looked aghast. "There's a *boat*?"

One of the major challenges of being a freelancer is learning to manage your time sensibly. Otherwise, it's not even a question of *missing* the boat...it's more like you never even knew there was one! Think of this chapter as a short course in freelance survival skills, the freelancer's equivalent of starting a fire with two sticks or knowing where to find the edible roots and berries. I'll teach you what you need to know to manage your time wisely and avoid both procrastination *and* burnout.

Performance Anxiety

If you have ever had trouble getting started, er, *working,* rest assured that you are in very good company. *Very* good company. Let me get real here—I dare you to name a freelancer who hasn't had *some* trouble buckling down to work Monday morning. How can you tell if you're a procrastinator? Take the following simple test.

You're a classic procrastinator if...

1. You're still figuring out if bell bottoms, love beads, and a Nehru jacket are the right look for you.
2. You're just about ready to buy one of those newfangled TV sets— you know, the ones that show programs in color.
3. You sent for your Woodstock tickets in 1969 and just noticed they haven't arrived yet.
4. You try to pay your bills the very same decade they're due.
5. You can't decide if you should vote for Nixon or Kennedy this year.

Beginning freelancers often fail to realize that even the most experienced self-employed people occasionally have difficulty getting down to work. Many successful freelancers have devised little *rituals*—little habits that provide structure—to help them overcome their hesitation and make it easier for them to get into their work.

Ritual Behavior

Some work rituals are as simple as turning on the radio and sharpening a pencil. Some are silly, like using the same coffee mug every day or eating three jelly beans before getting down to work. Other rituals involve hard-boiled eggs, whipped cream, and olives, but let's not go there.

Instead, let me give you a check list to use as you create your own rituals to help you get started working every morning. (We're not going to push for bright-eyed and bushy-tailed, or even cheerful. We're just talking getting down to *business.*)

238

Check each ritual you think might make it easier for you to get started.

1. I can't start working until I've had a cup of coffee, preferably from the donut shop.
2. I have to pour the coffee into a thermal mug. Can't drink the coffee from Styrofoam or cardboard.
3. I have to sharpen my pencils before I start working, even though I'm a self-employed visiting nurse and take notes in pen.
4. I have to get fully dressed, as though I were going to an office.
5. I can't start working until the mail carrier comes.
6. I have to exercise for precisely half an hour before I start working.
7. First, I have to read the morning paper, cover to cover.
8. I have to set up my CD player with precisely three sets of oldies.
9. I can't start working until the fat lady sings.
10. I have to spill a little chicken blood first.

Patterns Plus

Okay, so now we know that we're all creatures of habit. It's also vital that you discover your optimal work time and work patterns so that you can make it as easy as possible to be productive. How can you isolate your best time and place to work? Try filling out the following worksheet.

Answer each question to see what patterns make it easier for you to get started.

1. At what time of day do I work best?

   _____

2. At what time of day do I get the least work done?

   _____

3. Where do I get the most work done?

   _____

4. Where do I get the least work done?

   _____

5. How long can I work at one sitting without getting tired or running dry?

   _____

6. What music do I play when I get the most work done?

   _____

7. What light source works best for me?

   _____

8. What do I wear when I do my best work?

   _____

Now, use what you learned about settling into a work routine to get yourself motivated. Remember a key freelance mantra: No work, no pay.

Three Neat Ways to Get Started

Here are some more ideas to get you going. Pick the ones that work best for you, but I won't complain if you try them all!

1. *Assume the position.* Get yourself ready to work by doing working things. This is not the time to be running to the deli for a doughnut. Instead, sit at your workstation. Get your weapon of choice: computer, phone, medical equipment, power tools, and so on. Remember: It's almost impossible to start working if you're pumping iron or attending the Tuesday aerobics class or sacrificing a chicken.

Home Alone
One success-ful freelancer attributes much of her success to personal discipline. "I have an absolute rule," she said. "Get up, shower, and be dressed and ready to work by 9:00." When she didn't have this rule, she found that she was slipping into self-destructive work habits.

Remember, there's no law that says productive work must include a commute, a foam cup of bad coffee, and an office full of intrigue—or a boss cracking a whip. After all, the tradition of working at home is much older than the current tradition of working in an office.

2. *Make the mind-body connection.* I'm not a California crystal queen (I don't know my astrological sign and I *can* change a light bulb unaided), but I do believe that there's something to getting yourself in the mood to work. True confessions: Unless you're one sandwich short of a picnic, you don't really *want* to work. But you *have* to work, because you have a better chance of getting struck by lightning eight zillion times than winning the lottery or finding a very rich and affectionate lost uncle to support you in the style to which you would like to become accustomed.

Approach your day's work seriously, but without a sense of doom and gloom. Be positive, upbeat, and cheerful—even if a particular assignment has gone as sour as Scrooge and you're muttering "Bah, humbug!" at the neighborhood children. It may be a stretch, but you can put yourself in the mood to work. After all, as a freelancer, you have a big edge over the average office drone: You're doing what you want to do where you want to do it.

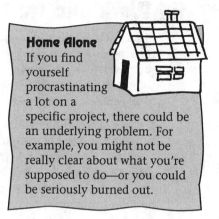

Home Alone
If you find yourself procrastinating a lot on a specific project, there could be an underlying problem. For example, you might not be really clear about what you're supposed to do—or you could be seriously burned out.

3. *Visualize yourself working.* Many successful freelancers say that they can work more effectively if they first imagine themselves working well. When you step in the shower in the morning, imagine yourself later in the day starting your job. Keep that picture in your mind as you brush your teeth, eat breakfast, and walk down the hall to your office. Think about it throughout the day when you feel your mind wandering or your energy flagging.

"What kind of New Age nonsense is this?" you may be thinking. "Are we back to the mind-body connection?" Try it, you doubting Thomas: Sit in a comfortable chair and close your eyes. Visualize yourself moving smoothly and easily from task to task. Then sit down and work for an hour. Stick with the method; it usually takes a few tries until you see progress.

Bet You Didn't Know

Many freelancers warm up to work by starting with something easy or routine, like making copies or answering e-mail. Your humble author (that's me!) starts every workday by answering and sending e-mail.

Last-Ditch Efforts

Self-discipline in freelancing has a lot more to do with habit and pattern than with an iron will or steely resolve. What successful freelancers have on their side is a schedule, a rhythm of work that works for them. Still having trouble? Try these ideas:

➤ Identify the problem that keeps you from working. Deal with the problem, and then go back to work.

➤ Set a regular time to work. Make it the same time every day.

➤ Force yourself to work for the specific amount of time you've set aside, even if you don't think you're producing anything usable. Work for the total time; no fudging!

➤ Keep your goals realistic. Decide to complete a section of a project today, not the entire project in one day.

All Work and No Play Makes Jack a Dull Boy

Then we have the other end of the spectrum—freelancers who overwork. At-home freelancers are notorious for it. A recent study showed that a third of these freelancers rank overwork as the biggest drawback to working at home. And the moonlighters among us may work a solid 40 hours a week at their salaried jobs and then kick in another 35+ hours a week trying to get their freelance careers off the ground.

If you're a full-time freelancer at home, without commutes and distractions, you can squeeze work out of every minute that you're not sleeping or eating. Even a part-time freelancer can easily slide into overwork. With your workplace only a step away, it's easy just to pop into the office for a few minutes of work after dinner—and not emerge until they're playing a test pattern on the TV. Or perhaps you take a few minutes to clear your desk on Saturday—and when you look up, it's Sunday.

Excuse *Me*

All freelancers will occasionally have to put the pedal to the metal to get the job done. Besides, many of us thrive on 36-hour days. But, especially if there's a family involved, you need to acknowledge the difference between a normal day's work and overtime. How can you tell if you're overworking? Take the following simple quiz to find out.

Put a check next to the items that apply to you. (No fair using this list to get ideas. Make up your own excuses to wear yourself down.)

_____ 1. It's a new account, so I need to devote more attention to it.

_____ 2. It's an old account, so how can I disappoint my stalwart customers? After all, they've always been there for me.

_____ 3. It's a friend; how can I say "no" to a friend?

_____ 4. It's the seasonal push. You know what *that's* like.

_____ 5. The work always comes in waves. It's a tidal wave this time.

_____ 6. It's a Friday, and I have to work through the weekend to get this done by Monday.

_____ 7. How can you say that I can't complete this assignment overnight? I am super(woman/man). Hear me (roar/soar/hit the floor).

_____ 8. It's an emergency, and they really need me to get this done.

_____ 9. The pay is outrageous; how can I pass up this one extra job?

_____ 10. Crisis on Planet X: Who knew my iguana would tree the neighbor's gerbil, leaving me two days behind?

Here's the truth: No one is indispensable. Not even you, super freelancer.

Cat on a Hot Tin Roof

Are you feeling a little stressed from overwork? Take the following simple test to find out. Check each item that applies to you.

You know you're overworked if...

_____ 1. Relatives that have been dead for years come visit you and suggest that you should get some rest.

_____ 2. You can achieve a "runner's high" by sitting up.

_____ 3. The sun is too loud.

_____ 4. You repeat the same sentence over and over again, not realizing that you have said it before.

_____ 5. You begin to explore the possibility of setting up an I.V. drip solution of espresso.

_____ 6. You wonder if brewing is really a necessary step for the consumption of coffee.

_____ 7. You can hear mimes.

_____ 8. You repeat the same sentence over and over again, not realizing that you have said it before.

_____ 9. You ask the drive-thru attendant if you can get your order to go.

_____10. You discover the aesthetic beauty of office supplies.

_____11. You begin to talk to yourself, then disagree about the subject, get into a nasty row over it, lose, and refuse to speak to yourself for the rest of the night.

_____12. You repeat the same sentence over and over again, not realizing that you have said it before.

_____13. Trees begin chasing you.

_____14. Antacid tablets become your sole source of nutrition.

Score Yourself

10 or more checked	Some days it's just not worth the effort to chew through the straps, eh?
6–9 checked	Stress? What stress? I always twitch like this.
3–5 checked	I'll slow down tomorrow. Cross my heart.
0–2 checked	They call me "mellow yellow."

The real reasons that many freelancers are afraid to slow down include money, status, and loss of identity. Pish-tosh. If you're good, the work will be there. Besides, no one ever had "I should have worked more" engraved on a tombstone.

Mind Your Own Business

We all think we're invincible. News flash: We're not. Watch your health. If you feel yourself getting sick, slow down. You'll make up the work later.

Home Alone

Store as much important information as possible on disk. This greatly reduces paper clutter.

Home Alone

Freelancers are most likely to overwork when their quarterly estimated tax payments are due. Having Uncle Sam breathe down your neck is a powerful incentive to take that one extra job. To prevent *this* particular reason for over-working, be sure to set aside enough money in your savings account to pay your taxes. See Chapter 21 for details.

Save Yourself

To prevent overwork, set regular hours and a dependable schedule. At the very least, a regular work schedule gives you time to have a life (or get one, if you've never gotten around to having one before). With a set schedule, you'll have to make a conscious choice to work like a pooch. Here are some additional suggestions to make your day more fruitful:

➤ Do real "it's-paying-money" work when you're most productive. Do work-related chores when you're least productive. For example, I write from 9:00 to 5:00, give or take. I do chores like filing after dinner, when my brain and butt hurt.

➤ Delegate and hire. Get an assistant to do routine office tasks and run errands. Teenagers are great for this.

➤ Keep a calendar to track important events.

➤ Organize your office. You know the drill: a place for everything and everything in its place.

➤ Be ruthless and eliminate clutter. If you don't need it, throw it out.

Why Buy the Cow When You Can Get the Milk for Free?

Unfortunately, when you work at home, people often assume that you're not really working. They suspect you're actually sitting on the divan eating bon-bons. (Does anyone ever really eat bon-bons? And what's a *divan*?)

Even if you *are* working, your friends, neighbors, relatives, clients, and even colleagues are often laboring under the delusion that you have plenty of time to do their bidding. It's astonishing how often freelancers are asked to walk a neighbor's dog when the neighbor is away or wait for people's deliveries while they're at the office—working. Ditto for attending time-wasting meetings, driving Aunt Maude to the doctor, or picking up a platter for the block party.

It's time for stern measures.

➤ **Stern measure #1:** Control the telephone. Monitor your telephone calls with your telecommunications system. Even a simple answering machine allows you to do this. My friends always chuckle when they make the cut and I pick up the call. One friend says, "It's *so* good to know that I'm still on the 'A' list." When I'm really deep in work, the only people I speak to are my husband (if he has gossip or a gift), my kids (if they are bleeding), and important clients. Remember, you can't get roped into doing stupid errands if you don't answer the phone.

Mind Your Own Business
Never, never turn off the phone. You're in your office working, not on Fantasy Island playing Robinson Crusoe.

➤ **Stern measure #2:** Don't socialize during work hours. No time to koffeeklatch.

➤ **Stern measure #3:** Attend only important meetings. If you have an agent, send the agent. After all, that's why you have an agent.

➤ **Stern measure #4:** Just say no. Someone else can walk Fido, water the lawn, or drop off the Rollerblades. Repeat after me: "No." See, that wasn't so hard, now was it?

Staffers will never admit it, but they usually get a lot more breathing room than freelancers. As a result, it's very important that we create a work routine that suits us individually. This involves setting up a schedule as well as setting limits. Learn when to say yes... and when to say no.

The Least You Need to Know

➤ Like breaking up, starting work is hard to do. Take steps to deal with your urge to procrastinate.

➤ Pay attention to your own style and create an environment you can work with.

➤ Too much work can be as bad as too little. Avoid overextending yourself.

➤ Learn to say *no* to distractions.

➤ Talk is cheap; work already.

Chapter 20

Working Without a Net

In This Chapter

➤ Learn to balance family and freelancing

➤ Discover ways to combat loneliness

➤ Figure out how to regulate work and cash flow

When Hank Aaron was up to bat for the first time in his major league career, the catcher for the opposing team tried to rattle him by saying, "Hey, kid, you're holding your bat all wrong. You should hold it with the label up so you can read it."

The young rookie for the Milwaukee Braves, who later went on to become the greatest home-run hitter of all time, was not at a loss for words. He simply replied, "I didn't come up here to read."

You know why you're up at bat, but that doesn't mean that everyone else does. In this chapter, learn how to balance family and home with the demands of being a freelancer.

Family Matters

Have you seen the magazine ads that show an attractive young mother in her tastefully decorated high-rise home office? There's a stunning view of the skyline in the background. Super Mom's immaculate office is crammed full of the latest high-tech gadgetry. With one hand, she's feeding a beautifully designed memo into her fax machine. With the other hand, she's burping the baby/wiping down the counter/grooming the pooch/answering the phone/cooking glistening red lobsters. What's wrong with this picture? For starters, it's about as realistic as *Jurassic Park*.

First of all, most home offices are less elaborate—and less immaculate. I could write a novel in the dust on my bookshelves; an archeologist could have a field day digging though the piles of Diet Coke cans, discarded doll shoes, and old newspapers in my office. (So that's where the three-prong adapter went!) Further, the only view I have is of the Schmidts' house next door. They are great neighbors, but Mt. Rushmore their garage isn't.

Take My Word For It

Cross-functional is a new term coined to describe a worker who must perform a variety of duties in an overwhelmed company. The term seems to hit the freelance/family conflict right on the nose.

Together, my fax machine and copier are older than my teenage son and if I try to do two things at once, something blows. I make a serious fashion statement in my spandex bike shorts from K-Mart and a T-shirt from a cereal giveaway. Where the magazine ads really fail, however, is in their implication that you can easily balance work and family. You can't, even if you freelance as a juggler.

Kid's Play

The average two-year-old is not well versed in role theory. A child doesn't look at his parent working at home and think, "Well, now my parent is busy being a freelance accountant. I better come back with my question at a later date." To a child, a parent is always a parent—and if home, always available.

Mind Your Own Business

Kids don't have the market cornered on a freelancer's time. Spouses, in-laws, and neighbors can be every bit as demanding—and far less cute.

Teenagers are simply larger two-year-olds. Here's a scenario for you: Your teenage daughter enters your office without warning and demands money. She's wearing shorts which are appropriate only for establishments with *Girls! Girls! Girls!* flashing in neon on the outside. She's shadowed by a lanky male creature who shakes your hand sullenly and looks like a serial killer. You decide a talk with your daughter on the concept of convents is in order. Needless to say, your concentration is shot.

A freelancing friend of mine was talking on the phone to an important client one day when the walls of her office began to vibrate. Here's what she said:

> *I thought it was an earthquake, perhaps, or an alien invasion. No, it was a CD of the rock group "Pearl Jam" thundering from my 15-year-old son's basement bedroom. To halt the pandemonium, I stomped on the floor like Mr. Ed and frantically tried to continue my business call. It was not my finest moment, but at least my client knows I can thump my foot and count to five.*

Hired Help

Children need constant attention. Working at home is not a substitute for child care. If you're a freelancer with one or more bundles of joy (small or large), you must manage day care and personal responsibilities in a way that will allow you to successfully meet your job responsibilities. And don't think it gets easier as the child gets older. Some teenagers require almost as much vigilance as a toddler, and a lot more car rides.

Take this message to heart: You *can* work a successful freelance business with a child or two in the house, but you will go out of your mind. Your work has to be done by someone, and it won't happen while you're playing Candyland, taking Sis to soccer practice, or driving Junior to the orthodontist. The sooner you realize this, the better off you'll be. Hire child care and taxi services. If you want to spend quality or quantity time with your children, be it cheering or chauffeuring, hire an office assistant, cleaning help, and a home shopper. Everyone suffers if you try to do it all.

What happens if you really can't afford to hire a lot of help? Maybe you're just starting out as a freelancer and your career hasn't taken off yet. In this case, you may want to barter work for child care. When my kids were small, for example, I used a lot of teenage babysitters. In exchange for child care, I helped them with their term papers, reports, and later, resumes and cover letters. We worked out an economic arrangement that suited us all.

Or, you may decide to freelance part-time until your children are older. If this is the case, accept only the most lucrative jobs from the most reliable clients. Establishing a solid base will make it easier for you to build up your freelance business later.

Home Alone
Some freelancers are able to work when their children nap. I was lucky this way. I often took my kids out in the morning so we could all exercise. In the afternoons, they slept two to three hours while I worked. (P.S. Nothing tires a kid out faster than swimming!)

Bet You Didn't Know

Being at home isn't all bad. Here's what one freelancer said about her teenagers: "There's just too much that can happen to teens who are home all alone during the summer and after school." When another freelancer moved his photography business into his home, his teenage sons fled to a friend's house. "I wish you were back out," they told their father. "It was so much easier for us to do what we wanted to do when you weren't home."

Homecoming

Your husband is on vacation. *You* think he's going to help you assemble the new shelves for your office; *he* has other ideas. So what does he do for a week? How about continuously pressing the channel changer on the remote until he comes across (a) a sports event of any kind, including Iranian bowling, or (b) *Baywatch*?

Then there's your brother-in-law. He's moved in with you while he "finds himself." Your largest single unsecured debtor, he periodically tells you that you are letting one of your biggest clients take advantage of you and he "wouldn't put up with such crap." Then he pulls a beer from your refrigerator and leaves.

It can be hard to ignore the six loads of laundry, towering weeds, and piles of bottles that need recycling. It can be frustrating when other family members don't pull their weight—or what you consider to be their weight. Then you get the out-and-out freeloaders. Throughout it all, the office shelves still have to be assembled; the dog still has to be walked.

Bet You Didn't Know

One of the advantages of getting older is that the more farsighted we get, the less often we need to dust. And you thought all you had to look forward to was the senior citizen's discount at "Franks a Lot."

Here's my advice, as a freelancer with more than 20 years' experience and a nice marriage of nearly 25 years' duration:

➤ Ignore the mess. Force yourself. Here's your mantra: "I've got work to do." Repeat it three times after me: "I've got work to do. I've got work to do. I've got work to do." The chores will be there tomorrow. I promise.

➤ Can't ignore it? Hire household help. It is well worth the outlay, especially when you're getting your freelance business started. You can't do it all. Even if you can, why would you want to?

➤ Count on yourself, not your family, to get your home in order. Yes, we're all in this together, we can make plenty of charts, we can have family powwows, and yadda-yadda-yadda, but you'll likely be wasting more time with all the negotiations than you'll gain.

Your husband, children, and shiftless brother-in-law all have their own lives. If they want to clean the bathroom grout with a toothbrush, they will. If they don't notice the mold but it's making your blood pressure rise faster than the Concorde, it's your problem—not theirs. Let it go, hire help, or do it yourself.

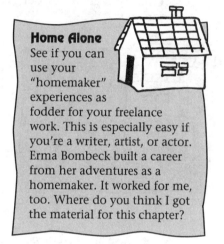

Home Alone
See if you can use your "homemaker" experiences as fodder for your freelance work. This is especially easy if you're a writer, artist, or actor. Erma Bombeck built a career from her adventures as a homemaker. It worked for me, too. Where do you think I got the material for this chapter?

Me, Myself, and I

Okay, so now I've cut you off from your friends, relatives, and neighbors. This leaves you with solitude and loneliness. I won't even let you scour the sink, rake leaves, or fix the plug in the CD player. How can you feel less lonely?

Here are some suggestions to help you combat loneliness:

➤ Be good to yourself. You deserve little treats and rewards for work well done. At the end of a project, see a movie, a show, or a concert. If the project was a whopper that paid big bucks, see Greece, Bora-Bora, or Paris.

➤ Get out every day. Even if it's a brief walk to the post office, get up and moving.

➤ Bundle errands and do them all together. That way, you're getting out, but you're still getting something done so you don't have to suffer from guilt pangs.

➤ Set up a support system of freelancers who live close by. If you don't know any such freelancers, run an ad and start your own local freelance organization. It's also a great way to network.

➤ Every once and a while, change your work routine to give yourself a break.

Be my little ray of sunshine. Keep a positive outlook and dump the self-pity. Remember that even freelancers who have a lot of outside contact can experience loneliness. You chose this life, and it is a good one.

Buns of Steel

It's a truth universally acknowledged: You get the most work done when you apply the seat of your pants to the seat of the chair. Unfortunately, sitting in one place for hours at a time isn't good for your overall health. Exercise is a great way to combat loneliness and boredom.

Home Alone
There are an amazing number of exercise shows on television. Pick one you like and shake your booty. It's easy, fun, and free.

Freelancers tend to be a sedentary lot (unless they're freelance personal trainers, of course). Make it your business to move your bones on a regular basis. Stretching your arms, wiggling your toes, and blinking do not count, you cheater. I'm talking some serious sweating. You'll feel better, look better, work better, and live longer. Here are some ideas:

➤ Take a daily walk, run, or jog. I take a walk every day with a delightful, supportive friend. She lets me vent my frustrations—while I race-walk 2–5 miles.

➤ Enroll in a fitness club. And then attend on a regular basis (It can also be a great place to network!)

➤ Take an exercise class at the local university or community college.

➤ Join a local team. My community has an "Over-the-Hill" baseball league for men age 40 and over. See what your town offers.

➤ Buy an exercise bike or a treadmill. Use it while you read the mail or newspaper or catch up on magazines.

Go With the Flow

Another big problem freelancers face is regulating the work and cash flow. One month you're swimming in jobs and don't have time to exhale; the next month you have time to watch reruns of *Gilligan's Island*, alphabetize your canned goods, and clean the lint from your navel.

As a result, your cash flow is equally erratic. In June you might get a check for $5,000— but it has to last for three months until the next client gets around to paying you. In the past few years this problem has gotten worse as corporations downsize. This uneven work and cash flow makes it especially hard to manage your personal and freelance life.

Even if you do manage to keep a good supply of the green stuff coming in, you can still run into problems. Here's an example. Freelance writer/editor Nancy Stevenson had a difficult time buying a house because of the uncertainty of the freelance life, although she makes an impressive income. Here's her story:

> I bought a house after having freelanced for a year; I had to put down 20 percent and give the bank tax returns, letters from clients, and so on to get a mortgage. It got to the point where I was sure they were going to ask me to spin straw into gold. As a freelancer I continued to have difficulty getting loans and credit, even after several years when I had a solid track record of income.

Experienced freelancers have found that there are three reliable ways to keep the work and cash flow steady. These three methods are:

1. Look for work even as you are working.

2. Do temporary work.

3. Have a part-time job.

Let's look at each method in detail to see its advantages and disadvantages for you.

Strategy 1: Doing the Hustle

To keep yourself solvent, always try to have a lot of work coming in. That means working on *getting* work even while you're *doing* work. Try these ideas:

Mind Your Own Business
Beware of companies that shift their payment schedule, even in midstream. It's not uncommon for a major corporation that used to pay every 30 days to begin paying every 60 or even 90 days.

Mind Your Own Business
One of the latest gimmicks? Some companies will only issue and sign a contract *after* the work has been completed. This gives the company months and months extra to hold the payment. Since you are working without a contract, you don't have any protection if the job goes sour.

➤ Take a few minutes once or twice a week to call clients and see what projects they're looking for now and in the immediate future. Then follow up immediately, even if it means taking a brief break from your current work.

➤ Continually develop proposals and submit them to likely clients.

➤ As you work on your current project, see whether you can recycle it into more work.

➤ Think about ways to rework former projects as new work as well.

➤ Keep your ear to the ground. Network by attending professional conferences and meetings.

Strategy 2: Temp Time

Mind Your Own Business

Reusing something is the freelancer's equivalent of hitting the lottery. Just be very careful that you don't violate the terms of any contract you have signed. Often, you can't produce anything for a set length of time (often one to three years) that will compete with the former project.

So what happens if you can't find freelance work for a few weeks or even months? Perhaps it's summer and all the beautiful employers are in the Hamptons soaking up the sun. Maybe there's been a merger in your field and everyone is sitting tight for a few months until the dust settles. Perhaps you have a firm promise for a job but the project is still under development. In the meantime, you still have to eat.

Many freelancers temp for a time. According to the National Association of Temporary and Staffing Services, professional temps (freelancers who turn to temping during dry spells) now collect 20 percent of the $7.6 billion industry payroll.

If you're lucky enough to have office and computing skills, you can very likely earn enough money to tide you over during downtimes by temping. A temp with excellent office skills can earn as much as $40 an hour at a Fortune 500 company. If your skills are marginal, however, your rates will be adjusted accordingly.

Home Alone

Many freelancers select a temp agency on the basis of the benefits it offers. Affordable group health insurance is often at the top of the list. You may want to put it on the top of *your* list as well.

In addition, the larger temp agencies offer a number of big-company advantages. Here are a few of the most important:

➤ You might be able to get free training in a skill you need, such as computers. This training can help you enhance your freelance career.

➤ Many large temp agencies allow employees to purchase health insurance at group rates. This can save you some serious bucks.

➤ Temp work tends to be steady. Having a good relationship with one or more temp agencies can tide you over the rough spots as you establish a freelance career.

➤ Working as a temp can give you the inside track to assignments in your freelance field. Even if it doesn't, you may still make valuable contacts through your temp work.

Strategy 3: Part and Parcel

In many ways, finding a part-time job gives you the best of all possible worlds: You have a steady paycheck and you have time to set up your freelance career and get it flying. But remember that you are looking for a paycheck, not a second career, so look for part-time jobs that leave you plenty of time to work on your *real* job—freelancing. Possible part-time jobs include working as a bookkeeper, furniture mover, chauffeur, or waitress, for example.

Part-time jobs don't have to be as predictable as the ones I listed above. You might have a steady gig as a baby-sitter, car parker, or dog walker, for instance. During the holidays, you can get part-time work as a store Santa or gift wrapper. Just be sure that the job doesn't wipe you out and make you unable to devote sufficient time to freelancing.

Getting the Credit You Deserve

Conservative bankers are a fact of life. As a result, freelancers often have more difficulty establishing credit than staffers who earn the same amount of money. Getting credit can be a real problem, as you learned from Nancy's story earlier in the chapter. What can you do? Here are some ideas:

➤ Pitch while you're rich. You sound and feel more confident and successful when you're busy. This applies to credit as well as work. When things are going well, you'll be a tougher negotiator with bankers as well as clients.

➤ Keep the money coming in, even if it's from temp jobs. Paychecks from any source can help you get the credit you need to keep your business afloat.

The Least You Need to Know

➤ It is possible to balance work and family. Be realistic, hire help, and learn to let go.

➤ One is the loneliest number. Remember to take care of yourself. Find a support group, and don't forget to exercise.

➤ Pitch while you're rich. To keep the work and cash flow steady, look for work even as you are working.

➤ In a pinch, do temporary work or take a part-time job.

Part 6
Economics 101

G.K. Chesterton and several other famous writers were asked what one book they would take with them if they were stranded on a desert island. "The Complete Works of Shakespeare," answered one writer. "I'd choose the Bible, instead," said another writer. Then Chesterton was asked what book he would select. "I would choose," replied the famous English man of letters, "Thomas's Guide to Practical Ship-building."

You're a sensible person. You never play "fetch" with a pit bull and you always wait two hours after a meal to go swimming. You lather, rinse, repeat. I'll bet you even floss. You know that you have to take care of yourself, especially where economic matters are concerned. In the following three chapters, you'll learn how to cope with the freelancer's financial facts of life: taxes, insurance, and retirement planning.

Cry Uncle: Taxes

In This Chapter

➤ Learn why it's important to clearly define your freelance status

➤ See how your business structure can affect your taxation rate

➤ Explore the marvelous world of deductions, including the fabled home office deduction

➤ Be sure to plan ahead

Have you seen the new freelancer's tax form? If not, here it is:

EZ Tax R Us

1. How much money did you make last year?...>_____

2. Send it in...>_____

3. If you have any questions or comments, please write them on the provided line ....>_____

There are only two sure things in life: death and taxes. There's not a whole lot I can do about the former (other than warning you against swimming after a big meal and playing catch with a pit bull), but I *can* help you cope with the freelancer's key financial fact of life: taxes. That's what you'll learn about in this chapter.

P.S. You really don't have to pay *all* your money in taxes. It just seems that way.

A Horse Is a Horse, of Course, of Course

The IRS doesn't much like freelancers because we make extra work for the bean counters. That's okay, because we really don't like *them* much, either, but in this situation the IRS has the muscle and we rarely do. That's why it's crucial to make sure that you meet their definition of a freelancer. Otherwise, you could be paying a lot more in taxes than you have to. You might be setting yourself up for an audit, to boot.

To be considered a freelancer by the IRS, you must meet the following two criteria:

1. You're in charge of your workday. You set your own schedule.

2. You use your own equipment and tools.

Oooo, Wilbur

Sounds easy, no? Ha! First off, more than a few employers have tried to claim that their staffers are really freelancers. This lets the boss off the hook when it comes to paying Social Security, unemployment, and worker's compensation taxes. Such a scam leaves the employees skewered like well-done shish-ka-bobs. But even the most well-meaning employers and employees can get trapped in a definition nightmare. Here's how. Imagine that you get a big, fat juicy freelance job that will last a year or so. You even get to work in the client's office, using the client's equipment. "Great," you say, "This saves me all the expense of buying equipment and I get some face time in, too." This sounds like a sweet deal, until you realize that the IRS isn't going to take such a chipper view of your work status.

Are you still a freelancer—or have you become an employee? Situations like this have caused the IRS to clamp down on freelancers. Freelancers must use their own equipment or tools and establish their own work hours to maintain their freelance status. This isn't the case when you're working on-site. In this instance, you're using the corporation's equipment and following their schedule. For example, if you're an editor, you can't work from midnight to 6 AM; you have to follow the company's 9–5 schedule.

Mind Your Own Business

Some companies hire on-site freelancers as a way to evade paying benefits and taxes. The IRS is wise to this scam. Now you are too. If you want to maintain your freelancer status, be very careful if you accept an in-house position.

Even if you've been nice rather than naughty, filing as a freelancer sets the red fla[g]
at the IRS home office. What can you do to cover your behind? Here are my top six

1. If you decide to file as a freelancer, play by the rules. Make sure you really *are* a freelancer.

2. Keep scrupulous financial records; hire a book-keeper or accountant if necessary.

3. Base your career in a home office. More on that later in this chapter.

4. Will Rogers claimed that income tax has made more liars out of the American people than golf. Take only legitimate deductions. Don't fudge.

5. Prepare your tax return correctly. If necessary, hire an accountant to do it.

6. Keep up-to-date on the tax laws. After all, it's *your* money.

Home Alone
IRS-phobic? Join the club… and hire an accountant to set up your books, prepare your taxes, and come with you if (God forbid) you get audited. Look for someone who specializes in a free-lancer's tax needs.

You Can Run but You Can't Hide

My husband has a degree in accounting, although that's not his career. As an executive in the publishing/entertainment industry, he works with a great many freelancers. Every year or so, he lives through the following scene. It usually takes place in a secluded corner of the office very late in the day. Here's how it goes:

Bonehead Freelancer: "Uh, could I talk to you in private?"

Beloved Hubby: "This is as private as it gets, unless you crawl into my pocket."

Bonehead Freelancer: "Uh, I have a problem. A bad one."

Beloved Hubby: "So give already, I want to make my train. Dinner's waiting." (Hubby is very compassionate with boneheaded freelancers.)

Bonehead Freelancer: "Uh, I hear you have a degree in accounting."

Beloved Hubby (looks at watch, taps his foot, snorts): "Yeah. So?"

Bonehead Freelancer: "I haven't paid my taxes in five years. What should I do?"

Beloved Hubby (as he runs for the door): "Get an accountant. Right now. And pay as much as you can as soon as you can. Like yesterday."

It *is* tempting to evade the whole tax thing. After all, the government does seem to have a lot of money, that pesky national debt aside. Why should Big Brother hit *you* up for your tithe? You're small potatoes in the grand scheme of things.

. That's the way the system works. We all fork over our share, no
we have to pay it when it's due. I'm not going to launch into a
nerica" (even though I *do* think this is the greatest country in the
e we are getting what we pay for. So whatever you do, pay your
ime.

..2?

~p asking my husband the Tax Maven how we can slash my tax bill. He always has
the same answer, "Make less and we'll pay less." As a freelancer, you want to be a success.
Being a success means making a profit. If you make a profit, Uncle wants his share—that's
where *income taxes* come in.

But that's not the end of the story, sorry to say. Depending on the type of freelance
business you run, you may also be faced with *sales tax* to collect and pay to the state (if
you live in a state that has a sales tax—not all do). If someone works for you,
you're getting into the wonderful world of *payroll taxes*
to collect and pay to the feds. There are other taxes, too,
which is why you'll supplement this overview with help
from an accountant or tax preparer who knows the
freelancer's needs.

Home Alone
You may wish
to access Nest
Egg IRS Tax
Information Center at
*nestegg.iddis.com/nestegg/
articles/taxctr.html*. This
Cyberspace site contains
articles on small business
taxes and IRS forms.

Further, all businesses are not taxed the same. How you
organize your business—sole proprietorship, partnership, corporation—affects your tax rate. It determines
which tax return you file, what tax rate you'll pay on
profits, and how the payments are treated. Here's an
overview of the tax structure for the three main ways
that freelancers can legally organize their business.

One Hand Clapping: Sole Proprietorships

As you learned in Chapter 14, if you freelance on your own and you don't incorporate,
the IRS considers you a sole proprietor. As far as Uncle Sam is concerned, you and the
business are one and the same. Here's how the tax game works in this instance:

➤ Report all your business income and expenses on your individual income tax return.

➤ Explain all your business income and expenses on a Schedule C or Schedule C-EZ
(the easy version, get it? It's the IRS version of a joke).

The first thing the IRS gives you when you open your business as a sole proprietor is a
slap in the face: 15.3 percent in Social Security and Medicare taxes. As an employee you

pay only half that—your employer coughs up the other half. On your own, you have to cough it all up.

The IRS does cut you a little slack, however. You only have to levy that 15.3 percent against 92.35 percent of your earnings, and you can take half of the tax amount as an adjustment on your personal return. But the bottom line is that an employee earning $50,000 a year would pay $3,825 in Social Security and Medicare taxes, while a sole proprietor with the same income would pay $6,076.

Mind Your Own Business

If you have no employees and business expenses of $2,500 or less, you may be able to file the simplified schedule called Schedule C-EZ.

Bet You Didn't Know

Be sure to claim all of your legitimate expenses, which can substantially reduce your tax gouge. For example, if you have $50,000 worth of income, your tax rate is 43.3 percent (15.3 percent in Social Security taxes plus 28 percent in income taxes). Each dollar of expenses saves you 43.3 cents.

Me and My Shadow: Partnerships

In many ways, a partnership is the same as a sole proprietorship as far as Uncle Sam is concerned. Each partner's share of the businesses' profit or loss is described on a form called Schedule K-1, part of form 1065. Since each partner reports his or her share of income separately, each partner is taxed at his or her rate.

For example, let's say that you and your buddy Siegfried form a partnership to sell underwater fire prevention kits. The first year, you make a profit of $60,000. (Underwater fire prevention is clearly a growth field.) You and Ziggy split the profit equally. Suppose you're in the 15 percent tax bracket. Now suppose that Ziggy has a sweet trust fund, a working wife, and a fat stock portfolio, so he's in the 31 percent tax bracket. Even though you both made the same amount of profit, Ziggy will be paying more than twice the tax rate on his share. Tough luck, Ziggy.

Bet You Didn't Know

The IRS rarely audits partnerships. If they do, they may audit both partners or only one.

Highway Robbery: Corporations

If you're incorporated, the whole tax scene changes. First of all, a corporation has its own tax, the "corporate income tax," whose rates are different from individual levies. Corporate tax rates currently run from 15 percent to 35 percent. Further, the corporation files its own return, Form 1120, while you file your own personal return.

Bet You Didn't Know

Doctors, lawyers, and consultants who have incorporated (so-called "personal service corporations") are socked at a flat rate of 35 percent. They can't use the graduated income tax rates, no matter how much profit they have.

The big deal here is the double whammy, a legalized form of highway robbery: double taxation. Income the corporation earns that isn't taken as salary is taxed as dividends. They're taxed twice: once when the corporation earns them and again when you earn them.

The S corporation is a variation on incorporation that changes your tax status. The IRS treats an S corporation more like a partnership, passing the corporation's income through its owners and taxing them directly. See your tax preparer to determine if this might be the right structure for your freelance business.

My advice? Keep things simple. Many freelancers rush to incorporate. In most cases, however, you're better off operating as a sole proprietorship filing a Schedule C. Using a corporation usually adds $500 to $2,500 a year in accountants' fees alone, not to mention state charter fees and minimum corporate taxes.

There Is Some Justice in the World: Deductions

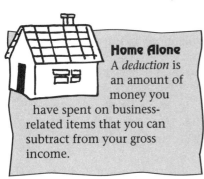

Home Alone
A *deduction* is an amount of money you have spent on business-related items that you can subtract from your gross income.

All is not lost, however, because you get *deductions*.

A *deduction* is an amount of money you have spent on business-related items that you can subtract from your gross income. Deductions are therefore very good things because they enable you to reduce your tax bite.

All business-related deductions are declared on a tax form called a Schedule C (Profit or Loss in a Business or Profession). This is filed along with the standard 1040 tax form that all taxpayers use.

Something for Nothing?

Some freelancers overpay their taxes because they are not aware of all the tions. Rozakis to your rescue! Here are some legitimate deductions freela

- ➤ Office rent or mortgage
- ➤ Real-estate taxes
- ➤ Insurance
- ➤ Commissions and fees
- ➤ Business entertainment
- ➤ Gifts and cards to clients
- ➤ Health insurance
- ➤ Work-related publications
- ➤ Office supplies
- ➤ Office furniture
- ➤ Repair service
- ➤ Equipment depreciation
- ➤ Retirement plans
- ➤ Accounting services
- ➤ Legal services
- ➤ Postage

- ➤ Office utilities
- ➤ Cleaning services
- ➤ Membership dues
- ➤ Education expenses
- ➤ Public relations
- ➤ Business travel
- ➤ License fees
- ➤ State sales tax
- ➤ Printing and copying
- ➤ Office equipment
- ➤ Tools needed for job
- ➤ Bank charges
- ➤ Financial planning
- ➤ Bank interest
- ➤ Moving expenses
- ➤ Transportation

News flash: Big Brother doesn't completely trust you. (I know, it's shocking but true.) As a result, business deductions are deductions only if you have the proof to support your case. If you can't cough up the receipt, you may have to cough up back taxes and a penalty.

Technically speaking, you don't need a receipt for a cash payment under $10. This could occur when you take a subway, bus, or cab to visit a client, for example. However, you must still document the expense in a log (or spreadsheet). You learned how to do this in Chapter 15.

Home Alone
For a complete rundown of freelance deductions you may not know about, call or write to the IRS for a free copy of their brochure, "Tax Guide for Small Businesses," #334. The telephone number is 800-829-1040.

The famous Schedule C. A thing of beauty, no?

SCHEDULE C (Form 1040) Department of the Treasury Internal Revenue Service (99)	**Profit or Loss From Business** (Sole Proprietorship) ▶ Partnerships, joint ventures, etc., must file Form 1065. ▶ Attach to Form 1040 or Form 1041. ▶ See Instructions for Schedule C (Form 1040).	OMB No. 1545-0074 19**97** Attachment Sequence No. **09**

Name of proprietor | Social security number (SSN)

A | Principal business or profession, including product or service (see page C-1) | B Enter principal business code
(see page C-6) ▶

C | Business name. If no separate business name, leave blank. | D Employer ID number (EIN), if any

E | Business address (including suite or room no.) ▶ ....
City, town or post office, state, and ZIP code

F | Accounting method: (1) ☐ Cash (2) ☐ Accrual (3) ☐ Other (specify) ▶ ....
G | Did you "materially participate" in the operation of this business during 1997? If "No," see page C-2 for limit on losses. ☐ Yes ☐ No
H | If you started or acquired this business during 1997, check here . . . . ▶ ☐

Part I Income

1	Gross receipts or sales. **Caution:** *If this income was reported to you on Form W-2 and the "Statutory employee" box on that form was checked, see page C-2 and check here* . . . . ▶ ☐	1	
2	Returns and allowances	2	
3	Subtract line 2 from line 1	3	
4	Cost of goods sold (from line 42 on page 2)	4	
5	**Gross profit.** Subtract line 4 from line 3	5	
6	Other income, including Federal and state gasoline or fuel tax credit or refund (see page C-2) . . .	6	
7	**Gross income.** Add lines 5 and 6 . . . . ▶	7	

Part II Expenses. Enter expenses for business use of your home **only** on line 30.

8	Advertising	8		19	Pension and profit-sharing plans	19	
9	Bad debts from sales or services (see page C-3) . .	9		20	Rent or lease (see page C-4): a Vehicles, machinery, and equipment .	20a	
10	Car and truck expenses (see page C-3)	10		b Other business property . .	20b	
11	Commissions and fees . .	11		21	Repairs and maintenance . .	21	
12	Depletion	12		22	Supplies (not included in Part III) .	22	
13	Depreciation and section 179 expense deduction (not included in Part III) (see page C-3) . .	13		23	Taxes and licenses	23	
				24	Travel, meals, and entertainment: a Travel	24a	
14	Employee benefit programs (other than on line 19) . . .	14		b Meals and entertainment . c Enter 50% of line 24b subject to limitations (see page C-4) .		
15	Insurance (other than health) .	15				
16	Interest: a Mortgage (paid to banks, etc.) .	16a		d Subtract line 24c from line 24b .	24d	
	b Other	16b		25	Utilities	25	
17	Legal and professional services	17		26	Wages (less employment credits) .	26	
18	Office expense	18		27	Other expenses (from line 48 on page 2)	27	

28	**Total expenses** before expenses for business use of home. Add lines 8 through 27 in columns . . ▶	28	
29	Tentative profit (loss). Subtract line 28 from line 7	29	
30	Expenses for business use of your home. Attach **Form 8829**	30	
31	**Net profit or (loss).** Subtract line 30 from line 29. ● If a profit, enter on **Form 1040, line 12,** and ALSO on **Schedule SE, line 2** (statutory employees, see page C-5). Estates and trusts, enter on Form 1041, line 3. ● If a loss, you MUST go on to line 32.	31	
32	If you have a loss, check the box that describes your investment in this activity (see page C-5). ● If you checked 32a, enter the loss on **Form 1040, line 12,** and ALSO on **Schedule SE, line 2** (statutory employees, see page C-5). Estates and trusts, enter on Form 1041, line 3. ● If you checked 32b, you MUST attach **Form 6198.**	32a ☐ All investment is at risk. 32b ☐ Some investment is not at risk.

For Paperwork Reduction Act Notice, see Form 1040 instructions. | Cat. No. 11334P | Schedule C (Form 1040) 1997

Schedule C (Form 1040) 1997

Part III   **Cost of Goods Sold** (see page C-5)   Page **2**

33   Method(s) used to value closing inventory: **a** ☐ Cost   **b** ☐ Lower of cost or market   **c** ☐ Other (attach explanation)

34   Was there any change in determining quantities, costs, or valuations between opening and closing inventory? If "Yes," attach explanation . . . . ☐ Yes   ☐ No

35 Inventory at beginning of year. If different from last year's closing inventory, attach explanation . . .	**35**	
36 Purchases less cost of items withdrawn for personal use	**36**	
37 Cost of labor. Do not include salary paid to yourself	**37**	
38 Materials and supplies	**38**	
39 Other costs	**39**	
40 Add lines 35 through 39	**40**	
41 Inventory at end of year	**41**	
42 **Cost of goods sold.** Subtract line 41 from line 40. Enter the result here and on page 1, line 4 . .	**42**	

Part IV   **Information on Your Vehicle.** Complete this part **ONLY** if you are claiming car or truck expenses on line 10 and are not required to file Form 4562 for this business. See the instructions for line 13 on page C-3 to find out if you must file.

43   When did you place your vehicle in service for business purposes? (month, day, year) ▶ . . . . . . / . . . . . . / . . . .

44   Of the total number of miles you drove your vehicle during 1997, enter the number of miles you used your vehicle for:

a Business . . . .   **b** Commuting . . . .   **c** Other . . . .

45   Do you (or your spouse) have another vehicle available for personal use? . . . . ☐ Yes   ☐ No

46   Was your vehicle available for use during off-duty hours? . . . . ☐ Yes   ☐ No

47a   Do you have evidence to support your deduction? . . . . ☐ Yes   ☐ No

   b If "Yes," is the evidence written? . . . . ☐ Yes   ☐ No

Part V   **Other Expenses.** List below business expenses not included on lines 8–26 or line 30.

. . . .		
. . . .		
. . . .		
. . . .		
. . . .		
. . . .		
. . . .		
. . . .		
. . . .		
48 **Total other expenses.** Enter here and on page 1, line 27	**48**	

⊛

here the Deduction Is

:-office deduction is a wonderful thing, but be careful. To qualify as a home
tax purposes, your space has to meet two tough tests. The space must be:

1. sed "exclusively and regularly" for business

2. Your principal place of business

I'm not being funny here; the IRS is as ruthless as Sherman marching through Georgia
when it comes to home-office deductions. For example, you can't deduct the kitchen just
because your desk is in the corner. You can't deduct the bedroom if you've installed a
computer, file cabinet, and office chair—it's still the room set aside for sleeping.

However, the tax code changes more often than Madonna's hair style. The newest twist?
After 1998, home offices will be deductible under more generous rules. With this change,
a home office will qualify as the principal place of business if it is used exclusively and
regularly by the taxpayer to conduct administrative or management activities—and if
there is no other fixed location where he or she conducts substantial administrative and
management activities of the business.

At one time, the IRS actually required freelancers to have a separate room for business.
They have since backed down on that one, but like a dog that's smelled a T-bone, the IRS
is hot on our trail. Be very careful here. IRS agents live for busting freelancers on home-
office deductions. If you're not sure if your space qualifies, talk to a pro.

But if you *do* meet the two requirements, the percentage of household expenses you may
deduct equals the percentage of your living space that you use as an office. For instance, if
you use 150 square feet of a 1,500 square foot house, you can deduct 10 percent of most
expenses. Here are some deductions you can take with a home office:

➤ Mortgage interest

➤ Casualty and theft losses

➤ Rent

➤ Insurance

➤ Security systems

➤ Cleaning

➤ Real estate taxes

➤ Depreciation

➤ Utilities

➤ General home repairs

➤ Snow removal

You can't use a home office to create a tax loss. You may only take deductions up to the
amount of profit your business in the space makes. But know that people who take a
home-office deduction are audited at a higher rate than people who don't.

Nothing for Something

Before you start turning cartwheels and shouting, "Whoopee! Deductions!" remember that how much a deduction is really worth depends on the tax bracket you're in. For example, if you're in the 31 percent bracket, for every dollar you spend on your freelance business, you'll only save about one-third in income taxes.

In addition, not all expenses are fully deductible. The IRS just chopped the entertainment deduction, for instance. Travel and entertainment (known in the trade as "T&E") are a dicey point for the IRS. They don't cut us much slack when it comes to networking. Here are some more recent sacrifices:

Expense	Restriction
Gifts	$25 each
Entertainment	Half of cost
Country club dues	Not deductible
Foreign conventions	Only if directly related to your business and a logical place to hold a convention in your field
Spouse travel	No dice—unless your spouse is your employee

Child Labor

Under certain circumstances, your children can each earn up to $4,000 from your business tax-free. (And you thought they were good-for-nothing louts.) When you claim your child as a dependent on your tax return, the IRS limits the standard deduction on your child's tax return to $650 or the child's earned income up to $4,000, whichever is greater. Earned income above that is taxed at your child's rate regardless of age. Here are two more advantages of child labor:

> **Take My Word For It**
> *Earned income* is money you get in a paycheck. *Interest income* is money earned as interest on a bank account or other investment.

1. You can save on Social Security by hiring your tykes. If you're a sole proprietor, the wages you pay to your children under the age of 19 are exempt from Social Security taxes. This makes the effective cost of employing your child less than that of a nonfamily member.

2. Kids can save tax-free. Your child can start a tax-deductible Individual Retirement Account (IRA). Under current rules, your child may deposit the lesser of $2,000 or 100 percent of earnings into an IRA and deduct the full amount. Combining the

$2,000 IRA contribution with the $4,000 standard deduction means that your child can earn up to $6,000 per year without paying federal income tax. Keep in mind, however, that an IRA is a long-term investment and your child will face nasty penalties if the funds are withdrawn before the child is 59 ½ years old.

Don't get any bright ideas here. Unless you want to lose your bacon to Uncle Sam, your children must be performing legitimate work at a pay level comparable to what you would be paying a person from outside the family. For example, don't hire your child to answer the telephone at $100 an hour if you would pay an outside worker $10 an hour for the same service. The IRS looks at these deductions more closely than a former ingenue scrutinizes her wrinkles.

Fork It Over Early and Often: Estimated Payments

The IRS collects from freelancers quarterly, not in one lump sum. "How can I possibly know what I'm going to earn?" you protest. You can't. That's why the IRS invented *estimated tax payments*. These guys think of *everything*.

Here's what one freelancer said about making estimated payments:

> *Obviously making estimated tax payments is important, but it can be especially tricky given the fluctuating nature of freelance income. My first year as a freelancer I made $75,000 and made appropriate estimated tax payments; the second year I made about $115,000 and owed about $9,000 in taxes above and beyond what I'd paid in. This year I'm just not going to work as hard and pay less in taxes! It's good advice to monitor what you're making for the year and up your estimates accordingly. I had no idea until tax time how much I'd made—I just knew I was exhausted. This year I'm keeping a running tally.*

To figure out what you have to pay, estimate your tax bill for the whole year and divide by four. Then make four equal payments on this schedule:

➤ April 15   ➤ June 15
➤ September 15   ➤ January 15

On April 15, you calculate how much you really made and adjust your payment accordingly. If you paid too much during the year, you gave the IRS a break they didn't deserve. If you paid too little, they can give you a stiff penalty (that we know *you* don't deserve).

More on that stiff penalty for underpayment. It's based on the amount you *should* have paid versus what you actually *did* pay. If your income isn't even during the year, you can base your estimated payments on when you receive the money. However, you must keep very accurate records. *Very.*

If you make the big chunk of change in the beginning of the year, you shouldn't have a problem if your income falls off in the second half because you should have paid most of what you need to. However, if you made most of your money in the second half of the year, be prepared to prove it to the IRS. Otherwise, you could get socked good.

Home Alone
The penalty for nonpayment is much less than the penalty for nonfiling. I don't recommend either course of action, but knowledge is power.

Confused? I don't blame you. This is the kind of thing that drives unsuspecting freelancers who used to file form 1040-EZ into the arms of the tax pros. And that's not such a bad place to be. Besides, their fees are deductible.

Grin and Bear It: Audits

Bad news: Most freelancers are sole proprietors. A sole proprietor is six times more likely to be audited than a freelancer who has incorporated.

Good news: Audits are not the end of the world. Worst-case scenario, you'll end up paying a little more. (I won't mention jail. Jail? What jail?)

If you *are* called for an audit and you can justify every one of your deductions, you have nothing to fear but fear itself. The experience probably won't be like a month in the country, but it won't be a root canal, either. If you've fudged a little here and hoodwinked a little there, you haven't been reading that carefully, now have you?

Here are some guidelines to tilt the scales in your favor if the IRS decides to call you in for a little two-step together:

➤ Try to get the audit on your home turf rather than the IRS office. This will make it easier to prove that you really do work at home. Also, you'll be more comfortable.

➤ Make sure you clearly understand what aspects of your return are being audited. Then take only those records and stick to that topic.

➤ Be sure your records are clear and well-organized.

➤ Have your tax preparer there, ready to explain everything.

➤ Be on time.

➤ Play nice. This is no time to cop an attitude.

➤ Don't suck up to the agent, either. You're not best friends.

➤ Answer questions; don't ask them.

➤ Loose lips sink ships. Never volunteer any information.

➤ Be there or be square. If you do nothing else, be sure to show up.

Even if the audit doesn't go your way, all is not lost. First, you can request an appeal by the auditor's superior. If that doesn't work, you can appeal the decision in tax court. Keep in mind that the IRS wins in more than 50 percent of the cases; individuals win only about 8 percent of the time. The rest of the decisions favor both sides.

 **Bet You Didn't Know**

The art of taxation consists in so plucking the goose as to obtain the largest amount of feathers with the least amount of hissing.

Plan Ahead

Okay, you know the drill: You make money, you pay taxes. This is a no-brainer. So how can you lessen the pain? The best way is through financial planning. "Moi?" you yelp. "Not moi!" Everyone has an excuse when it come to avoiding tax planning. Take the following quiz to see where you fit.

Pick the valid excuse:

> _____ 1. I'm too busy to do any of this tax planning stuff.
>
> _____ 2. I can't count at all. I even failed remedial math.
>
> _____ 3. The forms are more complicated than trying to mate porcupines.
>
> _____ 4. I don't have to do that. That's why there are tax planners.
>
> _____ 5. I'm the sensitive, artistic type. I don't do money.

Answer: Bong. They're all dopey. You have no excuse for not doing some basic financial planning to reduce your tax bite, or at least not be astonished when you get snagged.

Here are a handful of painless and super-easy ways to reduce your tax payments as a freelancer.

➤ *Maximize your deductions.* For example, do you want to see Mickey and Minnie? If so, try to combine your vacation at the Magic Kingdom with some legitimate business in Orlando. Then you have a deduction for the amount of time you spent on business.

➤ *Plan purchases.* If you need some new office equipment, buy it during a year when you earned a lot. You'll save more on taxes that way.

➤ *Pay ahead.* Do you need more deductions for a specific fiscal year? Why not pay your January rent in December?

➤ *Defer income.* Did you have a boffo year? If you want to reduce your income toward the end of the year, ask a client to put off paying you until the next year.

Bet You Didn't Know

If you want to defer income, don't put off cashing a check until the next year. The IRS is wise to this dodge. The money will appear on the client's tax forms and your 1099s anyway. And while we're at it, you won't get a 1099 if you earned less than $400 from a company. However, you must still report the income and pay the correct amount of tax on it.

Our tax code is more confusing than programming a VCR, using a cash machine, or raising a teenager. That's why it's important to know what you can and can't do on your own. I strongly recommend that you take a simple tax course (at a local college or through adult education) so you have a general idea of the tax situation. Then hire an accountant to take you through the process for a few years. *Then* you might be ready to try it on your own. But always consult an accountant when the tax code changes so you're up with the latest permutations in the law. I hear the food is lousy in jail.

The Least You Need to Know

➤ Make sure you meet the IRS's definition of a freelancer.

➤ The business structure you select can affect your tax payments in a big way.

➤ Deductions give you a break on the amount you have to pay. Plan ahead so you get the most possible deductions and the best ones, too.

➤ The wages of sin are death, but by the time taxes are taken out, it's just sort of a tired feeling.

Chapter 22

Plain Talk About Protecting Yourself: Insurance

In This Chapter

➤ Learn all about health insurance

➤ Don't forget disability and life insurance

➤ Insure your office, too

Novelist John O'Hara's wife divorced him allegedly because she discovered that writers were simply too difficult to live with. She believed they were quirky, moody, and unpredictable. However, soon after the divorce, she fell in love with another writer. When O'Hara read the announcement of his former wife's upcoming wedding, he sent her a telegram that read: "Heartiest congratulations and best wishes." Then he signed it, "Frying Pan."

Best intentions aside, you *can* end up in some hot spots.

Insurance is designed to cushion such trying times. This chapter is designed to help you save your bacon if you end up going from the frying pan into the fire.

An Ounce of Prevention: Health Insurance

To many freelancers, financial security means a good customer base, steady work, and an income that provides the necessities plus a frill or two.

But is that really all that freelancers need?

No, it's not. You're only financially secure if you're providing for your future needs as well as your current ones. That means protecting yourself with the benefits that employed professionals often take for granted: adequate health insurance and a retirement savings plan. Now, let's talk about insurance. We'll deal with planning for retirement in Chapter 23.

I'm not going to pound you over the head with reasons why you must have health insurance. You're a smart cookie; otherwise, you wouldn't have bought this book. Suffice it to say that my last routine physical examination would have cost me over $500 if I didn't have insurance; an exam for a false-alarm heart murmur ran $1,000. And I wasn't even sick in either case. I can't imagine what it costs to get sick. That's why I have health insurance; so I don't even have to think about it. And that's why you're going to make sure that you have health insurance, and good health insurance at that.

The Bad News

Going solo can wreck you. What most freelancers cruising the aisles of the office superstore don't realize is that some of the biggest—and most ruinous—sinkholes involve their insurance situation. You lose a bundle when you kiss your W-2 bye-bye. Don't scoff.

All those employee benefits you rarely thought about are worth about 40 percent of your salary, according to a study by Hewitt Associates, a benefits consultant firm in Lincolnshire, Illinois. You must earn more than 140 percent of your former salary to buy these benefits on your own. That's because as an individual you won't get as good a deal as your former company did. This is one place that freelancers get creamed. When it comes to buying insurance, you are penalized for working for yourself.

 **Bet You Didn't Know**

Mark Twain once said, "The only way to keep your health is to eat what you don't want, drink what you don't like, and do what you'd rather not."

The Worse News

For many freelancers, health insurance is a pitfall of epic proportions. Many freelancers end up pulling their hair out trying to get individual coverage. Choices are limited and the waiting period before pre-existing conditions are covered typically stretches to a year.

The second battle is finding good insurance at a decent price. One freelancer I know switched health plans three times last year because the premiums crept up faster than kudzu.

Finally, Some Good News

Everyone can get health insurance. You may have to pay through the nose for it, but you can get it. No one has to be a wallflower at *this* party.

Health insurance providers fall into two groups:

> **Mind Your Own Business**
> Keep up with the latest insurance legislation. In this field, the scores can *really* change.
> IS THAT CLEAR?

➤ *Fee-for-service.* This is the most common system, in which the health care provider (usually a doctor) treats you and bills you. In most cases, you can select your own doctor. Preventative care is generally not covered.

➤ *Managed care.* This includes the HMOs (Health Maintenance Organizations), PPOs (Preferred Provider Organizations), and POSs (Point of Service) plans. In managed care, health care providers treat patients through a specific plan.

With a managed care policy, your freedom of choice is restricted, but your costs are generally lower. Further, preventative care is often covered and you usually have less paperwork to deal with.

Some health insurance providers offer mixed plans, which let you go outside the plan's list of approved health care providers. Of course, you shell out more for this privilege, but you might be much happier with the care you receive.

Bet You Didn't Know

oH!

In eleven states (Alabama, Maryland, Massachusetts, Michigan, New Hampshire, New Jersey, New York, Pennsylvania, Rhode Island, Vermont, and Virginia) and the District of Columbia, the local Blue Cross and Blue Shield organization is the insurer of last resort. This means they have to accept your application for health insurance no matter what your health status might be. The good news? You will have health insurance. The bad news? The rates may be the same as or higher than a private insurance company. Further, BC/BS may be able to legally restrict coverage for any pre-existing condition.

Better Safe Than Sorry

As a freelancer, you can get your own individual health insurance, or you can get it through a group. In most cases, a group policy is less expensive (because the risk is spread over more people).

It is likely to take you several calls to find the health care policy that's right for you. How many calls? Try "more than you want to know." Nonetheless, be persistent. Also, keep in mind that various health services have different names in different areas of the country and the insurance laws are changing even as I type this.

You can get a head start by calling the National Insurance Consumer Hotline at 800-942-4242. The hotline is staffed by licensed insurance agents who will answer your questions, send out brochures, and refer consumer complaints to the correct sources. You can also get local numbers from them.

Here are some things to consider when you shop for insurance:

➤ *Savings in numbers.* In my experience, the best way to get health insurance is to join a group that offers coverage to its members. You can start by comparing plans offered by the Independent Business Alliance (800-450-2422), the National Association for the Self-Employed (800-232-6273), and trade groups to which you belong.

You must maintain your membership in the group to be eligible for its insurance. Be cautious here: Some "associations" are just a flimsy excuse to sell the insurance and the "association" is making a hefty profit on you.

➤ *Go national.* There are several national organizations and government agencies you can contact for information. Here are two:

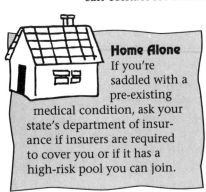

Home Alone
If you're saddled with a pre-existing medical condition, ask your state's department of insurance if insurers are required to cover you or if it has a high-risk pool you can join.

Health Care Financing Administration
6325 Security Boulevard
Baltimore, MD 21207

Group Health Association of America
1129 20th Street NW
Suite 600
Washington, DC 20036-3403

➤ *Sign of the moose.* In addition to various professional groups, different fraternal and religious organizations offer group health insurance to their members.

➤ *Payroll payoff.* If you have a client for whom you do steady work, another option is to ask to be put on their part-time payroll. Many companies offer part-timers a group health plan. Usually you have to work a minimum of 20 hours a week to qualify.

➤ *It's the law!* If you had a full-time job with health insurance before you went freelance, you may wish to keep this insurance from your full-time job through COBRA. By law, you must be able to keep your insurance through your previous employer's plan for 18 months after leaving your job. However, this coverage can be pricey, since you're now footing the entire bill yourself.

➤ *Medicare.* If you're 65 or older or have certain disabilities, you are eligible for Medicare, the federal health insurance program. Many freelancers on Medicare supplement their benefits with additional coverage. Contact your state insurance department or an insurance agent for more information.

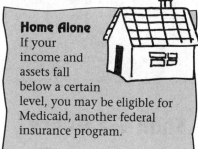

Home Alone
If your income and assets fall below a certain level, you may be eligible for Medicaid, another federal insurance program.

Dollars and Sense

There are three terms you need to know as you shop for health insurance: premium, deductible, and co-payment. The *premium* is the amount you pay each month. The *deductible* is the total amount you must pay each year before the insurance kicks in. The *co-payment* is the amount you pay for each office visit or service after you have satisfied your deductible.

Use the following two guidelines as you're shopping for insurance:

1. In general, the higher your deductible and co-payment, the lower your monthly premium will be.

2. The most cost-effective decision is to take the plan with the highest deductible you can reasonably afford.

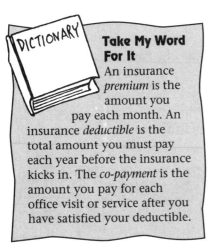

Take My Word For It

An insurance *premium* is the amount you pay each month. An insurance *deductible* is the total amount you must pay each year before the insurance kicks in. The *co-payment* is the amount you pay for each office visit or service after you have satisfied your deductible.

To figure out what deductible you can reasonably afford:

➤ Anticipate your medical needs for the coming year.

➤ Estimate your income.

➤ Factor in the amount you can afford to pay for any unexpected medical problems.

As a freelancer, your financial status can change faster than a movie starlet's bust line. As a result, you should also find out how often the health insurance policies you're considering allow you to change your level or type of coverage. According to the policy, will the insurance be able to double your rates next year? Does the insurer have the right to drop you flat on your face if you make too many claims? Be sure to read the fine print on your policy.

Shall We Dance?

You've done all your legwork and you know your health insurance options. Now it's time to make your choices. Which company are you going to use? Which policy the company offers best suits your health care needs and budget?

Use the following worksheet to help you weigh your options. See how closely your priorities match up with the policy and its provisions.

On the following lines, rank the ten items listed below from most to least important.

Most important	Important	Least important
_____	_____	_____
_____	_____	_____
_____	_____	_____
_____	_____	_____

➤ Cost of the premium

➤ Cost of the deductible

➤ Cost of the co-payment

➤ Ability to choose your own doctors

➤ Ability to choose your own hospitals

➤ Mental health coverage

➤ Restrictions

➤ Security of coverage

➤ Company reputation

➤ Prescription drug plan

Don't Lose Your Head: Disability Insurance

"Winfield goes back to the wall. He hits his head on the wall and it rolls off! It's rolling all the way back to second base! This is a terrible thing for the Padres!"

—Jerry Coleman, Padres radio announcer

Even professional athletes can get injured, though they rarely lose their heads! What does this say about the chances we weekend warriors have of escaping a cut or scrape—not to mention a beheading?

As a result, you should consider *disability insurance,* which provides you with some level of income if you become physically unable to work. Disability insurance is crucial for single freelancers who would have no other source of income if they stopped working. It may also be important for married freelancers or those in other types of relationships, depending on their partner's income.

> **Take My Word For It**
> *Disability insurance* provides you with some level of income if you become physically unable to work.

What about Worker's Compensation or unemployment insurance, you say? As a freelancer, you can't benefit from either of them. A freelancer in Indiana had this to say about the current insurance situation for freelancers in her state:

> As a freelancer, I can't even get disability insurance in my state, though they're working on legislation for it. This means if I get disabled, I'm up a tree. Insurance companies won't give this to you because you have no "regular" income to base the disability amount on.

Fortunately, disability insurance is available to freelancers in most states, and is often much easier to get than health insurance. It usually costs less, too. That's because the cost of replacing someone's income is much more predictable than paying all their medical bills.

The *elimination period*—the period after your illness or injuries occur but before you start to collect benefits—works like a deductible in health insurance. The longer the period, the cheaper the policy.

Mind Your Own Business

Shop carefully for disability insurance. Under some policies, you would have to assume another occupation if you became injured and could no longer perform your previous job. Other policies, however, would pay your disability forever.

In general, rates for disability insurance depend on two factors:

➤ What percentage of your previous income the plan provides when you're disabled

➤ When you start getting paid

When you consider your position on disability insurance, start by figuring out how long you can go without a paycheck and how much income you need to survive. Take into account how much you have saved and what backup (spouse's income, trust fund, wealthy folks, etc.) you can tap.

To find disability insurance, start with an insurance broker who specializes in this kind of coverage. You can also call the Independent Business Alliance and the National Association for the Self-Employed for their plans.

The Game of Life: Life Insurance

If you have dependents who depend on you for financial support, you may also want to buy life insurance. There are two types of policies:

➤ *Term life:* This policy pays your beneficiaries a certain amount upon your death (assuming your premiums are paid up). With term insurance, you are insured only for the *term* of the insurance—hence the name. In other words, if you buy a five-year term policy and don't die within the five years, the insurance company keeps your money. (Hey, but you're still alive.)

➤ *Cash value:* This policy acts as an investment with certain tax advantages as well as paying out when you die (also called *whole life*).

Term insurance is cheaper than cash value insurance, but term is a terrible investment. However, it is a good choice if you know that you're only going to need the coverage for a specific length of time. People with young children often buy term life insurance, for instance. They know they will no longer need the policy when their children are independent (which better be around ages 18–22).

Because rates and plans vary, you need to shop around. See if any organization you belong to offers life insurance to its members. If so, you're apt to get better rates.

And while we're on the topic of insurance, more and more people are purchasing long-term-care insurance. This type of insurance covers the cost of home-based health care or nursing-home care. It may seem a waste of money to a young, fit freelancer, but keep in mind that the premiums don't rise as you get older, so if you start paying when you're 30 years old, you'll pay the same rate when you're 60. Be very careful with this type of insurance, however, since the policies can be very tricky. Shop carefully and deal with a reputable company.

Cataloging: Do You Know What You Own?

Quick—how many books do you have in your office? What is the serial number on your computer? Printer? Fax? Where did you put the three extra printer cartridges, the ones that cost $100 each? Busy freelancers tend to store things in a hurry, often cramming them into closets just before a new project arrives. "Have to clear some floor space," you mutter once a week, and things do go 'a flying.

Every few months you may reassure yourself with a brave, "I'll sort the closet/drawer/shelves in a few weeks," but the weeks stretch into months. By then, you're too afraid to reach into the closet. Lord knows *what's* living there.

Spring Cleaning

Bite the bullet, plunge in, and take the closet test. Even beginning freelancers have often built up an impressive stock of books and supplies. Complete the Office Inventory Worksheet on the following page to start sorting your supplies. Describe each item in as much detail as necessary. Here are some details to include:

➤ Size: height, weight, depth, length

➤ Color

➤ Condition

➤ Brand name

➤ Serial numbers and other identification marks (especially important on office equipment)

➤ Age

➤ Cost

➤ Source (name of store where purchased)

Home Alone
While you're at it, why not take out the guarantees, warranties, and instruction booklets for all your office machines. Then store all this information in one central place.

Take a complete inventory of your office by completing this worksheet. If you need more space, add additional sheets of paper.

Office Inventory Worksheet

Computers (make and model) _____

_____

Printers (make and model) _____

_____

Telephones and answering machines (make and model) _____

_____

Photocopiers (make and model) _____

_____

Radio (make and model) _____

_____

Stereo (make and model) _____

_____

Television (make and model) _____

_____

Software _____

_____

Books (especially expensive reference texts) _____

_____

Supplies _____

_____

Art _____

_____

Furniture _____

_____

You Could Look It Up

Okay, you've spent a weekend figuring out what's in your office. Now it's time to arrange the items in an easy-to-read inventory.

Home Alone Save and attach your sales receipts to this inventory.

Office Inventory

Item	Source	Date of Purchase	Cost	Current Value
1.				
2.				
3.				
4.				
5.				
6.				
7.				
8.				
9.				
10.				
11.				
12.				
13.				
14.				
15.				

What Do You Mean It's Not Covered?

Now that you know what you have, it's time to insure it. Most standard home-owners policies insure home office business equipment for up to $2,500 only. This isn't carte blanche to insure your office up the wazoo, however.

How much insurance do you need? Enough to replace what you've got. It's as simple as that. This brings us to a discussion of replacement value versus actual (or depreciated) value.

➤ With *replacement value,* you are insured for the full cost of replacing the item. For example, if your computer currently sells for $2,000, you get $2,000 to replace it in the event that it is destroyed by some means covered in your policy. (A visiting toddler shoving a Pop Tart into the B drive is usually not covered. Don't ask; it's still a sore point in this house.)

285

➤ With *actual (or depreciated) value,* you get the value of the item minus depreciation. Say you've had your computer two years. The insurance company might calculate the depreciation at $500. The company will then pay you $1,500, not $2,000. That's not enough for you to replace the machine.

I recommend replacement-value coverage. That way, you get to replace your office equipment right away, without having to dip into your own pocket.

Even if you have several policies on your property, you can still collect only the amount of your actual cash loss. All the insurers share the payment proportionally. For example, suppose that you're carrying two policies—one for $20,000 and one for $30,000—on a $40,000 building. Let's say a fire causes damages to the building amounting to $12,000. The $20,000 policy will pay $4,800; the $30,000 policy will pay $7,200.

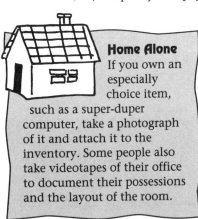

Home Alone

If you own an especially choice item, such as a super-duper computer, take a photograph of it and attach it to the inventory. Some people also take videotapes of their office to document their possessions and the layout of the room.

Further, homeowners' policies usually don't cover you for accidents involving your business, something you'll need if a messenger delivering a business letter trips on a crack in your sidewalk and decides to sue the pants off you. To cover yourself here, you'll need extended liability insurance.

You should also check into a policy endorsement. For a nominal annual cost, a policy endorsement will increase your coverage of business-related property and provide you with a small amount of liability protection. The amount depends on the insurer. If you think you need more insurance, you can buy a separate business owner's policy to cover inventory and other possible losses.

Some freelancers buy their insurance through an insurance broker, who shops around and gets them information on a variety of insurers. This system is common throughout the United States. It saves a lot of time and makes it easy to comparison-shop.

Regardless of the way you buy your insurance, you need it. We all think "It can never happen to me"—but we all know that it can. My sister had a flood of Biblical proportions when an upstairs toilet cracked and flooded the house for seven days while they were away on vacation. The damage topped $100,000. A very close friend had two floods; another just lost her house in a fire. This is not the place to scrimp.

The Least You Need to Know

➤ You must have health insurance. Group insurance usually gives you the most bang for your buck.

➤ You may wish to consider life insurance and disability insurance, too.

➤ Don't forget to insure your office and its contents.

Chapter 23

Caveat Investor

In This Chapter

➤ See why you need a nice, big, fat retirement account

➤ Learn how to get one through Keoghs, IRAs, and different investment vehicles

➤ Start planning for your retirement now!

Ben Franklin once said, "Money begets money and its offspring begets more." To illustrate this point, Franklin left a legacy of $5,000 to the city of Boston, stipulating that the interest from the money must be allowed to accumulate for 100 years. Between 1791 and 1891 the fund grew from $5,000 to almost $400,000. After the first century was up, the city of Boston built a school with part of the money and invested the remaining $92,000. By the middle of the 20th century, the money had grown to just under $1 million. That's not chump change.

Staffers have pensions; freelancers have freedom...but no pension. That's why you've got to sock it away for that rainy day when you'll be an old geezer doing the rumba in Miami Beach. It's never too early to start your retirement fund—even if you're only in your 20s (you kid, you). That's what you're going to learn all about in this chapter.

I'll teach you all about Keoghs, retirement plans tailored just to freelancers, and IRAs, retirement plans that freelancers can use. That way, when we meet in Miami in 30 years, you'll be picking up the tab for the Early Bird Special and driving me around in your shiny Caddy.

Wrinkled but Running

➤ Forty-seven percent of all Americans ages 30–49 say they won't be prepared for retirement.

➤ Half of all households (including baby boomers) have less than $1,000 in net financial assets.

These are not reassuring facts. Different people age at different rates and the variations expand with age. But one thing is sure: Unless you play chicken with tractor-trailers on the interstate, odds are you're going to live longer than you think. In fact, on average, people live 14 years longer today than they did 50 years ago.

This is great when it comes to catching up on late-night television, but it might be a problem money-wise. Everyone knows we have a "problem" with Social Security. Maybe someone will (yawn) fix it, but I'm not holding my breath. In essence, America committed itself to subsidizing the retirement of its older citizens when they were a small proportion of the population, when they didn't live beyond age 65, and when our standard of living was doubling roughly once every 30 years. But things are vastly different today.

America will soon resemble Florida, where nearly 20 percent of the population is over age 65. Further, living standards rise about one-eighth as fast as they did 30 years ago. The generosity of our earlier commitments is thus seriously mismatched with our ability to pay for them.

Nor is that the worst of it. Most Americans pay more in Social Security taxes than they do in income taxes, but contrary to popular belief, these funds are not set aside as a nest age for the future. Instead, they are scooped up to pay for current retirees. There *is* some money left over, but the Treasury uses those funds to pay other federal government expenses. As a result, the U.S. Treasury is sitting on a mountain of IOUs—to the tune of $17 trillion!—that will fall due just when *you're* ready to retire. Ain't life grand?

What does all this mean for you? It means that you'd better have your own retirement plan, because as sure as the sun will come up tomorrow, you can't depend on Social Security to pay for your cookies and milk when you're a happily retired freelancer.

 **Bet You Didn't Know**

A recent survey found that most baby boomers think they are more likely to see a UFO than a check from Social Security—and they may be right.

The Rich Are Made, Not Born

Who are America's typical millionaires? The tycoons you see tickling each other's palms at the races are actually pretty rare. Generally, the typical American millionaire owns a chain of convenience stores, deals in scrap-metal…or is your friendly neighborhood freelancer. Keep reading to find out how the average millionaire can be *you*.

Money Talks, Nobody Walks

Start by taking stock of your financial situation. How can you tell if you're on the track to becoming wealthy? Take out your calculator or fingers and toes and complete the following:

1. Your age _____

2. Your annual income before taxes

   _____

3. Age × annual income _____

4. Divide by 10 _____

5. Double the number _____

This is what your net worth should be *now* to get you on the fast track to a comfortable retirement. For example, if you're 50 years old and you make $50,000 a year, you should have $500,000 in net worth.

If your numbers match these figures, pass go, collect $200, and go on to the next chapter. You've obviously figured it out. If not, read on.

> **Mind Your Own Business**
> Be sure to double-check your numbers as you calculate your net worth. I once told my accountant that I had $90,000 in office-supply deductions. I had misplaced the decimal a bit…to the tune of $89,100. I had really spent $900. Since I'm math-impaired, I had no clue that $89,100 worth of paper clips, pencils, and paper would fill my house, garage, and probably most of the neighborhood.
>
> IS THAT CLEAR?

Ouch! That Smarts!

As you know, freelancers have to be especially savvy about planning for their retirement because they don't have the benefit of employer-sponsored retirement plans. Mistakes count big when you're working without a net. How many of these financial boo-boos do you make?

➤ You deposit your freelance checks in your checking account and forget about them. Your balance earns little or no interest. While your back is turned, inflation gnaws away at your money.

➤ You faithfully sock your money in a passbook savings account. See #1.

➤ You never get around to balancing your checkbook and so rack up hefty fees for rubber checks. This also does a number on your credit rating.

➤ Acting on a tip, you buy 5,000 shares of stock. The tip is good, but you never get around to tracking the stock. As a result, you don't get around to selling until the stock tanks. Bye-bye profit. Hello loss.

➤ You sell your stock at the wrong time and get socked with heavy-duty capital gains.

➤ To stay one step ahead of inflation, you shift your money to a brokerage account. Too pressed to deal with it, you let the broker have his head. Bad move; the broker is a dope.

Starting to see a pattern? Read on to find out how you can become penny- *and* pound-wise. It's not that difficult; I promise!

Daddy Warbucks

You know me well enough by now to know that I'm nothing if not helpful. Most American millionaires are people who learned to live below their means and saved, saved, saved. Here's how you can join their ranks, without eating Gainesburgers or wearing potato sacks. Use the following suggestions to help you achieve a comfortable retirement:

➤ Start saving now. The earlier you begin saving, the more you'll benefit from the magic of compound interest, and the more your savings will grow.

➤ It's never too late to start saving. Put away at least 15 percent of your income every year. Start with 5 percent when you're in your 20s, then move to 10 percent, and finally kick it up as high as you can.

➤ To find the money to sock away, live below your means. Drive that old car awhile longer; take books out of the library rather than buying them. You don't have to be Scrooge, but you don't have to be profligate, either.

➤ Pay your bills on time. This will cut down on late fees.

➤ Beware of ATM fees. These can add up faster than Liz Tayor's ex-husbands.

➤ Pitch the extra plastic. Get one or two cards with low interest rates, low (or no) yearly fees, and good benefits. My Visa card, for example, racks up points that we've used for free trips to Hawaii, Arizona, and Puerto Rico.

 **Bet You Didn't Know**

According to an article in *Newsday*, the average American has eight credit cards. Consider that many people carry a balance from month to month on each one and you can see how easy it is to get in over your head.

➤ Put your money somewhere where it will grow without your having to pay taxes on it immediately. Later in this chapter, I discuss how to do this with Keogh and IRA plans.

➤ Don't overpay your taxes; you'd be astonished how many freelancers do. Review your estimated tax payment schedule.

➤ Try to prepay your mortgage, if you have one. If you can't eat the whole debt (who can?), make one or more extra payments a year. For example, on a $100,000-, 10.5-percent, 30-year mortgage, paying $500 extra a year will save you over $50,000 in interest and knock six years off your mortgage.

➤ Don't prepay bills. Keep your money working for you.

➤ Keep a record of where you've invested your money. There are several excellent and very easy-to-use spreadsheet programs available for this purpose. This makes tracking your investments much easier.

➤ Make a solid financial plan. Check it with financial planners you trust.

➤ Review your plan often and make changes as needed to adjust for changes in your lifestyle.

➤ It's not enough to have a financial plan; you also have to follow it. Invest the amount you allocated; save what you decided you can afford.

➤ Keep up with financial news. Read financial magazines and newspapers. Know what's happening in the world of money.

Now, let's zero in on the Number One way to assure a comfortable retirement: tax-deferred saving. For freelancers, nothing (and I mean nothing) beats putting off the tax bite as long as you can.

Living on Easy Street

Keoghs and IRAs are the best way for freelancers to build a retirement fund. Keoghs are designed specifically for the self-employed; IRAs are available to many people who work and do not have other sources of pension funding.

Keoghs and IRAs are such great retirement plans for freelancers because they offer outrageous tax advantages. Further, setting up a Keogh or IRA is no more difficult than opening a savings account. Here are some more guidelines you should know:

➤ You can invest money in an IRA and Keogh account using almost any method of investing (stocks, bonds, certificates of deposit, etc.) except collectibles and investments made with borrowed funds.

Home Alone
In some cases, you can deduct your Keogh contribution the year before you make it. To take a deduction for 1998, for example, a valid Keogh plan must exist in 1997. See your accountant for more details.

➤ These plans allow you to switch your money from investment vehicle to investment vehicle to take advantage of changing rates of return.

Let's take a closer look at IRAs and Keogh accounts.

The Most Bang for Your Buck: Keogh Retirement Plans

Keoghs are the ultimate way for freelancers to set aside money for retirement. A Keogh is like getting four cherries in a row at the slots. That's because a Keogh plan gives you four distinct tax benefits:

1. You get a tax deduction for your *Keogh contribution*, the amount you put into your Keogh every year.

2. You don't pay any tax on the contribution you make for your own benefit, even though you have an absolute right to collect eventually. This is better than the usual rule, which taxes employers immediately on any amount they will collect only in the future.

Bet You Didn't Know

Don't wait for the perfect moment to invest in stock; that moment will never come. Instead, use a simple investment strategy called "dollar cost averaging." To do this, invest a fixed amount every month, whether the price of the stock (or mutual funds, etc.) is going up or down. In the long run, you'll end up with more shares at medium rather than high prices.

3. Investment earnings on amounts you contribute to your Keogh are not taxable until you or your heirs take them out. This is better than the usual trust rules, in which someone is taxed now on the trust's income.

4. Amounts you collect at retirement or that your heirs collect after you've shuffled off this mortal coil can qualify for reduced tax liability. This is another good break.

To qualify for a Keogh:

➤ You must be self-employed.

➤ Your self-employment must be profitable.

There are two basic types of Keogh plans: a *defined-contribution Keogh plan* and a *defined-benefit Keogh plan*.

Here's the rundown:

1. *Defined-contribution Keogh plans:*

   A *money-purchase plan* requires a self-employed person to contribute a specific percentage of net income to the plan each year. The maximum you can contribute is 25 percent or up to $30,000.

   A *profit-sharing plan* allows a self-employed person to contribute, on an optional basis, up to 15 percent of net income up to $30,000.

2. *Defined-benefit Keogh plans:* These plans allow you to decide the amount of your retirement income. You make contributions to meet that goal. You may be allowed to claim a larger deduction than would have been available under a defined-contribution Keogh.

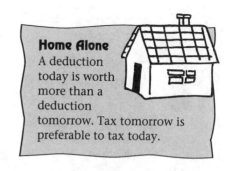

Home Alone
A deduction today is worth more than a deduction tomorrow. Tax tomorrow is preferable to tax today.

The ABCs of IRAs

Beginning January 1, 1982, any worker or self-employed person who is under 70 $\frac{1}{2}$ years of age became eligible to open an Individual Retirement Account. Even if you already have a Keogh, you can have an IRA as well.

Why is an IRA such a good deal? As with a Keogh, your contributions are fully deductible from your taxable income. For example, if you put the full $2,000 in your IRA, you may reduce your taxes by as much as $1,000, depending on your tax bracket. In most states, you also get to deduct your IRA contribution from your state taxes. Further, what you earn on your IRA investment goes untaxed until you withdraw it.

Here are some other things you should know about IRAs:

➤ The most you can contribute to an IRA is $2,000 a year.

➤ You do not have to contribute the full $2,000 every year.

➤ Once you open an IRA, you may skip contributions entirely for a year or more and still stay within the rules.

➤ There is no minimum contribution you must make to open an IRA, although a specific financial institution may impose its own minimum in order to open an account with them.

➤ You have until the April 15 federal income tax filing deadline to open an IRA account and put money into it.

Mind Your Own Business

Pick one name for your retirement accounts and stick with it. For example, I have all my retirement accounts under the name "Laurie Rozakis, Ph.D." This not only distinguishes my business accounts from my nonbusiness accounts, but also helps prevent possible confusion down the line.

➤ You must start withdrawing money when you reach age 70 ¹/₂ or risk a stiff penalty.

➤ Look into the newest IRA. Called the Roth IRA, it's keyed to income.

➤ You can withdraw your money early from an IRA, but there are penalties.

Wall Street Wizard

You can invest your Keogh money or IRA money just about any way you like. Below are the most popular choices, arranged from least to most risky.

Now, some of us like risk; some of us don't. Select the investment options that suit your financial goals and level of comfort. You can set up these accounts through your bank or through an investment firm.

➤ *Savings Bonds.* Savings bonds are no longer as staid as an old Chevy. Okay, they're not sexy, but they *do* offer fairly competitive rates. You'll never make a financial killing with savings bonds—but you'll sleep easy at night. Further, they're simple and can be purchased for as little as $25.

If you have munchkins who might want a college education eventually, savings bonds bought after 1989 pay federally tax-free interest if used for your child's college tuition (depending on your income level). Call 800-US-BONDS for the current interest rate (in Washington, DC, the number is USA-8888).

➤ *CDs, a.k.a. Certificates of Deposit.* Certificates of deposit give you a higher rate of interest if you are willing to surrender your money for a specific length of time, anywhere from seven days to ten years. Like savings bonds, they're safe and easy. CDs are offered with fixed or variable rates. Bear in mind that you will incur a substantial penalty for early withdrawal.

➤ *Money Market Mutual Funds.* Money market mutual funds are mutual funds that invest solely in short-term debt securities, such as Treasury bills, commercial paper, and certificates of deposit. Unlike stock and bond mutual funds, the price of money funds doesn't fluctuate wildly. As a result, there's no risk of loss if the stock market goes nova. The interest rate for money market funds varies, but you'll usually get one to three points higher than passbook accounts. The minimum investment is usually $1,000 to $5,000. Most money market funds carry check-writing privileges, and the funds are completely liquid. You can have your money any time you want.

➤ *U.S. Treasury Bills.* This is another easy and safe investment. T-bills operate much like savings bonds. The face value of a T-bill is $10,000, but the actual price is determined at auction. (Most bidders are banks and other financial institutions.) This means you buy a $10,000 bill at discount. When the bill matures, you receive the full face value. T-bills mature in three, six, and twelve months. The minimum investment is $10,000, with $5,000 increments.

Home Alone
Check the reference section of the library for *The Do-It-Yourself Guide to Investment Information* and *Nelson's Directory of Investment Managers*. Both provide in-depth information on investing.

An account is set up for you at the Federal Reserve and credited or debited as you buy more securities or they reach maturity. The rates are tied to the stock market. All income from Treasury bills is exempt from state and local taxes, but not from federal taxes. T-bills are easily sold, but you risk losses if you're forced to sell prematurely.

➤ *U.S. Treasury Notes.* These are very similar to T-bills, but mature in two to ten years and pay a fixed rate of interest twice a year. The longer the note's maturity, the higher the interest rate.

➤ *Treasury Bonds.* Sold in $1,000 denominations, Treasury bonds mature in ten to thirty years. Like U.S. Treasury notes, they pay interest twice a year.

Call the Bureau of Public Debt at 202-287-4088 for the current interest rate or check *The Wall Street Journal* or other financial papers. The easiest way to make these investments is through a stockbroker.

IS THAT CLEAR?

Mind Your Own Business
Never use your emergency cash reserve money to buy T-notes or T-bonds because they are not liquid enough for that. T-bills, in contrast, are more liquid because their rates are short-term and fluctuate less.

➤ *Ginnie Mae Certificates.* These are pools of home mortgages, packaged and guaranteed by the Government National Mortgage Association (GNMA). You need $25,000 to buy a single Ginnie Mae; additional certificates can be purchased in increments of $5,000.

These are tricky and often misunderstood investments. Yes, they are government guaranteed, but only against late mortgage payments and foreclosures. There's no guarantee of a specific yield or fixed maturity, since the value rises and falls just like any other bond.

Home Alone
U.S. Industry Fund Directory and *Moody's Handbook of Dividend Achievers* are additional sources of investment information.

For a free pamphlet on investing in Ginnie Maes, write to GNMA, Suite 1600, 451 Seventh Street SW, Washington, DC 20410.

➤ *Stock Mutual Funds*. Don't have the time to follow the bulls and bears? Most busy freelancers find that the best way to take advantage of the abundance of stocks and bonds is to invest in mutual funds. You get full-time, professional investment management, often for a minimum investment of $500 or less.

Home Alone
More information on mutual funds is available in the following volumes: *Mutual Fund Encyclopedia*, *Individual Investors Guide to Low-Load Mutual Funds*, and *Mutual Fund Buyer's Guide*.

The cost of running a fund is called the "load." All funds are not created equal; some have much higher loads than others. Look for *no-load* or *low-load* mutual funds—you'll get a much higher return for your money. So you can make a reasoned choice, know that the average stock fund has an expense ratio of 1.3 percent ($130 per each $10,000 in assets).

Write for *The Guide to Mutual Funds*, a list of stock funds and their phone numbers published by the Investment Company Institute, 1600 M Street NW, Suite 600, Washington, DC 10036. The pamphlet costs $5.

Mind Your Own Business
Watch the cost of broker's fees; these can really eat into your profit. There are several excellent discount brokers. Charles Schwab is probably the most famous.

➤ *Individual Stocks and Bonds*. You can build your own portfolio by selecting the investment vehicles that suit your needs. Some people, for example, buy stock according to their conscience; others pick stocks for their growth potential. The choice is yours.

➤ *Asset Allocation Funds*. These funds invest in several asset categories at once, such as U.S. stocks, bonds, money market instruments, foreign securities, real estate, and metals. Thus, by choosing one fund, you get instant diversity.

Bet You Didn't Know

Consult financial and business periodicals, which you can often get for free in the public library. (Savvy freelancers learn to look for free things. Free is good.) Here are some of the best publications: the *New York Times*, *The Wall Street Journal*, the *Value Line*, *Donoghue's Money Letter*, *Low Price Stock Survey*, *Investor's Business Daily*, *Morning Star*, *Money*.

Field of Schemes

In the 1600s, people believed that toads were poisonous, and anyone who mistakenly ate a toad's leg instead of a frog's leg would die. Rather than swearing off frog's legs, people sought a cure for the "fatal" food poisoning. Performing in public, charlatans would sometimes hire an accomplice who would pretend to eat a toad, at which point his employer would whip out an instant remedy and "save" his helper's life. Anti-toad medicine sales were understandably brisk.

Con artists are getting more creative and sophisticated with their scams, according to the Federal Trade Commission and the North American Securities Administration Association. This is especially true when it comes to investments. The stock market's unprecedented run-up in recent years is responsible for much of the rise of these crimes. As one securities regulator noted, "People think high returns are possible, so the phony pitches have become more believable."

Home Alone
You may also wish to consult *Complete Words of Wall Street, Market Share Reporter,* and *Walker's Manual of Unlisted Stocks* for more facts on investing.

Though swindlers have tried to empty the pockets of small investors through direct mail solicitation, classified ads, and even the Internet, the most common way to lure victims is still over the phone. The sales pitches run the gamut from phony gold mines, oil wells, and fraudulent public works to projects in developing countries.

Recent outlandish investment swindles include snail farms in Iowa, ostrich ranches in Idaho, and movie projects in Hollywood. One recent get-rich scheme involved frozen cow embryos in Ohio. There are Ponzi schemes to invest in phony cellular or digital technology companies, too.

Although there is no foolproof way to determine the legitimacy of an investment opportunity, you can try to protect yourself in these ways:

➤ Contact the securities' regulating agencies or the Better Business Bureau of the state in which the company operates.

➤ Realize that companies that sell securities to the public must be registered with the Securities and Exchange Commission or state regulators.

➤ Make sure that the broker is licensed. All brokers must be licensed.

➤ Beware of telemarketers. Telemarketed investment schemes are popping up like mushrooms after a rainstorm. Telemarketers prey on everyone, not just the obvious marks.

Home Alone
If you get a phone call from a telemarketer and you tell the seller never to call you again, and they do, they have broken the law and can be slapped with a heavy fine.

Bet You Didn't Know

There's good news in tax shelters today. An Australian court has ruled that monkeys working on sheep ranches may be listed as dependents on income tax forms...and I was so worried about that.

Here's a final word of advice: If it sounds too good to be true, don't invite it home for dinner. Investment scams pop up faster than best friends at a lottery winner's birthday party. That's cause for caution, not terror. With some research and common sense, you can invest prudently and safely.

The Least You Need to Know

➤ Don't rely on Uncle Sam to support you in your old age. Start setting aside money now.

➤ Millionaires are made, for the most part, not born. What are you waiting for?

➤ Tax-deferred savings can't be beat. Keoghs and IRAs are the two tax-deferred retirement programs for freelancers.

➤ How you invest your retirement savings is up to you. Find out as much as you can about what's available, assess your needs and comfort level, and put your money to work.

Part 7
Top of the Heap

Recently, I called a company and asked to speak to Bob. The person who answered said, "Bob is on vacation. Would you like to hold?"

Know the feeling? Maybe it seems like your freelance career is on perpetual hold. Or maybe you're so busy you've forgotten the meaning of the word "vacation." In either case, this section is for you. Here you'll learn how to revive a sagging freelance business or expand a booming one. You'll get the scoop on hiring help and find out how to polish up old skills and acquire new ones. Finally, you'll get a chance to evaluate whether or not freelancing is really for you.

HELP!

Expansion League

Question: How can a freelancer tell that it's time to make some changes in his or her business?

Answer: That's what this chapter is all about!

Nothing stays the same forever. This is terrible when it comes to your waistline, but great when it comes to your freelance business. Change is common in all businesses, but especially for freelancers. *Every* freelance business must change to survive.

The day comes to every freelance business when it must expand. Sometimes it's because the freelancer has too much business; other times, it's because the freelancer has too little to do. First, let's explore what happens when too much of a good thing assails a freelancer.

Boomtown Meltdown

Oglop Smedley, like most freelancers, was grateful to be on his own. At times, he couldn't believe he had created such a sweet life for himself. While others were Dilbert-ing their lives away in a 4×4 cubicle, Smedley was happily ensconced in his cozy home office. He was so happy, in fact, that he became utterly consumed with his work. At 5:00 PM, when normal worker bees were flying home to the hive, Smedley was still plugging away at his computer. After a quick take-out meal, Smedley was back to the salt mine, home office version. And when the other drones were relaxing with the 11:00 news, Smedley was still at work.

See Smedley work. See Smedley overachieve. See Smedley's head melt down like a nuclear power plant.

You can tell it's time to expand when you become Smedley, lured into maniacal overwork by the tantalizing siren song of the freelancer, "I can do it! I'm Super Freelancer!" Not to worry; I have some solutions for you.

Help Can Help

Start with this mantra:

> Do the things you do the best
> And hire someone to do the rest.

Remember what you learned in Chapters 19 and 20 about running your life as a freelancer? When your business gets too big to handle, it may be time to consider hiring help and delegating specific responsibilities. Start by asking yourself these questions:

➤ What kind of help will I need?

➤ How much help do I need?

➤ Will a little support from the spousal-unit and the tykes be enough, or will I need more than they can give?

Here are some options to consider if you find yourself acting like poor Freelancer Smedley:

1. Hire a regular employee to work full-time.

2. Hire one or more employees to work part-time.

3. Hire part-timers to complete specific tasks, such as accounting, secretarial work, and deliveries. This not only saves you space but can cut down on your taxes, too. Check with your accountant for details.

4. Farm out some of your extra work to other independent contractors. These will most likely be people you have met through networking or contacted through advertising.

5. Hire short-term help from a temporary agency. While you might pay more for this type of assistance, the temp agency hires, fires, and pays these people. That's one, two, three fewer tasks that you have to do!

Looking for Mr./Ms. Goodbody

If you're looking for help, you don't want just a warm body to take up space and give you the illusion of help—you want just the *right* employee. Before you can find that perfect employee, you have to analyze a number of different factors. Use the following worksheet to help you narrow your search.

Mind Your Own Business

IS THAT CLEAR?

Be sure to consider whether you have the space in your office to accommodate additional workers. Further, do you want people coming into your home every day? Farming out work allows you to maintain your privacy and lighten your work load.

1. What do I want the person to do?

   _____

2. What experience does the person need to complete these tasks well?

   _____

3. What skills should the person have?

   _____

4. What will the person's schedule be?

   _____

5. What salary am I willing to offer?

   _____

In addition to considering these factors, screen applicants to make sure that their personality and attitude are compatible with yours. You don't want to end up as half the odd couple, battling with a slob or a neatnick.

Now, write a job description. This helps both you and the applicant know exactly what's required of the position. You can place the advertisement in a newspaper or magazine. In addition, here are some other sources to try:

➤ Your local college placement office

➤ The senior citizens' center

➤ Job-training programs

➤ Word-of-mouth and networking

Mind Your Own Business

If you decide to place a classified advertisement to attract applicants, don't include your telephone number or address. Instead, use a box number provided by the newspaper. This lets you screen applicants and check out their references before you set up interviews. Only interview applicants you would seriously consider hiring.

Mind Your Own Business

Local zoning restrictions may limit the number of people you can hire—or even if you're allowed to hire any help. Review your local zoning laws to find the limits on employees.

Headless Body Found in Topless Bar!

Just when things get a little slow on TV, a fresh scandal occurs to keep us happy. Watergate had its moments, and Chuck and Camilla were worth a few chuckles. Then there was Nannygate, the scandal over a prospective attorney general's decision to overlook the federal law regarding hiring employees. That little oversight cost her the job and sent scores of employers off to check their records. We can all take a lesson from this little imbroglio—when you hire someone, make sure to follow the rules. And here they are:

➤ When you decide to hire an employee, first obtain a federal employer identification number from the Internal Revenue Service.

➤ At the same time, send away for the most recent federal publication concerning employees, the Employer's Tax Guide. This covers the federal regulations that apply to the employer-employee relationship.

➤ Be sure to check the laws regarding hiring legal and illegal aliens, if this situation applies to your freelance business.

➤ Pay whatever employee taxes are required.

➤ Consult an accountant or attorney to make sure you are in compliance with all the laws.

Sizing Things Up

If you're a freelance writer like me, you may never have to leave home. I've been working from my home office for close to two decades and I have no plans to decamp. I have just enough work to keep me busy and happy. Since I have all my manuscripts and much of my research material on floppy disks, I have plenty of room. Further, I've been able to farm out tasks that I don't have the time to do, such as accounting, so I'm the only body in here.

But what happens if your business has grown so much that you and your little elves are tripping over each other's toes? Perhaps you can't turn around without bumping into a pile of papers, product, or people. If this description fits your current situation, it might be time to fly the coop. Think about taking larger quarters—outside home.

Squeeze Play

Before deciding to move to larger quarters, consider the following remedies. They can save you time and money:

➤ *Make a clean sweep.* Maybe the reason you're feeling a little squeezed is that you haven't cleaned up your office since the Great War. (Was that 1914 or 1812?) Be ruthless. Clear the desk. Clear the floor. You'd be surprised how much useless stuff you can ditch when you set your mind to it. Donate it. Trash it. Whatever you do, get it out of your house. Remember: no guts, no glory.

If you're feeling really brave, aim for a paperless office. Scan your files on disks. Then throw out the paper files and keep the disks.

➤ *Rent a warehouse.* Consider storing excess product in a warehouse. You may also wish to warehouse books, files, and papers that you just can't bear to part with. I recommend using a real warehouse rather than someone's basement, attic, or garage. Basements flood, attics get musty, and I once found a really dead opossum in my garage. Warehouses are safer bets for storing important items.

➤ *Get professional help.* Hire a designer to revamp your office. For example, the designer may be able to save you a surprising amount of space by adding a different desk, shelves, and bins. Even changing the lighting can save you valuable space.

➤ *Add on.* If all else fails, you might be able to enlarge your office space by breaking through a wall or adding on a room. I had a handyman remove the closets on the other side of my office. Then we pushed the wall back and I gained about five feet of space. This gave me much more wall space for bookshelves.

Home Alone
The bite for enlarging your office may not be as bad as you think, because you may be able to deduct the cost of structural changes on your tax return through depreciation. Check with your tax preparer or accountant.

Leaving the Nest

Tech Support: "What does the screen say now?"

Person: "It says, 'Hit ENTER when ready.'"

Tech Support: "Well?"

Person: "How do I know when it's ready?"

How can you tell if you're ready to move out of your home office to larger space? If none of the ideas you just read work for you, then short of becoming the incredible shrinking freelancer, you have no choice but to move to larger quarters. Before you start packing your pencils, think about the bottom line. Yes, moolah, folding money, cash. Much as you'd like to move your office to larger quarters, you might not be able to pay the freight. Use the following worksheet to evaluate your individual situation.

Item	Estimated Cost
1. Rent	_____
2. Decorating expenses	_____
3. Furniture costs	_____
4. Phone installation	_____
5. Wiring	_____
6. Moving costs	_____
7. Mailings to notify customers	_____
8. New checks	_____
9. New business cards	_____
10. Commuting costs	_____
11. Eating out	_____
12. Parking fees	_____
Total cost	_____

Home Alone
Don't assume that commercial rents are comparable to residential rents. Instead, look through the commercial real estate ads in your local newspaper to get realistic figures.

Do some research, add it all up, and see where you stand—before you go where you might not be able to afford to stay. Always figure high rather than low. That way, what's the worst that will happen? You'll end up with a little extra money.

Not Waving but Drowning

Economically speaking, all freelancers have their ups and downs. Fluctuations in our balance sheet are often the result of changes in the economy or the natural rhythms of our particular business. For example, in the summer many staffers take vacations, so freelance assignments tend to taper off until September.

But what if you're just not making enough money all the time? What if you have days, weeks, or even months of downtime? There are several possible reasons for your work drought. Here are some of the most important ones:

➤ You're lazy. (Is that what they mean by tough love?)

➤ You're charging too much and scaring away all the customers.

➤ You have the wrong product or service.

➤ Your marketing is poor.

➤ You haven't been actively seeking new business.

➤ Your skills are weak.

To figure out which reasons apply to you, you have to assess your own situation honestly. As a general rule, I'm not one for soul-searching (though I am *very* good at breast-beating and Monday-morning quarterbacking), but here's one instance where you can run but you can't hide. I can provide you with some of the most common reasons you might not be getting work, but only you can see which ones apply to you and you alone.

Growing Pains

Assuming that you've got your nose to the grindstone and your prices are as right as rain, it's time to dig a little deeper into the problem. Start by going back to the customer profile you crafted for your business plan in Chapter 7. Examine it as you answer the following questions. Be truthful, now. I'm looking over your shoulder.

Circle *yes* or *no* to answer each question.

---

1. Do you get positive feedback from your customers?
   Yes   No

2. Do you have a lot of repeat business?
   Yes   No

3. Is your product or service high quality?
   Yes   No

4. Is your product or service required in your area?
   Yes   No

5. Are you meeting your customers' needs?
   Yes   No

6. Do you continue to solicit business even as you're working?
   Yes   No

---

7. Do you review your marketing plan on a regular basis?

   Yes   No

8. Do you ask customers for feedback? Do you follow their suggestions?

   Yes   No

9. Do you have the skills or equipment you need to accept most of the jobs you are offered?

   Yes   No

10. Do you keep up with trends and innovations in your field?

    Yes   No

Home Alone

In freelancing, 20 percent of your clients cause 80 percent of your aggravation. Getting rid of those rotten clients can improve your business by freeing up the time you need to concentrate on soliciting new business and brushing up on your skills.

If you answered *yes* to most of these questions, the problem most likely isn't with the quality of your work. In that case, you may just need to come at things from a slightly different angle. More on this coming up.

Too many *no* answers might mean that you've lost interest in your work. Read on for some suggestions, and be sure to check out Chapter 25 for more help.

Onward and Upward

Doctor, doctor, what can I do? We know you have a problem; now it's time to take Dr. R's cure. It's time to expand, bubba. No, I'm not saying you should eat enough Ding-Dongs to make your butt the size of a FedEx truck.

Instead, what you have to do is analyze your situation to see where you might expand your business to breath new life into it. I've designed the following questionnaire to make it easier for you to develop new areas of expertise. So sharpen that #2 pencil and get cracking. You can eat *one* Ding-Dong to make your task easier.

1. My present freelance business is

   _____

2. Here are three businesses or services that are closely related to my present freelance business:

   a._____

   b._____

   c._____

3. Here are three less-closely related businesses or services that I feel comfortable doing:

   a._____

   b._____

   c._____

4. The three most promising choices are

   a._____

   b._____

   c._____

5. Here are some resources I could use to find out more about these three choices (include people as well as print sources):

   a._____

   b._____

   c._____

Once you have narrowed down your choices, follow the steps you learned in Chapter 7 to write a new business plan. This will enable you to assess the feasibility of your proposed expansion. Figure out how much the expansion will cost, calculate the return on your investment, and decide if this is the right move for you.

One of the wonderful aspects of freelancing is its constant challenges. To stay in the game (not to mention on top of it), you have to adapt to changing conditions, hire help if you need it, and be prepared to explore new ideas and learn new skills.

The Least You Need to Know

➤ No dinosaurs need apply; freelancers must adapt to changing conditions or risk becoming extinct.

➤ If you're busier than a mosquito in a nudist colony, you may have to expand and hire some help.

➤ If your freelance career has flatlined, it's time to explore ways to revitalize your business.

I CAN TAKE THAT PROJECT.

Chapter 25

Keep That Sparkle in Your Step

An older couple met their demise in an auto accident and were transported to Heaven. As they were waiting to be processed, they began to look all around.

The wife was amazed at the beauty, the peace, and the contentment she felt. She commented over and over about what a nice place Heaven was and how fortunate she felt to be there.

The husband huffed, "If it weren't for you and your damned oat-bran muffins and health-food crap, we'd have been here 15 years ago."

Freelancing can be heaven on earth...and you don't even have to eat oat-bran muffins! In this chapter, you'll discover ways to keep yourself challenged so you continue to enjoy your life as a freelancer.

The Sweet Smell of Success

The Roper Organization recently surveyed 2,000 adults and asked them to rank the things that gave them the most satisfaction. Here are the items. How would you rank them?

Work	1._____	Greatest satisfaction
Friends	2._____	
Family	3._____	
Music	4._____	
Reading	5._____	
Home	6._____	
Television	7._____	Least satisfaction

Here are the survey results:

1. Family
2. Television
3. Friends
4. Music
5. Reading
6. Home
7. Work

Notice where work ranks: dead last. Now, this is not to say that you can't get a great deal of pleasure from your freelance career. I do, and I sincerely hope that you will enjoy your career as much. But what can you do to make sure that you still enjoy your career years down the road, when you're well established? How can you keep yourself happy, challenged, and fresh? Read on to find out!

oH!

Bet You Didn't Know

According to a survey in *The Bottom Line*, police officers, fire-fighters, doctors, and other health care professionals have among the most stressful jobs in America. What's the most stressful job? Circus roustabout! (Doesn't that make you feel better about deciding to become a freelancer instead?)

A Table for One

Before I was a freelance writer, I taught high school English for more than a decade. Last week I attended the retirement bash given for my former department chairman. For more than five hours, we roasted and toasted this fine man with songs, poems, speeches, testimonials, and jokes. The balloons shimmered in the light and my friend glowed with happiness well deserved.

This got me to thinking about my own retirement. Even though it's a million years off, what happens when this freelancer hangs up her mouse and covers her keyboard? Will my clients gather together to fete me? It's not likely. After all, they don't even know each other!

One of the problems with being a freelancer is the lack of appreciation. Oh sure, you get those nice checks, but the shiny medals and testimonial dinners are few and far between. No gold watch, either. It's even rare to get a thank-you letter or a phone call of appreciation. And don't wait for the promotion. Your rank—Freelancer, First Class—is the same at the end of your career as it was at the beginning.

Some freelancers don't require kudos; others feel aggrieved by the lack of gratitude. That's the nature of the beast. As long as your clients keep coming back, you know they like your work, but don't sit up nights waiting for a festive cheese platter to come in the mail. How can you keep yourself cheerful and challenged without the support of an appreciative audience?

Let's look at how one of history's best-selling freelancers, William Shakespeare, kept himself amused. Here are the top ten plays that Shakespeare chose *not* to publish:

10. *Henry VIII, I Am, I Am*
 9. *Fast Times at Verona High*
 8. *Romeo & Steve*
 7. *Six Degrees of Francis Bacon*
 6. *Stratford-upon-Avon 90210*
 5. *Om'let*
 4. *King Gump*
 3. *Romeo & Michelle's High School Reunion*
 2. *Twelfth Night, Children Stay Free*

And the Number One play Shakespeare chose not to publish...

 1. *Big Macbeth and Fries*

Home Alone
In addition to offering personal challenges, learning new skills provides greater job security. The more you can do, the more work you'll have.

As this list shows, we all have our off days. One of the best ways to keep your freelance life exciting is to challenge yourself by trying new areas. Here are some of the methods that work best for me and my colleagues.

All the Right Moves

A freelance researcher who started a decade ago would be lagging behind today unless he or she knew how to find information on the World Wide Web. Books are far from dead, but I keep hearing a few wracking coughs from that direction. Our smart researcher took some extra training in "Information Retrieval Services" to know how to surf the Net like a pro. She enjoyed learning the new skills and got some choice freelance assignments as a result of them.

I'm a relatively young coot, but when I started my career as a freelance writer, computers were things that occupied an entire floor in the Pentagon. We wrote our manuscript on these machines called "typewriters," using carbon paper to make multiple copies. Today, it's virtually impossible to be a freelance writer and not have good computer skills. To stay challenged and competitive, nearly all freelance writers are computer-literate. Most are comfortable cruising the Internet and communicating through e-mail, too.

To keep yourself from snoozing off from boredom, you have to make sure you have hot skills, especially after you've been freelancing for several years. Of course this is true of staffers as well, but their lack of knowledge can be more easily covered by cooperative co-workers, especially if the slacker knows where the bodies are buried. As a lone eagle, you don't have anyone to cover your, uh, gaps.

Home Alone
If you don't want course credit, you can sometimes audit a class and save big bucks. Some colleges charge as little as $25 for auditors. If you're a Gray Panther, you may be even better off: Many community colleges allow people over age 55 to take classes for a reduced fee.

Here are some ways to get the skills you need to keep yourself fresh:

➤ *Take assignments in related fields*. I did some work for IBM on a teachers' manual for a computer-writing program. I've done piles of teachers' manuals, but never one on computer writing. I learned new skills and made important new contacts in a related field.

➤ *Take jobs in fields you don't know*. This is a gamble, because you're doing on-the-job training. Nonetheless, if you're a self-starter, a quick study, and a good researcher, you can often acquire fresh skills by branching out into new areas.

For example, I have a Ph.D. in English and American literature and more than 20 years' experience teaching writing, literature, speech, and so on. I've lectured on my specialties around the world; I've published scores and scores of books in these fields. As a recognized expert in these areas, I'm in demand as a consultant, too.

I am *not* an expert in math, however. To keep myself challenged, I've written parts of several math books. These projects forced me to read, network, and expand in whole new areas.

➤ *Take college courses.* Check out the colleges and universities in your area to see what they offer that you may need.

➤ *Take adult education classes.* These are offered through your school district.

➤ *Work in-house briefly.* Consider taking a staff job to learn a new skill that you can use in your business.

➤ *Read the latest publications in your field.* Include trade journals, newspapers, and magazines.

➤ *Be nice to yourself.* Don't work yourself into a frazzle. Be sure to schedule decent vacations and make time for friends and family.

➤ *Don't be afraid to take a break.* A friend of mine is taking a year off from his job as a freelance editor to teach high school in Istanbul. Life's too short to fill it with "If I only had the time I could have..." Do it.

Freelancer Overboard

You can spend your entire career as a freelancer and have a happy and fulfilled life. Sometimes, however, your personal situation changes and you have to reassess your career choices. Maybe you're not having fun any more; maybe you find it difficult to keep selling yourself. Perhaps you miss the camaraderie of an office or need the structure an office schedule provides. It could be that your personality and temperament are not suited for the freelance life. Whatever the reason, there's no such thing as virtual freelancing. You have to try it to see if you like it.

A friend of mine tried freelance writing and editing when he lost his job with a New York publisher. At first, he was thrilled with the concept. After all, freelancing offered more freedom and no commuting. He would have more time to spend with his family and on his hobbies, too. Here's what he had to say about the experience:

It only took a few months to realize that freelancing wasn't for me. I had enough work to make the same salary I had earned as a staffer—my connections are great—but I hated the "all or nothing" flow. One week I didn't have enough to do; the next week I was drowning in assignments. It was very difficult to plan my time because I could never be sure what would happen the following week. Rather than having more time with my family, I found that I was with them less. I wanted the structure of an office, where I could work 9 to 5 five days a week.

Mind Your Own Business
Be wary of taking an in-house job and also trying to keep your current freelance clients. Don't get stretched so thin you can't do anything well.

Soon after, this editor took another staff job. He had to try freelancing to know that it wasn't right for him.

Still other freelancers alternate freelance work with staff jobs, depending on their goals at each point in their lives. A dear friend spent five years freelancing after the company where she was an executive relocated to a distant state. She took a staff job when her family situation changed and she needed more security than freelancing could offer.

Maybe freelancing isn't the problem at all—maybe it's the specific freelance career that you've selected. You might be perfectly well-suited for life as a freelancer in a different field. For example, you might have developed a career as a freelance makeup artist, but you may be happier as a freelance hairdresser, wigmaker, or interior designer. Look carefully at the freelance specialty you have selected. Could *that* be the problem?

Hello, I Came to Say I Cannot Stay

How can you tell if it's time to leave freelancing and take a staff job? Fortunately, there are some clear signs that it may be time to reassess your career choices. Complete the following worksheet to see whether it might be time to bail out.

Write *yes* or *no* to answer each question.

_____ 1. I can't make enough money to pay the bills. Anyone's bills.

_____ 2. Savings? What are savings?

_____ 3. I haven't had a vacation since Elvis left the room.

_____ 4. I'm watching too much daytime TV.

_____ 5. I like daytime TV.

_____ 6. I may be a candidate for daytime TV.

_____ 7. I put off doing my work so long that I've made procrastination into an art form.

_____ 8. I feel as nervous as a teenager waiting for a date.

_____ 9. Lonely, I'm Mr. Lonely.

_____ 10. I'm so bored that I look forward to watching paint dry.

_____ 11. I rarely bother to get dressed, even for the UPS man.

_____ 12. My job isn't giving me much pleasure anymore.

Score Yourself

8–12 marked yes	The ship's sinking, cap'n. Time to bail.
5–7 marked yes	You need a night out, a dye job, or a new toaster—not a career change.
1–4 marked yes	Don't worry. Be happy.

Stress and depression are clear signs that something's wrong. So are a string of seemingly minor health problems: sinus infections, aches and pains, bumps and bruises. I'm a firm believer that no career is worth your health. If you find that freelancing is taking a toll on your mind and body, it's time to rethink your choices. Freelancing, like soap on a rope, is not for everyone. There's no shame in discovering this. And you're better off recognizing that you need a different lifestyle *before* you crash and burn.

Mind Your Own Business
Remember that there are ups and downs in everyone's career. You may just be hitting a low point. Consider giving freelancing at least three more months before you bail.

IS THAT CLEAR?

Jumping Ship

Aside from death and taxes, nothing in life is permanent. If you're feeling a little burnt around the edges, you might want to consider taking a staff job and reassessing your priorities. Perhaps you just need a change of pace and some time in an office again. Or, you can take an temporary in-house freelance job for three, six, or nine months. This will give you time to sort the matter through while you are getting a salary, more structure, companionship, and benefits.

But what happens if you're sure that freelancing isn't for you? In that case, it's time for a graceful exit. I have some great exit lines, but unfortunately they all pertain to death, not leaving a career. Instead, I offer you these guidelines for shuttering your freelance business:

➤ Be sure to notify everyone that you are folding up your tents and leaving.

➤ Give plenty of notice. No last minute, "Oops, I'm out of here" dashes for the door, please.

➤ Play nice. Resist the urge to tell your worst client where he or she can stick it. You never know who you'll meet where.

➤ If possible, finish all your jobs so you don't leave any clients high and dry.

➤ If you can't complete all your work, consider turning unfinished projects over to someone you'd trust with your life, child, or Corvette.

Home Alone
Depending on the nature of your freelance business, you may wish to sell it. Obviously, this isn't going to work with a freelance writer, but it is feasible with a freelance electrician, plumber, or insurance broker, for example.

➤ Even if you do complete every job, you may wish to give each of your clients a referral to a fellow freelancer. This builds good will in several ways.

➤ Save all your files and your Rolodex. Someday you may return to freelancing.

➤ Keep in touch. Some of your freelance clients might become clients in your staff position.

You Should Live and Be Well

You've gotten this far, kiddo, so the odds are that freelancing might be the career of choice for you. If so, congratulations! Life will be sweet.

However, you know me by now. I simply must have the last word. How could I resist a few parting morsels of advice before I send you happily on your way? So, here are my suggestions to you:

➤ Always keep soliciting new work. Right now, I'm writing three major projects. I feel like Little Jack Horner with his finger in a lot of pies. Nonetheless, I sent out two new book proposals this week. Never forget: Contracts fall through and promises are broken. Cover yourself by continually drumming up new work.

➤ Network. Stay in touch with everyone, even people who can't help you right now. Things change. People shift jobs often. You never know where a contact will end up.

➤ Be nice. It costs nothing and can pay off big.

➤ Keep your skills fresh. Learning new things makes you happier and in greater demand as a freelancer.

➤ Keep good records. Save receipts and organize them.

➤ Watch the bucks. The work flow is uneven.

➤ Set aside money for your retirement.

➤ Get health insurance.

➤ Take care of yourself. Eat right, exercise, and watch your health.

➤ Have fun. Freelancers are notorious for overworking. Leave time to play and smell the petunias.

The Least You Need to Know

➤ Prevent burn-out by keeping yourself challenged.

➤ If freelancing isn't for you, bow out gracefully.

➤ You're not the prisoner of Zenda. Plug away, but make time for fun, too.

➤ Good luck and best wishes!

Index

A

accounts payable/accounts
  receivable, 183
acquiring customers
  conversations, professional,
    94-96
  initial contact, 93-94
  record-keeping, 96
  self-promotion, 93
  sources, 90
      co-workers, 88-89
      Internet, 91-93
  targeting customers, 92-93
  unsuccessful contacts, 96
actual value of
  equipment, 286
adjustable fee considerations,
  150-151
ads
  classified ads, 201-202
      hiring employees, 304
  display ads, 201-202
  programs, 202
  radio, 203
  TV ads, 203
  yearbook ads, 202
  Yellow Pages, 202-203
advantages of freelancing, 35
  comforts of home, 34-35
  family time, 31
  flexibility, 29-30
  productivity, 32
  values, determining, 33-34
  variety of work, 32-33

advertising
  business cards, 197
  follow-up guidelines, 222
  Internet, 221
  marketing plans, 199-201
  methods
      brochures, 203-204
      bumper stickers, 205
      calendars, 205
      classified ads,
        201-202, 304
      competitors'
        strategies, 203
      decals, 205
      direct mail
        advertising, 204
      magnets, 205
      pamphlets, 204
      postcards, 204
      programs, 202
      radio, 203
      T-shirts, 205
      tips, 201
      TV ads, 203
      yearbook ads, 202
      Yellow Pages, 202-203
  naming businesses
      competitors'
        strategies, 201
      copying names, 196
      family names, 195
      guidelines, 195
      image, 194
      importance, 194
      misunderstandings,
        195-196

  resumes
      chronological
        resumes, 198
      sample, 198-199
      skills resumes, 198
agents, 230-235
  appropriate situations,
    230, 232
  business managers, 233
  contracts, 234
  defined, 230
  finding, 233
  freelancer/agent
    relationships
      dissolving, 234-235
      guidelines, 234
  *Guide to Literary Agents &
    Art/Photo Reps*, 233
  hidden fees, 232
  one-time deals, 231
  responsibilities, 230-231
  Society of Authors'
    Representatives, 233
alarm systems, 138
Amazon.com (bookstore) Web
  site, 220
American Association of
  Home-Based Businesses,
  The, 218
American Express Web
  site, 221
American Society of
  Journalists and Authors, 42
analytical skills, 53
answering machines, 128
anxiety, career uncertainty,

20-22
associations
American Association of
Home-Based Businesses,
The, 218
American Association of
University Women, 217
American Society of
Journalists and
Authors, 42
Editorial Freelancers
Association, 42, 78
Group Health Association
of America, 278
Independent Computer
Consultants
Association, 70
National Association for the
Self-Employed, The, 218
National Association of
Temporary and Staffing
Services, 254
audits, 261
guidelines, 271-272
partnerships, 263
authors, American Society of
Journalists and Authors, 42
avoiding mistakes,
choosing careers
duplicating current
situations, 63
suitable careers, 62
trends, 62-63

B

background knowledge,
essentials, 50-52
backing up work, computers,
125-126
balancing workflow, 252-255
credit, 255
job-hunting, 253
lack of work, 306-308
part-time jobs, 255
temporary services, 254
family/career, 248
children, 248-249
baby-sitters, 249

household chores,
250-251
writing about, 251
barter systems, 158
bartering, 182
beepers, office essentials, 130
benefits, 35
co-payments, 279
comforts of home, 34-35
deductibles, 279-280
disability insurance,
281-282
family time, 31
flexibility, 29-30
Group Health Association
of America, 278
health insurance, 276-281
Blue Cross and Blue
Shield, 277
considerations, 280-281
costs, 276-277
drawbacks, 276-277
importance, 276
Medicaid, 279
pre-existing
conditions, 278
providers, types, 277
resources, 278-279
independence, 30
life insurance, 282-283
premiums, 279
productivity, 32
retirement plans, 288-294
importance, 288
IRAs, 291-294
Keoghs, 291-293
mistakes, avoiding,
289-290
net worth,
determining, 289
tips, 290-291
values, determining, 33-35
variety of work, 32-33
bill-paying services, freelance
careers, 69
blue-collar workers, 13
book-keeping
essentials, 182
expenses, categorizing, 183
fears, 181
handwritten records, 186

importance, 181-182
income, categorizing, 183
invoices, 187
IRS, 186
methods, 184
sample, 184-185
reasons for failure, 180
receipts, 186-187
setting up, 182-187
expenses,
categorizing, 183
income,
categorizing, 183
methods, 184
samples, 184-185
single entries, 182
updating records, 187
books
*Business Plan Guide for
Independent Consultants,
The*, 71
*Complete Words of Wall
Street*, 297
Employer's Tax Guide, 304
*Guide to Literary Agents &
Art/Photo Reps*, 233
*How to Open and Operate a
Home-Based Craft
Business*, 71
*How to Start a Service
Business*, 71
*How to Start and Run Writing
and Editing Business*, 69
*Individual Investors Guide to
Low-Load Mutual
Fund*, 296
Literary Market Place, 80
Making It On Your Own, 88
Market Share Reporter, 297
*Mutual Fund Buyer's
Guide*, 296
*Mutual Fund
Encyclopedia*, 296
*Upstart Guide to Owning and
Managing a Desktop
Publishing Service, The*, 69
*Walker's Manual of Unlisted
Stocks*, 297
breaking into freelancing,
24-25
briefcases, 136

brochures
    advertising methods,
        203-204
    "Tax Guide for Small
        Businesses," 265
    "Selecting the Legal
        Structure for Your Firm,"
        172
budgets
    adjustable fees,
        considerations, 150-151
    assistance, 189
    equipment purchases,
        considerations, 123-124
    expenses
        adjustable fees,
            considerations, 150-151
        calculating rates,
            determining, 145-147
        categorizing, 183
        tax deductions, 269
    financing, 188
    lack of work, raising
        fees, 152
    losses, 188
    profits, 188
        determining rates, 148
    types, 187
    see also record-keeping
bumper stickers, advertising
    methods, 205
bundled software, 120
businesses, *see* home offices
business cards, 131-133
    advertising, 197
    considerations, 130-131
    costs, 131-132
    essentials, 131
    logos, 133
    networking, 197
    pictures, 219
    tips, 132-133
    typeface, 132
business names, 194-196, 201
    competitors' strategies, 201
    copying names, 196
    family names, 195
    guidelines, 195
    image, 194
    importance, 194
    misunderstandings,
        195-196

*Business Plan Guide for Indepen-
    dent Consultants, The*, 71
business plans
    essentials, 79-85
        competitor profiles,
            80-82
        customer profiles, 80
        financial statements,
            84-85
        location of business,
            82-83
        marketing strategy, 84
        organizational structure,
            83-84
        overview, 79
        sales forecasts, 82
    purpose, 76-77
    researching fields, 77-78
business structures, 8
    legal structures
        business names, 167
        changing, 170
        considerations, 171
        corporations, 168, 264
        determining, 170
        partnerships,
            167-168, 263
        "Selecting the Legal
            Structure for Your
            Firm," 172
        sole proprietorships,
            166-167, 262-263
buying
    equipment, 122
        budget considerations,
            123-124
        comparison
            shopping, 124
        money-saving tips, 123
        needs assessments, 122
        researching options,
            122-123
    supplies, 135-136

C

calendars, advertising
    methods, 205
calls
    answering machines, 128
    cellular phones, 129-130
    telecommunications
        systems, 128-130

    telephone lines, 129
    voice mail, 128
cards, business
    advertising, 197
    considerations, 130-131
    costs, 131, 132
    essentials, 131
    logos, 133
    networking, 197
    pictures, 219
    tips, 132-133
    typeface, 132
careers
    appropriate careers,
        determining, 64
    niches, filling, 66-67
    others' input, 64
    possibilities, 63, 68-71
    suitable careers, 62
    trends, 62-63
    writing, 68-69
    common, 11-12
    researching, business
        plans, 77-78
caterers, freelance careers, 69
cellular phones, 129-130
certificates of deposit
    (CDs), 294
chairs
    chair mats, 111
    ergonomics, 110-111
challenging yourself, 313-316
    changing fields, 315-316
    college courses, 314-315
    in-house work, 315
    projects, 314
    trade journals, 315
Chamber of Commerce, 77
    zoning laws, 104
charitable events, public
    relations, 212-213
children
    balancing family/career,
        248-249
    baby-sitters, 249
    hiring, 269-270
    IRAs, 269
chronological resumes, 198
classified ads
    advertising methods, 201
    costs, 202
    hiring employees, 304

clients
    acquiring, 88-90
        conversations,
            professional, 94-96
        co-workers, 88-89
        initial contact, 93-94
        Internet, 91-93
        record-keeping, 96
        self-promotion, 93
        sources, 90
        targeting customers,
            92-93
        unsuccessful contacts, 96
    confidentiality, 96
    freelancer/client
        relationships, 308
        confidentiality, 96
        conflicts, 226
        conflicts of interest, 10
        good relationships,
            225-226
        harassment, 229-230
        initial contact, 231-232
        Internet, 91-92
        raising fees, 163
        record-keeping, 96
        reputation, building, 224
        self-promotion, 93
        uncontrollable
            incidents, 229
        unfulfilled contracts,
            227-228
    profiles, 80
    rapport, building, 88
    reputation, 228
    targeting customers, 92-93
co-payments, health
    insurance, 279
collecting payments
    completed work only, 253
    deadlines, 159
    invoices, 159-160, 187
    late payments, 160
    legal action, 161
    promptness, 158-159
    receiving payments,
        161-162
    shifted schedules, 253
    structuring payments, 228
    see also fees

color consultants, freelance
    careers, 69
comforts of home, 34-35
commercial properties
    advantages/
        disadvantages, 107
    rent, 306
communication
    freelancer/client, 44
    skills, 53
community groups,
    networking, 217
competitors
    advertising strategies, 203
    fees, 149
    marketing strategies, 201
    profiles, business plans,
        80-82
*Complete Words of Wall
Street*, 297
CompuServe Web site, 221
computer consultants,
    freelance careers, 70
computers
    advantages, 116-117
    considerations, 112,
        123-124
    cyberphobia, 117-118
    disadvantages, 118-119
    hardware basics, 119-120
    Internet access, 121
    magazines, 122
    outdated equipment, 119
    setting up, 124-125
    software basics, 119-120
    start-up costs, writing, 69
    tax deductions, 119, 123
    use guidelines, 125-126
confidentiality, 96
conflicts
    conflicts of interest, 10
    dealing with, 226
    guidelines, 226
consignment, working on, 158
consultants, freelance careers,
    70-71
    resources
        *Business Plan Guide for
            Independent Consultants,
            The*, 71
        *How to Start a Service
            Business*, 71

National Entrepreneurs
    Opportunity Network,
    Information
    Exchange, 70
contacts
    alumni associations, 218
    appointments,
        scheduling, 222
    civic groups, 217
    community groups, 217
    importance, 215-216
    meal dates, 216
    record-keeping, 219
    referrals, 219-220
    trade associations, 218
    volunteer work, 219
    World Wide Web
        (WWW), 218
contracts
    advantages, 172
    agents, 234
    essential elements, 173
    first, 231
    guidelines, 174
    invoices as contracts, 175
    negotiable elements,
        173-174
    reusing material, 254
    sample, 175-177
conversations, acquiring
    customers, 94-96
corporate anorexia, 19
corporations, 168-170
    advantages, 169
    considerations, 170
    disadvantages, 169
    S corporations, 170
    taxes, 264
correspondence, *see* thank-you
    notes; phone calls
courier services, 136-137
craft businesses, *How to Open
    and Operate a Home-Based
    Craft Business*, 71
credit, regulating work
    flow, 255
credit cards
    accepting, 84
    financing methods, 188
customer profiles, 80
customers, *see* clients
cyberphobia, 118

D

daily fees, calculating, 149
deadlines
    meeting, 224
    payment collection, 159
decals, advertising
    methods, 205
decorating, 83
deductibles, health insurance, 279-280
deductions, taxes
    computers, 119, 123
    expenses, 269
    home offices, IRS classification criteria, 268
    Keogh retirement plans, 292-293
    legitimate deductions, 265
    sole proprietorships, 167
    T&E (travel & entertainment) budgets, 226, 269
    tax brackets, 269
    "Tax Guide for Small Businesses," 265
deficits, 188
desires/needs
    determining, 312
    workers in workplace, 23-24
desktop publishing
    freelance careers, 68-69
    Upstart Guide to Owning and Managing a Desktop Publishing Service, The, 69
difficult clients
    guidelines, 227-228
    harassment, 229-230
direct mail advertising, 204
disadvantages of freelancing, 39-42, 46
    communication, lack of, 44
    control of projects, lack of, 43-44
    hours, 40
    loneliness, 41-42
    record-keeping, 41
    responsibilities, 45-46
    unfulfilled promises, 45
    work uncertainty, 42-43

disc jockeys, freelance
    careers, 69
discipline, 53
discount coupons, promotions, 214
discounts for clients, 150-151, 214
display ads, 201-202
disputes
    conflicts of interest, 10
    dealing with, 226
    guidelines, 226
Doing Business As form, 167

E

e-mail (electronic mail), 91
earned income, 269
economic anxiety, 20-22
editing
    freelance careers, 68-69
    resources
        Editorial Freelancers Association, 42, 78
        How to Start and Run Writing and Editing Business, 69
Editorial Freelancers Association, 42, 78
employees
    hiring
        classified ads, 304
        considerations, 302-303
        employer responsibilities, 304
        options, 302-303
        screening applicants, 303
        sources, 303
        zoning restrictions, 304
employers
    leaving
        acquiring customers, 88-89
        guidelines, 89-90
    responsibilities, hiring employees, 304
    see also clients
Employer's Tax Guide, 304
Entrepreneurial Edge Online Webzine, Web site, 116

envelopes,131
equipment
    answering machines, 128
    beepers, 130
    cellular phones, 129-130
    computers, 119-122
        considerations, 123-124
        hardware, 119-120
        magazines, 122
        software, 119-120
    envelopes, 131
    fax machines, 121
    fire extinguishers, 138
    flashlights, 139
    insurance, 285-286
        actual value, 286
        considerations, 285-286
        homeowners' insurance, 286
        replacement value, 285
    inventories, 285
        essential information, 283
        Office Inventory Worksheet, 284
    motion sensor floodlights, 139
    photocopiers, 121
    purchasing, 122
        budget considerations, 123-124
        comparison shopping, 124
        money-saving tips, 123
        needs assessments, 122
        researching options, 122-123
    scanners, 122
    security, 137-139
    smoke detectors, 139
    stationery, 131, 133
    supplies, 133-136
    tax deductions, 119, 123
    telecommunications systems, 128-130
    telephone lines, 129
    voice mail, 128
    Web sites, 136
ergonomics, 110-111
errand services, freelance careers, 69

estimated tax payments, 270-271
ethical issues
    confidentiality, 96
    conflicts of interest, 10
evaluating services, 307-308
exercises, overcoming
    loneliness, 252
expanding businesses, 302-309
    considerations, 308-309
    hiring employees
        classified ads, 304
        considerations, 302-303
        employer
            responsibilities, 304
        options, 302-303
        screening applicants, 303
        sources, 303
        zoning restrictions, 304
    lack of work
        reasons, 306-307
        service evaluation, 307-308
    moving, 305-306
    remodeling offices, 305
    space-saving tips, 303, 305
expenses
    adjustable fees, considerations, 150-151
    calculating rates, 145-147
    categorizing, 183
    tax deductions, 269

F

failure of businesses, 180
family
    balancing family/career, 248-251
        children, 248-249
        household chores, 250-251
        writing about, 251
    benefits of freelancing, 31
    business names, 195
    children
        balancing family/career, 248-249
        hiring, 269-270
        IRAs, 269

fax machines, 121
fears, 181
Federal Trade Commission (FTC), 297
fee-for-service health care, 277
feedback, 52
fees, 145, 150
    adjustable fees, considerations, 150-151
    agents, 232
    barter systems, 158
    collecting payments
        deadlines, 159
        invoices, 159-160
        late payments, 160
        legal action, 161
        promptness, 158-159
        receiving payments, 161-162
        structuring payments, 228
    competitors' rates, 149
    considerations, 144-145
        adjustable fees, 150-151
    consignment, working on, 158
    contracts
        advantages, 172
        agents, 234
        essential elements, 173
        firsts, 231
        guidelines, 174
        invoices as contracts, 175
        negotiable elements, 173-174
        reusing material, 254
        sample, 175-177
    daily fees, 149
    determining
        competitors' rates, 149
        expenses, calculating, 145-147
    difficult clients, 228
    flat fees, 150
    lack of work, raising fees, 152
    long-term projects, 149-150
    monthly fees, calculating, 149
    negotiating, 152-154
    profit margins, 148

raising fees, 152
    freelancer/customer relationships, 163
    guidelines, 162-163
    lack of work, 152
short-term projects, 149-150
speculation, working on, 156-157
structuring payments, 228
time management, 151-152
weekly fees, calculating, 149
fields, choosing
    appropriate careers, determining, 64
    niches, filling, 66-67
    others' input, 64
    possibilities, 63, 68-71
    suitable careers, 62
    trends, 62-63
    writing, 68-69
    common, 11-12
    researching, business plans, 77-78
financing
    corporations, 169
    sources, 188
fines,
    taxes, 271
    zoning laws, 104
fire extinguishers, 138
flexibility
    benefits of freelancing, 29-30
    schedules, 12
flow of work, regulating, 252-255
    credit, 255
    job-hunting, 253
    lack of work, 306-308
    part-time jobs, 255
    temporary services, 254
forms
    Doing Business As form, 167
    taxes
        Schedule C sample form, 266
        Web site, 262
freelancing
    blue-collar workers, 13

breaking into freelancing, 24-25
characteristics, 7-8
fields
   appropriate careers, determining, 64
   common, 11-12
   niches, filling, 66-67
   others' input, 64
   possibilities, 63, 68-71
   suitable careers, 62
   trends, 62-63
   writing, 68-69
   researching, business plans, 77-78
increase, 5-6
IRS classification
   criteria, 260-261
reasons
   career uncertainty, 20-22
   overworked, 22
   retirement, early, 19
   stress in workplace, 22
   unmet needs/desires, 23-24
trendy terms, 9
typical profile, 12-13
U.S. rate, 7, 13
vs. telecommuting, 10
vs. working for others, 8-9
white-collar workers, 13
FTC (Federal Trade Commission), 297
furniture
   considerations, 111-112
   essentials, 110
   lights, 112
   seating, ergonomics, 110-111
   special needs, 113

G-H

Ginnie Mae Certificates, 295
giveaways, promotions, 215
good relationships with clients, guidelines, 225-226
government regulations, corporations, 169
greeting cards, public relations, 212

growth rate, 7, 13
Guide to Literary Agents & Art/ Photo Reps, 233

handwritten records, record-keeping, 186
harassment, dealing with, 229-230
Health Care Financing Administration, 278
hiring employees
   classified ads, 304
   considerations, 302-303
   employer responsibilities, 304
   options, 302-303
   screening applicants, 303
   sources, 303
   zoning restrictions, 304
home equity loans, 188
Home Office Computing magazine, 122
home offices, 35
   answering machines, 128
   beepers, 130
   briefcases, 136
   business plans, writing, 82-83
   cards, business
      considerations, 130-131
      essential information, 131
      tips, 132-133
   cellular phones, 129-130
   closing, 317
      guidelines, 317
   commercial properties
      advantages/ disadvantages, 107
      rent, 306
   computers
      advantages, 116-117
      considerations, 123-124
      cyberphobia, 117-118
      disadvantages, 118-119
      hardware, 119-120
      magazines, 122
      outdated equipment, 119
      setting up, 124-125
      software, 119-120

      tax deductions, 119, 123
      use guidelines, 125-126
   considerations, 107-108
      family activities, 109
      furniture, 111-112
   courier services, 136-137
   daily tasks, 84
   decorating, 83
   envelopes, 131
   expanding
      considerations, 308-309
      employer responsibilities, 304
      finding employees, 303
      hiring employees, 302-304
      lack of work, 306-308
      moving, 305-306
      remodeling offices, 305
      screen applicants, 303
      space-saving tips, 303, 305
   fax machines, 121
   furniture
      considerations, 111-112
      essentials, 110
      lights, 112
      seating, ergonomics, 110-111
      special needs, 113
   insurance, 285-286
   Internet access, 121
   inventories, 285
      essential information, 283
      Office Inventory Worksheet, 284
   IRS classification
      criteria, 268
   lights, 112
   location, 105
      commercial properties, 107, 306
      considerations, 106-108
      family activities, 109
   motion sensor floodlights, 139
   naming businesses
      competitors' strategies, 201
      copying names, 196

family names, 195
guidelines, 195
image, 194
importance, 194
misunderstandings,
195-196
organizational structure
business names, 167
changing, 170
considerations, 171
corporations, 168, 264
determining, 170
partnerships,
167-168, 263
"Selecting the Legal
Structure for Your
Firm," 172
sole proprietorships,
166-167, 262-263
photocopiers, 121-122
preferences/requirements,
105-106
remodeling, 109, 305
scanners, 122
seating, 110-111
security, 137-139
smoke detectors, 139
special needs, 113
stationery, 131, 133
storage space, 113
supplies, 133-136
tax deductions, 268
telecommunications
systems, 128-130
telephone lines, 129
voice mail, 128
Web sites, 136
wiring, 125
zoning laws
common zones, 102
fines, 104
guidelines, 104-105
hiring employees, 304
illegal businesses,
103-104
local laws, 103
remodeling homes, 109
see also equipment
homeowners' insurance, 286
hours
balancing family/
career, 248

children, 248-249
household chores,
250-251
writing about, 251
considerations, 239-240
disadvantages, 40
maintaining set schedules,
244-245
overworking, 242-244
procrastination, 238
rituals, 238-239
schedules
considerations, 239-240
maintaining set sched-
ules, 244-245
overworking, 242-244
procrastination, 238
rituals, 238-239
self-discipline strategies,
240-241
self-discipline strategies,
240-241
household chores
balancing family/career,
250-251
how-to books
*How to Open and Operate a
Home-Based Craft
Business,* 71
*How to Start a Service
Business,* 71
*How to Start and Run
Writing and Editing
Business,* 69

I

illegal businesses, zoning laws,
103-104
image consultants, freelance
careers, 69-70
in-home health care workers,
freelance careers, 69
in-house jobs, 315
incentives (sales)
discount coupons, 214
essential elements, 213
follow-up guidelines, 222
giveaways, 215

methods
ads, 201-202
brochures, 203-204
bumper stickers, 205
calendars, 205
classified ads, 201
competitors'
strategies, 203
decals, 205
direct mail
advertising, 204
magnets, 205
pamphlets, 204
postcards, 204
programs, 202
radio, 203
T-shirts, 205
tips, 201
TV ads, 203
yearbook ads, 202
Yellow Pages, 202-203
multiple purchase
offers, 215
sample products/
services, 215
trial offers, 214
income
categorizing, 183
earned income, 269
interest income,
defined, 269
level, taxes, 263
regulating workflow,
252-255
credit, 255
job-hunting, 253
part-time jobs, 255
temporary services, 254
see also fees; taxes
Independent Computer
Consultants Association, 70
*Individual Investors Guide to
Low-Load Mutual Fund,* 296
Individual Retirement
Accounts (IRAs), 291-292
children, 269
guidelines, 293-294
industry layoffs, 21

initial contact with clients, 231-232
insurance, 41
  Blue Cross and Blue Shield, 277
  co-payments, 279
  deductibles, 279-280
  disability insurance, 281-282
  Group Health Association of America, insurance, 278
  health insurance, 276-277
    considerations, 280-281
    costs, 276-277
    drawbacks, 276-277
    Medicaid, 279
    Medicare, 279
    pre-existing conditions, 278
    providers, types, 277
    reasons, 276
  life insurance, 282-283
  office equipment insurance
    actual value, 286
    considerations, 285-286
    homeowners' insurance, 286
    replacement value, 285
  premiums, 279
  resources, 278
interest income, defined, 269
interests, Interest Inventory, 48-50
interior designers, freelance careers, 69
Internal Revenue Service (IRS)
  audits, 261
    guidelines, 271-272
    partnerships, 263
  classification criteria
    freelancers, 260-261
    home offices, 268
  Nest Egg IRS Tax Information Center Web site, 262
  see also taxes
Internet
  accessing, 121
  acquiring customers, 91-92
  advertising, 221

newsletters, 209
  "Working from Home" CompuServe forum, 91
interpersonal relationships
  agent/freelancer relationship
    dissolving, 234-235
    guidelines, 234
  client/freelancer relationships, 94
    conflicts, 226
    conflicts of interest, 10
    good relationships, 225-226
    harassment, 229-230
    initial contact, 231-232
    raising fees, 163
    reputation, building, 224
    uncontrollable incidents, 229
    unfulfilled contracts, 227-228
interpersonal skills, 51
inventories
  equipment, 285
    essential information, 283
    Office Inventory Worksheet, 284
  Interest Inventories, 48-50
  Personal Inventory, 72-73
investing
  CDs (certificates of deposit), 294
  Complete Words of Wall Street, 297
  Ginnie Mae Certificates, 295
  Money Market Mutual Funds, 294
  mutual funds resources, 296
  publications, 296
  retirement plans
    CDs (certificates of deposit), 294
    Ginnie Mae Certificates, 295
    mistakes, 289-290
    Money Market Mutual Funds, 294

net worth, determining, 289
  publications, 296
  savings bonds, 294
  scams, 297-298
  stock mutual funds, 296
  stocks, 292
  tax shelters, 298
  tips, 290-291
  Treasury Bonds, 295
  U.S. Treasury bills (T-bills), 295
  U.S. Treasury Notes, 295
  savings bonds, 294
  scams, 297-298
    avoiding, 297
  stock mutual funds, 296
  stocks, 292
  tax shelters, 298
  Treasury Bonds, 295
  U.S. Treasury bills (T-bills), 295
  U.S. Treasury Notes, 295
invoices, 187
  as contracts, 175
  deadlines for payment, 159
  guidelines, 159-160
  keeping, 187
  late payments, 160
    legal action, 161
  numbering, 196
  promptness of payment, 158-159
  receiving payments, 161
  see also record-keeping
IRAs (Individual retirement accounts), 291-292
  children, 269
  guidelines, 293-294
IRS (Internal Revenue Service), 186
  audits, 261
    guidelines, 271-272
    partnerships, 263
  classification criteria
    freelancers, 260-261
    home offices, 268
  Nest Egg IRS Tax Information Center Web site, 262
  see also taxes

J-K-L

jobs
    career uncertainty, 20-22
    in-house jobs, 315
    job sharing, 182
    part-time jobs, regulating
        workflow, 255
    stressful jobs, 312
journalists, American Society
    of Journalists and
    Authors, 42

Keoghs (retirement funds),
    291-293
    qualification criteria, 292
    taxes, 292, 293
    types, 293

lack of work, 306-308
    considerations, 307-308
    expanding businesses,
        306-307
laptop computers, 120
layoffs, top industries, 21
leaving
    freelancing, 317
    workplace, acquiring
        customers, 88-89
legal aspects
    agents' contracts, 234
    contracts
        advantages, 172
        agents, 234
        essential elements, 173
        firsts, 231
        guidelines, 174
        invoices as
            contracts, 175
        negotiable elements,
            173-174
        reusing material, 254
        sample, 175-177
    difficult clients, 228
    naming businesses
        competitors'
            strategies, 201
        copying names, 196
        family names, 195

guidelines, 195
image, 194
importance, 194
misunderstandings,
    195-196
organizational structure
    business names, 167
    changing, 170
    considerations, 171
    corporations, 168, 264
    determining, 170
    partnerships,
        167-168, 263
    "Selecting the Legal
        Structure for Your
        Firm," 172
    sole propietorships,
        262-263
partnerships, 167-168, 273
payment collection,
    161-162
sole proprietorships,
    166-167
    advantages, 166-167
    disadvantages, 167
    taxes, 167, 262-263
taxes
    audits, 261, 271-272
    corporations, 264
    Employer's Tax Guide, 304
    estimated payments,
        270-271
    freelancer classification
        criteria, 260
    necessity, 261
    Nest Egg IRS Tax Infor-
        mation Center Web
        site, 262
    payroll taxes, 262
    penalties, 271
    reducing payments,
        272-273
    S corporations, 264
    sales taxes, 262
    sole proprietorships, 167,
        262-263
zoning laws
    common zones, 102
    fines, 104
    guidelines, 104-105
    hiring employees, 304

illegal businesses,
    103-104
local laws, 103
remodeling homes, 109
see also taxes
letterhead, 131
letters of agreement
    advantages, 172
    essential elements, 173
    guidelines, 174
    invoices as contracts, 175
    negotiable element,
        173-174
    reusing material, 254
    samples, 175-177
liability, corporations, 169
lights, home offices, 112
Literary Market Place, 80
loans, 188
local zoning laws, 103
location of business
    business plans, essentials,
        82-83
    commercial properties
        advantages/disadvan-
            tages, 107, 304
    considerations, 105-108
        family activities, 109
logos, business cards/
    stationery, 133
loneliness
    disadvantages of
        freelancing, 41-42
    overcoming
        exercises, 252
        strategies, 251-252
long-term projects, fee
    considerations, 149-150
lowering fees, 145

M

magazines, 122
magnets, advertising
    methods, 205
mailing lists, 204
maintaining set schedules,
    244-245
makeup artists, freelance
    careers, 69

Making It On Your Own, 88
managed health care,
  advantages/
  disadvantages, 277
manager, business, 233
managing time, fees, 151-152
Market Share Reporter, 297
marketing
  advertising
    ads, 201-202
    brochures, 203-204
    bumper stickers, 205
    calendars, 205
    classified ads, 201
    competitors'
      strategies, 203
    decals, 205
    direct mail
      advertising, 204
    magnets, 205
    pamphlets, 204
    postcards, 204
    programs, 202
    radio, 203
    T-shirts, 205
    tips, 201
    TV ads, 203
    yearbook ads, 202
    Yellow Pages, 202-203
  agents, 232
    appropriate
      situations, 230
    business managers, 233
    contracts, 234
    defined, 230
    finding, 233
    freelancer/agent
      relationship, 234-235
    *Guide to Literary Agents &
      Art/Photo Reps*, 233
    hidden fees, 232
    one-time deals, 231
    responsibilities, 230-231
    Society of Authors'
      Representatives, 233
  business plans,
    essentials, 84
  freelance careers, 71
  Internet guidelines, 221

naming businesses
  competitors'
    strategies, 201
  copying names, 196
  family names, 195
  guidelines, 195
  image, 194
  importance, 194
  misunderstandings,
    195-196
plans
  considerations, 199-201
  strategies, 84-85
promotions
  discount coupons, 214
  essential elements, 213
  follow-up guidelines, 222
  giveaways, 215
  multiple purchase
    offers, 215
  sample products/
    services, 215
  trial offers, 214
strategies, business plans,
  84-85
massage therapists, freelance
  careers, 69
meal dates, networking, 216
medical claims assistants,
  freelance careers, 69
Medicare taxes, 263
Money Market Mutual
  Funds, 294
money-saving tips, equipment
  purchases, 123
monthly fees, calculating, 149
moving, expanding
  businesses, 305-306
multiple purchase offers,
  promotions, 215
mutual funds, resources, 296

N

naming businesses, 167
  competitors' strategies, 201
  copying names, 196
  family names, 195

guidelines, 195
image, 194
importance, 194
misunderstandings,
  195-196
National Association for the
  Self-Employed, The, 218
National Association of
  Temporary and Staffing
  Services, 254
National Entrepreneurs
  Opportunity Network,
  Information Exchange, 70
National Insurance Consumer
  Hotline, 278
negotiating, 52
  agents, necessity of, 232
  contracts, 173-174
  fees, 152-154
Nest Egg IRS Tax Information
  Center Web site, 262
net worth, determining, 289
networking
  acquiring customers, 90
    conversations,
      professional, 94-96
    client/freelancer
      relationship, 94
    initial contact, 93-94
    record-keeping, 96
    self-promotion, 93
    unsuccessful contacts, 96
  alumni associations, 218
  appointments,
    scheduling, 222
  business cards, 197
  civic groups, 217
  community groups, 217
  importance, 215-216
  meal dates, 216
  methods
    alumni associations, 218
    appointments,
      scheduling, 222
    civic groups, 217
    community groups, 217

co-workers, 88-89
  importance, 215-216
  Internet, 91-92
  meal dates, 216
  record-keeping, 219
  referrals, 219-220
  trade associations, 218
  volunteer work, 219
  World Wide Web
    (WWW), 218
record-keeping, 219
referrals, 219-220
resumes, 198
  chronological
    resumes, 198
  guidelines, 198
  sample, 200-201
  skills resumes, 198
targeting customers, 92-93
trade associations, 218
volunteer work, 219
World Wide Web
  (WWW), 218
newsletters, 209
news stories, 209
numbering invoices, 196

Office Inventory
  Worksheet, 284
office politics, 50
offices, 35
  answering machines, 128
  beepers, 130
  briefcases, 136
  business plans, writing,
    82-83
  cards, business
    considerations, 130-131
    essential
      information, 131
    tips, 132-133
  cellular phones, 129-130
  closing, 317
    guidelines, 317
  commercial properties
    advantages/
      disadvantages, 107
    rent, 306

computers
  advantages, 116-117
  considerations, 123-124
  cyberphobia, 117-118
  disadvantages, 118-119
  hardware, 119-120
  magazines, 122
  outdated equipment, 119
  setting up, 124-125
  software, 119-120
  tax deductions, 119, 123
  use guidelines, 125-126
considerations, 107-108
  family activities, 109
  furniture, 111-112
courier services, 136-137
daily tasks, 84
decorating, 83
envelopes, 131
expanding
  considerations, 308-309
  employer
    responsibilities, 304
  finding employees, 303
  hiring employees,
    302-304
  lack of work, 306-308
  moving, 305-306
  remodeling offices, 305
  screen applicants, 303
  space-saving tips,
    303, 305
fax machines, 121
fire extinguishers, 138
flashlights, 139
furniture
  considerations, 111-112
  essentials, 110
  lights, 112
  seating, ergonomics,
    110-111
  special needs, 113
insurance, 285-286
Internet access, 121
inventories, 285
  essential
    information, 283
  Office Inventory
    Worksheet, 284
IRS classification
  criteria, 268
lights, 112

location, 105
  commercial properties,
    107, 306
  considerations, 106-108
  family activities, 109
motion sensor
  floodlights, 139
naming businesses
  competitors'
    strategies, 201
  copying names, 196
  family names, 195
  guidelines, 195
  image, 194
  importance, 194
  misunderstandings,
    195-196
organizational structure
  business names, 167
  changing, 170
  considerations, 171
  corporations, 168, 264
  determining, 170
  partnerships,
    167-168, 263
  "Selecting the Legal
    Structure for Your
    Firm," 172
  sole proprietorships,
    166-167, 262-263
photocopiers, 121-122
preferences/requirements,
  105-106
remodeling, 109, 305
scanners, 122
seating, 110-111
security, 137-139
smoke detectors, 139
special needs, 113
stationery, 131, 133
storage space, 113
supplies, 133-136
tax deductions, 268
telecommunications
  systems, 128-130
telephone lines, 129
voice mail, 128
Web sites, 136
wiring, 125
zoning laws
  common zones, 102
  fines, 104

guidelines, 104-105
hiring employees, 304
illegal businesses,
103-104
local laws, 103
remodeling homes, 109
see also equipment;
workplace
one-time deals, agents, 231
organizational structure
business names, 167
business plans
essentials, 83-84
changes, 170
considerations, 171
corporations, 168
advantages, 169
considerations, 170
disadvantages, 169
S corporations, 170, 264
taxes, 264
determining, 170
partnerships, 167-168
audits, 263
disadvantages, 168
taxes, 263
"Selecting the Legal Structure for Your Firm," 172
sole proprietorships,
166-167
advantages, 166-167
disadvantages, 167
taxes, 167, 262-263
organizations
American Association of
Home-Based Businesses,
The, 218
joining considerations, 218
National Association for the
Self-Employed, The, 218
National Association of
Temporary and Staffing
Services, 254
service organizations, 213
Society of Authors'
Representatives, The, 233
overworking, 242
prevention tips, 244
reasons to freelance, 22
schedules, 243-44

P

pamphlets
advertising methods, 204
"Selecting the Legal Structure for Your Firm," 172
part-time jobs, regulating
workflow, 255
partnerships, 167-168
taxes, 263
payments, collecting
completed work
only, 253
contracts, first 231
deadlines, 159
invoices, 159-160, 187
late payments, 160
legal action, 161
promptness, 158-159
receiving payments,
161-162
shifted schedules, 253
structuring
payments, 228
taxes
estimating, 270-271
penalties, 271
see also fees
payroll taxes, 262
PC World magazine, 122
penalties
taxes, 271
zoning laws, 104
Personal Inventory, 72-73
personal shoppers, freelance
careers, 69
personal trainers, freelance
careers, 69
personality traits, 29
common, 10-11
essentials, 52-55
pet-sitting services, freelance
careers, 69
phone calls
answering machines, 128
cellular phones, 129-130
telecommunications
systems, 128
telephone lines, 129
voice mail, 128

photocopiers, 121-122
photographers, freelance
careers, 69
plans
business plans
essentials, 79-85
purpose, 76-77
researching fields, 77-78
marketing, considerations,
199-201
retirement plans
importance, 288
IRAs, 291-294
Keoghs, 291-293
mistakes, avoiding,
289-290
net worth,
determining, 289
stocks, 292
tips, 290-291
postcards, advertising
methods, 204
premiums, health
insurance, 279
press releases, 209
private investigators, freelance
careers, 69
procrastination, 238
productivity, 32
professional organizations
American Association of
Home-Based Businesses,
The, 218
joining considerations, 218
National Association for the
Self-Employed, The, 218
National Association of
Temporary and Staffing
Services, 254
Society of Authors'
Representatives, The, 233
professionalism
agent/freelancer
relationship 234
conflicts, 226
correspondence, 224
client/freelancer
relationships, 308
difficult clients
guidelines, 227-228
harassment, 229-230

good relationships, 225-226
harassment, 229-230
initial contact, 231-235
reputation, building
    guidelines, 224
uncontrollable incidents
    guidelines, 229
profits, 188
    partnerships, 168
programs, advertising
    methods, 202
promotion
    agents, 232
        appropriate
            situations, 230
        business managers, 233
        contracts, 234
        defined, 230
        finding, 233
        freelancer/agent
            relationship, 234-235
        *Guide to Literary Agents &
            Art/Photo Reps*, 233
        hidden fees, 232
        one-time deals, 231
        responsibilities, 230-231
        Society of Authors'
            Representatives, 233
    sales promotions
        discount coupons, 214
        essential elements, 213
        follow-up guidelines, 222
        giveaways, 215
        methods, 201-205
        multiple purchase
            offers, 215
        sample products/
            services, 215
        trial offers, 214
public relations
    charitable events, 212-213
    greeting cards, 212
    importance, 208
    newsletters, 209
    news stories, 209
    press releases, 209
    speaking engagements, 213
    thank-you notes, 209

Q-R

quality of work, 224
radio, advertising
    methods, 203
raising fees
    difficult clients, 228
    freelancer/customer
        relationships, 163
    guidelines, 162-163
rapport, building, 88
rate of freelancers, 7, 13
rates
    adjustable fees,
        considerations, 150-151
    agents, 232
    barter systems, 158
    collecting payments
        deadlines, 159
        invoices, 159-160
        late payments, 160
        legal action, 161
        promptness, 158-159
        receiving payments,
            161-162
        structuring
            payments, 228
    competitors' rates, 149
    considerations, 144-145
        adjustable fees, 150-151
    consignment,
        working on, 158
    contracts
        advantages, 172
        essential elements, 173
        guidelines, 174
        invoices as
            contracts, 175
        negotiable elements,
            173-174
        reusing material, 254
        sample, 175-177
    contracts, first, 231
    daily fees, 149
    determining
        competitors' rates, 149
        expenses, calculating,
            145-147
    difficult clients, 228
    flat fees, 150

lack of work, raising
    fees, 152
long-term projects, 149-150
monthly fees
    calculating, 149
negotiating, 152-154
profit margins, 148
raising fees,
    freelancer/client
        relationships, 163
    guidelines, 162-163
    lack of work, 152
short-term projects,
    149-150
speculation, working on,
    156-157
    advantages, 156
    disadvantages, 156-157
    selling tips, 157
time management, 151-152
unfulfilled contracts, 228
weekly fees,
    calculating, 149
reasons for failure, 180
reasons to freelance
    career uncertainty, 20-22
    overworking, 22
    retirement, early, 19
    stress in workplace, 22
    unmet needs/desires, 23-24
    workplace changes, 19
    see also advantages
receipts, 166-167
record-keeping
    contracts, 174
    customer contacts, 96
    disadvantages of
        freelancing, 41
    equipment inventories, 285
        essential
            information, 283
        Office Inventory
            Worksheet, 284
    essentials, 182
    expenses, categorizing, 183
    fears, 181
    handwritten records, 186
    importance, 181-182
    income, categorizing, 183
    IRS, 186

methods, 184
  sample, 184-185
networking, 219
payment collection
  deadlines, 159
  guidelines, 159-160
  late payments, 160
  legal action, 161
  promptness, 158-159
  receiving payments, 161
reasons for failure, 180
receipts, 186-187
setting up
  expenses,
    categorizing, 183
  income,
    categorizing, 183
  methods, 184
  sample, 184-185
single entries, 182
tax audits, guidelines,
  271-273
updating records, 187
reducing payments
  taxes, 272-273
referrals, 219-220
regulating workflow, 252-255
  credit, 255
  job-hunting, 253
  part-time jobs, 255
  temporary services, 254
relationships
  agent/freelancer
    dissolving, 234-235
    guidelines, 234
  client/freelancer
    conflicts, 226
    conflicts of interest, 10
    good relationships,
      225-226
    harassment, 229-230
    initial contact, 231-232
    Internet, 91-92
    raising fees, 163
    record-keeping, 96
    reputation, building, 224
    self-promotion, 93
    uncontrollable
      incidents, 229

unfulfilled contracts,
  227-228
remodeling
  home offices, 109-110, 305
  zoning laws, 109
rent, commercial
  property, 306
repair services, freelance
  careers, 69
replacement value,
  equipment, 285
reputation, 88
  building, 224
  customers, 228
researching
  competitors' rates, 149
  fields, 77-78
resources
  associations
    American Association of
      Home Based Businesses,
      The, 218
    American Society of
      Journalists and
      Authors, 42
    Editorial Freelancers
      Association, 42, 78
    Group Health Associa-
      tion of America, 278
    Independent Computer
      Consultants
      Association, 70
    National Association for
      the Self-Employed,
      The, 218
    National Association of
      Temporary and Staffing
      Services, 254
  books
    *Business Plan Guide for
      Independent Consultants,
      The*, 71
    *Complete Words of Wall
      Street*, 297
    Employer's Tax Guide, 304
    *Guide to Literary Agents &
      Art/Photo Reps*, 233
    *How to Open and Operate
      a Home-Based Craft
      Business*, 71

    *How to Start a Service
      Business*, 71
    *How to Start and Run
      Writing and Editing
      Business*, 69
    *Individual Investors Guide
      to Low-Load Mutual
      Fund*, 296
    Literary Market Place, 80
    Making It On Your Own,
      88
    Market Share Reporter, 297
    *Mutual Fund Buyer's
      Guide*, 296
    *Mutual Fund
      Encyclopedia*, 296
    *Upstart Guide to Owning
      and Managing a Desktop
      Publishing Service,
      The*, 69
    *Walker's Manual of
      Unlisted Stocks*, 297
  brochures
    "Selecting the Legal
      Structure for Your
      Firm," 172
    "Tax Guide for Small
      Businesses," 265
  Health Care Financing
    Administration, 278
  investment
    information, 296
  magazines, 122
  National Entrepreneurs
    Opportunity Network,
    Information Exchange, 70
  National Insurance
    Consumer Hotline, 278
  Web sites
    Entrepreneurial Edge
      Online Webzine, 116
    Nest Egg IRS Tax Infor-
      mation Center , 262
    "Working from Home"
      CompuServe forum, 91
restrictions
  zoning
    common zones, 102
    fines, 104
    guidelines, 104-105

illegal businesses,
103-104
local laws, 103
remodeling homes, 109
resumes, 198-199
chronological resumes, 198
guidelines, 198
networking, 198
sample, 200-201
skills resumes, 198
retirement plans
importance, 288
IRAs, 269, 291-294
Keoghs, 291-292
qualification criteria, 292
taxes, 292
types, 293
mistakes, 289-290
net worth,
determining, 289
stocks, 292
tips, 290-291
see also investing
reunion planners, freelance
careers, 69
reusing material, 254
rituals, work schedules,
238-239

S

S corporations, 170
taxes, 264
safes, office security, 138
sales, forecasting, 82
sales taxes, 262
samples
contracts, 175-177
record-keeping methods,
184-185
resumes, 200-201
sample products/services
promotions, 215
tax forms, 266
savings bonds, 294
SBA (Small Business
Administration), 66, 172
scams, investments, 297-298

scanners, 122
Schedule C tax form
samples, 266
schedules
balancing family/
career, 248
children, 248-249
household chores,
250-251
writing about, 251
considerations, 239-240
flexibility, 12
hours, 40
maintaining set schedules,
244-245
overworking, 242-244
procrastination, 238
rituals, 238-239
self-discipline strategies,
240-241
tax payments, 270-271
workload, 33
SCORE (Service Corps of
Retired Executives), 189
screening applicants,
expanding businesses, 303
seating, ergonomics, 110-111
Securities and Exchange
Commission (SEC), 297
security
alarm systems, 138
essentials, 137
fire extinguishers, 138
flashlights, 139
motion sensor
floodlights, 139
safes, 138
smoke detectors, 139
"Selecting the Legal Structure
for Your Firm," 172
self-discipline strategies
schedules, 240-241
self-employment
increase, 5-6
U.S. rate, 7, 13
self-esteem coaches, freelance
careers, 69
self-promotion
acquiring customers, 93
cards, business, 197

resumes, 198-199
chronological resumes,
198
guidelines, 198
sample, 200-201
skills resumes, 198
see also agents
selling
advertising
brochures, 203-204
bumper stickers, 205
calendars, 205
classified ads, 201
competitors'
strategies, 203
decals, 205
direct mail
advertising, 204
display ads, 201-202
Internet, 221
magnets, 205
pamphlets, 204
postcards, 204
programs, 202
radio, 203
T-shirts, 205
tips, 201
TV ads, 203
yearbook ads, 202
Yellow Pages, 202-203
agents, 232
appropriate
situations, 230
business managers, 233
contracts, 234
defined, 230
finding, 233
freelancer/agent relationship, 234, 234-235
*Guide to Literary Agents &
Art/Photo Reps*, 233
hidden fees, 232
one-time deals, 231
responsibilities, 230-231
Society of Authors'
Representatives, 233
barter systems, 158-159
businesses, 317
consignment, working
on, 158

contracts
  advantages, 172
  essential elements, 173
  guidelines, 174
  invoices as
    contracts, 175
  negotiable elements,
    173-174
  reusing material, 254
  samples, 175-177
freelance careers, 71
marketing
  follow-up action, 222
  Internet, 221
promotions
  discount coupons, 214
  follow-up action, 222
  giveaways, 215
  multiple purchase
    offers, 215
  sample products/
    services, 215
  trial offers, 214
public relations
  charitable events,
    212-213
  greeting cards, 212
  importance, 208
  newsletters, 209
  news stories, 209
  press releases, 209
  speaking
    engagements, 213
  thank-you notes, 209
sales taxes, 262
speculation, working on,
  157
Service Corps of Retired
  Executives (SCORE), 189
service organizations, 213
  speaking engagements, 213
services
  adjustable fees,
    considerations, 150-151
  barter systems, 158
  collecting payments
    deadlines, 159
    invoices, 159-160

late payments, 160
legal action, 161
promptness, 158-159
receiving payment,
  161-162
consignment, working
  on, 158
contracts
  advantages, 172
  essential elements, 173
  guidelines, 174
  invoices as
    contracts, 175
  negotiable elements,
    173-174
  reusing material, 254
  samples, 175-177
evaluating, lack of work,
  307-308
expanding
  considerations, 308-309
  employer
    responsibilities, 304
  hiring employees,
    302-304
  lack of work, 306-308
  moving, 305-306
  remodeling offices, 305
  screening applicants, 303
  space-saving tips,
    303, 305
fees
  competitors' rates, 149
  considerations, 144-145,
    150-151
  contracts, first, 231
  daily fees, 149
  determining, 145-147
  flat fees, 150
  long-term projects,
    149-150
  monthly fees, 149
  negotiating, 152-154
  raising, 152, 162-163
  short-term projects,
    149-150
  weekly fees, 149
lack of work, 306-307
  evaluating services,
    307-308
long-term projects, fee
  considerations, 149-150

profit margins, 148
sales taxes, 262
short-term projects
  fee considerations,
    149-150
speculation, working on,
  156-157
  advantages, 156
  disadvantages, 156-157
  selling tips, 157
setting up
  equipment, 124-125
  organizational structure
    business names, 167
    changing, 170
    considerations, 171
    corporations, 168, 264
    determining, 170
    partnerships,
      167-168, 263
    "Selecting the Legal
      Structure for Your
      Firm," 172
    sole proprietorships,
      166-167, 262-263
  record-keeping system
    expenses,
      categorizing, 183
    income,
      categorizing, 183
    methods, 184
    sample, 184-185
  see also home offices
sexual harassment, 229-230
short-term projects, fee
  considerations, 149-150
single entries, defined, 182
sites
  Amazon.com
    (bookstore), 220
  American Express, 221
  CompuServe, 221
  Entrepreneurial Edge
    Online Webzine, 116
  office supplies, 136
skills
  analytical skills, 53
  broadening, 313-314
    changing fields, 315-316
    college courses, 314-316
    in-house work, 315

projects, 314
  trade journals, 315
communication skills, 53
  essentials, 50-52
  insufficient, 51-52
  interpersonal skills, 51
  technical fields, 52
skills resumes, 198
Small Business Administration
  (SBA), 66, 172
smoke detectors, 139
Social Security taxes
  children, hiring, 269
  sole proprietorships, 262
Society of Authors'
  Representatives, The, 233
software
  basics, 119-120
  bundled software, 120
sole proprietorships, 166-167
  advantages, 166-167
  disadvantages, 167
  taxes, 167, 262-263
space-saving tips
  expanding businesses,
   303, 305
speaking engagements
  public relations, 213
special needs
  home offices, 113
speculation, working on,
  156-157
  advantages, 156
  disadvantages, 156-157
  selling tips, 157
starting businesses
  business plans
   essentials, 79-85
   purpose, 76-77
   researching fields, 77-78
   see also home offices
stationery, 131, 133
stocks, 292
  stock mutual funds, 296
  *Walker's Manual of Unlisted
   Stocks*, 297
storage space, 113
store-opening consultants
  freelance careers, 70-71

stress
  stressful jobs, 312
  workplace, reasons to
   freelance, 22-24
structuring businesses
  legal structures
   business names, 167
   changes, 170
   considerations, 171
   corporations, 168, 264
   determining, 170
   partnerships,
    167-168, 263
   "Selecting the Legal
    Structure for Your
    Firm," 172
   sole proprietorships,
    166-167, 262-263
supplies, 133-136
  buying tips, 135-136

T-U-V

T&E (travel & entertainment)
  budgets, tax deductions, 226,
  269
T-shirts, advertising
  methods, 205
targeting customers, 92-93
"Tax Guide for Small
  Businesses," 265
taxes
  1099s, 273
  audit guidelines, 271-272
  audits, 261
  corporations, 264
  deductions, 41
   computer equipment,
    119, 123
   expenses, 269
   home offices, 268
   Keogh retirement plans,
    292-293
   legitimate deductions,
    265
   T&E (travel & entertain-
    ment) budgets,
    226, 269

tax brackets, 269
  "Tax Guide for Small
   Businesses," 265
  Employer's Tax Guide, 304
  estimated payments,
   270-271
  freelancer classification
   criteria, 260-261
  Medicare, 263
  necessity, 261
  Nest Egg IRS Tax
   Information Center
   Web site, 262
  payroll taxes, 262
  penalties, 271
  reducing payments,
   272-273
  S corporations, 264
  sales taxes, 262
  Schedule C sample
   form, 266
  Schedule C-EZ, 263
  Social Security, 262
   children, hiring, 269
  sole proprietorships,
   166-167
   advantages, 167
   disadvantages, 166-167
   taxes, 167, 262-263
tax shelters, 298
technical fields, essential
  skills, 52
technology
  advantages, 12
  answering machines, 128
  beepers, 130
  cellular phones, 129-130
  computers, 123-124
   advantages, 116-117
   disadvantages, 118-119
   hardware, 119-120
   outdated equipment, 119
   setting up, 124-125
   software, 119-120
   use guidelines, 125-126
  cyberphobia, 117-118
  fax machines, 121
  Internet access, 121
  magazines, 122
  photocopiers, 121-122
  purchasing, 122-126

budget considerations,
123-124
comparison
shopping, 124
money-saving tips, 123
needs assessments, 122
researching options,
122-123
scanners, 122
security, 137-139
setting up, 124-125
tax deductions, 119, 123
telecommunications
systems, 128-130
use guidelines, 125-126
voice mail, 128
Web sites, 136
telecommunication systems,
128-130
telecommuting vs.
freelancing, 10
telephones
answering calls, 128
cellular phones, 129-130
lines, 129
temporary services, 20, 254
term life insurance, 282
thank-you notes, public
relations, 209
time management, 151-152
tour operators, freelance
careers, 69
travel & entertainment (T&E)
budgets, tax deductions,
226, 269
travel consultants, freelance
careers, 69
Treasury Bills (T-bills), 295
trends, choosing careers, 62-63
trial offers, promotions, 214
TV ads, advertising
methods, 203
typeface, business cards, 132

U.S. Treasury Bills
(T-bills), 295
uncertainty of work
disadvantages of
freelancing, 42-43
workflow, regulating,
252-255

credit, 255
job-hunting, 253
part-time jobs, 255
temporary services, 254
unethical conduct
confidentiality, 96
conflicts of interest, 10
unsuccessful contacts,
acquiring customers, 96
updating records, 187
*Upstart Guide to Owning and
Managing a Desktop Publishing
Service, The*, 69

values, determining, 48
benefits of freelancing,
33-35
Interest Inventory, 48-50
voice mail, 128
volunteer work, 219

W-X-Y-Z

*Walker's Manual of Unlisted
Stocks*, 297
weekly fees, calculating, 149
white-collar workers, 13
wiring home offices, 125
work
conflicts of interest, 10
flow, regulating, 252-255
credit, 255
job-hunting, 253
lack of work, 306-308
part-time jobs, 255
temporary services, 254
nature of, 8-9
quality of work,
reputation, 224
schedules, 33
considerations, 239-240
maintaining set sched-
ules, 244-245
overworking, 242-244
procrastination, 238
rituals, 238-239
self-discipline strategies,
240-241
working for others vs.
freelancing, 8-9

"Working from Home"
CompuServe forum, 91
working on speculation, *see*
speculation, working on
workplace
career uncertainty, 20-22
changes, 19
leaving
acquiring customers,
88-89
guidelines, 89-90
worksheets, Office Inventory
Worksheet, 284
World Wide Web
(WWW), 119
advertising, 221
networking, 218
sites
Amazon.com
(bookstore), 220
American Express, 221
CompuServe, 221
Entrepreneurial Edge
Online Webzine, 116
Nest Egg IRS Tax
Information
Center, 262
office supplies, 136
writing
about balancing family/
career, 251
freelance careers, 68-69
plans, business
essentials, 79-85
purpose, 76-77
researching fields, 77-78
press releases, 209
resources
*How to Start and Run
Writing and Editing
Business*, 69
Literary Market Place, 80

yearbook ads, 202
Yellow Pages, advertising,
202-203
zoning issues, 102-105, 109,
304